To our parents:
Donald J. Devinney, Johann R. Devinney;
Billy Marks Hightower, M.D., and Hilma Seay Hightower

Contents

Preface

The program for economic integration put forth by Lord Cockfield in his *White Paper on Completing the Internal Market* in 1985, and subsequently endorsed by both the European Community Commission and the twelve member governments of the European Community, is, in many respects, a singular event in European history. The Single European Act, the formal endorsement of the 1992 Single Europe Program, obligates EC members to abdicate a host of home government rights and responsibilities, either directly to the European Community bureaucracy or indirectly through the formal recognition of the laws and decisions of other European Community governments. The scope of such an exercise cannot be overemphasized, particularly given the depth of divisions that have kept the European continent at war for most of recorded history.

What is the Single Europe Program? What does it imply for the future of European and world markets? From "Euro-idealists" we hear discussion of a future "United States of Europe"—federal state of European nations with common economic and social policies. From "Euro-skeptics" we hear discussion of a future bureaucratic utopia with social and economic policy strings being tugged by Brussels mandarins. From jittery officials in America, Japan, and elsewhere we hear discussion of "fortress Europe," its guns trained on more efficient non-European producers in politically sensitive industries.

All of this is, of course, pure speculation. At present, no one truly knows what the "single European market" will look like or what the year 1992 will bring. And what changes Europe will have made by the early years of the 1990s will be affected by the changes in the economic climate while the program is being developed. However, although the European Community's current undertaking represents something of a unique historical endeavor, it is not without analogs from the recent past and educated speculation about its probable purposes and potential results is not without some scientific validity.

The purpose of the present book is to examine, in a rigorous and rational manner, the recent move toward a more integrated European Community. Although many readers are no doubt concerned about what a single European market means to their specific firm, industry, or interest group, we will avoid the tendency to prognosticate on "how you can profit from 1992." Instead, we will be focusing our examination on what we consider to be the fundamental economic, political, and social factors behind the European Community's recent endeavor. Having provided a substantive basis for understanding why the European Community and its member governments have decided to play the 1992 card, we can then more carefully formulate a rational forecast of what it bodes for the 1990s and beyond.

The book is structured to satisfy both individuals with some European experience as well as those who know nothing about the European Community and the functioning of its institutions. Chapter 1 provides an overview of our thinking on the root causes of and probable outcomes from the Single Europe Program. Chapter 2 is meant as an overview of the history and institutions of the European Community and will prove helpful for individuals wanting some institutional background before reading further. Chapter 3 is an overview of the Single Europe Program, a discussion of the official purposes of the program, and a look at progress to date. Chapter 4 presents a critical analysis of the 1992 program, looking first at why such an enterprise might be launched and how it has been sustained to date. Chapter 5 is a look at the most recent discussions in the European Community with regard to monetary union. We will argue that, in the end, the extent to which the Single Europe Program serves as a true stepping-stone toward a European federal system will be determined by the progress toward monetary union. Chapter 6 will end our discussion by giving an overview of the analysis and some speculation on the structure of European markets after 1992. Chapter 7 will close the discussion with a short look at the limits of European integration.

We also have attempted to provide the reader with a comprehensive data source on 1992 and the European Community. This includes a comprehensive bibliography along with a set of appendixes outlining the status of the current single market directives, current information on the European Community, and a checklist of questions useful in determining a 1992 strategy.

Acknowledgments

As with most projects of this scope, the authors represent a small portion of the people who are devoting themselves to its completion. We could not possibly name all of the corporate, government, and academic figures who have taken time to discuss their thoughts with us, have listened patiently to our ideas, and have worked tirelessly to provide us with the information we have requested. We thank all of them for their patience and expertise. Special thanks go to the individuals at Deutsche Bundesbank, the Bank of England, the Bruges Group, the U.S. Department of Commerce, the International Trade Commission, the International Federation of Robotics, the Boston Consulting Group, Lucky-Goldstar Economic Research Institute, and the European Institute for Advanced Studies in Management for their time, patience, and information. The European Community Delegation in Washington provided outstanding services without which this book could never have been completed. Personal thanks go to the outstanding staff at the Walker Library at Vanderbilt University, particularly Sylvia Graham and Carol Dickerson, for their unquestioning devotion to finding us what no doubt appeared to them the most meaningless esoterica and to colleagues and students at both Vanderbilt University and the University of Hamburg. Finally, we thank J. Dewey Daane for his help in getting this project going, Lee Anne Gay for research assistance, Cordy Cates for expert secretarial work, and Jane Birmingham for her editorial assistance.

1

European Economic Integration: An Overview

To the extent that it commanded virtually universal assent, the mission of European unification in the Twentieth Century has been to break down the barriers that separate from each other people with an increasing appetite for cooperation.

—Kenneth Minogue, Europe's Historical Passion For Cooperation

In 1985 Lord Cockfield completed the *White Paper on Completing of the Single Market*.[1] This document outlined a program whereby barriers to intercountry trade between the member states of the European Community (EC) would be selectively removed by December 31, 1992. This document was unique because it did more than simply put forth a vision of European economic integration in abstract terms; it methodically put that vision into operation. Three hundred directives were aimed at what were considered to be the most troublesome restrictions to the free movement of people, capital, and goods across EC borders.

The *White Paper* and the Single European Act, the legal document formalizing the Single Market Program, codified a process that has come to be called "1992." EC bureaucrats and statesmen argue that the move toward broader economic integration by 1992 is not simply a deadline but a process, a continuation of the dreams of men like Winston Churchill and Jean Monnet who saw Europe's nightmare and looked to a more progressive and positive future. The process called *1992* is occurring in front of our eyes and will continue to occur into the 1990s and the early part of the twenty-first century.

The psychological magnitude and administrative scope of 1992 should not be underestimated. This endeavor represents nothing short of the single largest and most complex peaceful transfer of government sovereignty to an extragovernmental authority ever seen. The closest analogy, and certainly a false one—the replacement of the Articles of Confederation by the Constitution of the United States—pales in comparison to the present European undertaking. Even in 1789, the United States was basically one culture with one language. The countries of the European Community represent a *minimum* of twelve cultures and twelve languages. Most of these nations, or their predecessors, have spent a large part of recorded history at war with one another.

The single market program of the EC has spawned something of a consulting and public relations bonanza. Hardly a day goes by that another 1992 seminar is not taking place in a major European capital and books and papers are flowing from the academic gristmill. Brokerage firms have developed mutual funds to capitalize on the profitability of companies that supposedly will be unleashed by the liberalization of European markets. Every major corporation, either currently operating in Europe or thinking of moving into the European market in the near term, has its own 1992 study group. The United States trade representative and commerce secretary both consider the study of 1992 a top priority, and the Japanese Ministry of Trade and Investment (MITI) is studying the EC project intensely. Major business magazines and newspapers have devoted entire sections to 1992. United States merger and acquisition specialists have expanded operations in Europe, taking advantage of their comparative superiority in the art and technique of corporate restructuring. At times one is left wondering if the 5 to 6 percent increase in gross domestic product (GDP) predicted from the liberalization of European trade barriers is simply the spoils of the consulting activity generated by the confusion and anxiety surrounding 1992.

Yet, in spite of, and perhaps because of, the 1992 hype, the European Community's pursuit of a more fully integrated and efficiently functioning market is something of an enigma to observers both inside and outside the Community. On paper, we appear to be seeing a level of European cooperation that statesmen in prior decades would have viewed as extraordinary. Yet one is left with the sense that something is not quite right. In the 1970s and early

1980s, the EC appeared as little more than a forum for acrimonious debate over budgetary transfers and agricultural subsidies. Although the move toward a single European market has not been completely smooth (witness the debate surrounding the Jacques Delors Trade Union Council speech and Margaret Thatcher's "response" at Bruges, Belgium), the atmosphere of cooperation that appears to exist is in stark contrast to the almost pathetic wrangling that existed only five to ten years ago. Is this the same EC? Or is it a "new and improved" EC?

This dilemma raises a rather interesting question about 1992. Why have leading European statesmen done such a volte-face? Are we seeing, in the words of John McGee, "a free[ing of] the European economy from self-imposed regulatory constraints"?[2] A laissez-faire renaissance in Europe? Alternatively, is 1992, in ex-prime minister Thatcher's words, an attempt "to suppress nationhood and concentrate powers at the centre of a European conglomerate"?[3] the building of the ramparts of the future "fortress Europe"? In reality it is both—and neither. This superficially schizophrenic aspect of the Single Europe Program has led so many observers astray. In seeking to categorize the program as either pro– or anti–free market many observers have unnecessarily ignored the forces causing the observed confusion behind the program's purpose. Nineteen ninety-two is a shell that contains many conflicting interests. Also, completing the internal market involves more than economics and trade. Economics and trade are why the game is being played and they represent the stakes, but 1992 is first and foremost a political enterprise.

In questioning what 1992 will bring, either globally, within Europe, or with respect to specific industry and political groups, it is important to understand what has driven European governments to embrace the 1992 program versus the alternatives that were potentially available to solve their perceived problems. More simply, we need to ask why European statesmen are choosing to play the economic unification game now. This question is even more perplexing in light of normal political reality. Why would the leaders of twelve separate, albeit similar, nations willingly abdicate important governmental powers, and hence the ability to satisfy their own political constituencies, to an authority that former British industry secretary Nicholas Ridley described as "seventeen unelected reject politicians . . . pandered to by a supine parliament,"[4] that faces no direct, and few indirect, penalties from ignoring the interests of powerful intracountry interest groups? After all, negotiators are rarely congratulated for what they have given up at the bargaining table.

In attempting to discover why the EC has resurrected free trade and economic unification we also need to determine the problem for which 1992 is the chosen solution. Governments and politicians do not give up power easily and have traditionally only done so under duress. Customarily, they try to solve perceived problems through government action, that is, spending, rather than seeking policies that are meant to reduce government aid or interference, in spite of all the rhetoric to the contrary.[5]

As noted earlier, 1992 is a process, but it is one that is made up of many other processes, some convergent, some divergent. Also, the 1992 process is taking place in a political arena that is not structurally different from the political arena of the past thirty years. Certainly, the players and stakes have changed, and cards are being played today that players of thirty years ago had hardly an inkling about, but the game is still the same. There is no evidence that politicians who support a more powerful European Community receive any more popular support today than they did in the 1960s or 1970s (see chapter 4). In the recent election of the European Parliament, the EC's assembly of member state representatives, most parties ran under banners proclaiming their allegiance to a greater and more open Europe. For example, the West German Christian Democratic party campaigned with the pro-1992 slogan, *"Grosses Europa, Grosses Zukunft"* (greater Europe, greater future). Yet the European Parliament elections failed to create the ground swell of support expected. The 56 percent voter turnout rate was low by European standards, and rather than confirming support for laissez-faire policy, the election made big winners of the left-of-center parties, such as the communists, the socialists, and the Greens, who command a two-seat majority in the Parliament.[6]

In our search for the causes and consequences of the Community's Single Europe Program, we are seeking the answers to four key questions. First, why is 1992 occurring now? Could economic unification have been as easily achieved sometime in the past or perhaps postponed into the future? Second, why is the Single Europe Program structured as it is? Third, what does its structure and timing tell us about the nature of the program? Fourth, what do the answers to the first two questions imply about the winners and losers of this geo-economic restructuring? Why are the losers losing and the winners winning? Only by knowing the why and the how of 1992 can we even begin to speculate in an educated manner about its ultimate outcome.

Playing the Unification Card—the "Why Now?"

In the words of Richard M. Nixon, "nothing unites Europeans like a common threat." The 1970s and 1980s saw rapid economic and social changes throughout the world, most noticeably in America and the Far East. In the Pacific, the economies of Japan, Korea, Hong Kong, Malaysia, and Thailand were rapidly industrializing, with Japan in the lead. By the late 1970s, Japan began structurally affecting a host of conventional industries, including automobiles, steel, and machine tools. In the 1980s, facing its own rising labor costs, Japan's position in the more labor-intensive conventional industries was ceded to countries like Korea, and Japan began to dominate a host of more technologically sensitive industries including semiconductors and telecommunications. Although the expansion of the Far Eastern economies was primarily at the expense of the Americans, Western Europe soon found many of its key industries under increasing pressure. In America, economic stagnation exacerbated by the growth of the export-driven Asians and debt-burdened South Americans was putting heavy strains on the world's leading economy. To make matters even worse, an unprecedented technological revolution was expanding commercially and changing production processes in some of the world's basic industries while at the same time fostering new high-technology industries. Change was inevitable. The only issue was how to manage that change.

In the United States, the economic upheavals of the late 1970s and early 1980s, in conjunction with the technological revolution, led to a massive debate about the management of United States business. The more libertarian element argued for a reduction in government interference in business and a changing of the tax structure. The more interventionist element emulated Japan's MITI and argued for the formulation of a United States industrial policy.

While Congress, the president, and academics debated, much of the change that was necessary was already under way. Corporations were challenging the regulatory structure both in Washington and through the courts. Businesses with antiquated capital and organizational structures were under severe pressure to restructure their operations or suffer the consequences. Within a few short years many corporations were reduced to mere vestiges of their former selves while others became stronger as a result of the trauma. The regulatory structures in telecommunications and airlines were virtually dismantled while the regulation of financial institutions rapidly eroded under competitive pressures. In addition, because of the mobility of the United States labor force, workers in declining industries or sections of the country soon found their way to jobs in more promising regions and industries.

The magnitude of this European decline can be seen most readily in figure 1–1. In terms of relative gross domestic product (GDP), the twelve countries of the EC accounted for slightly more than 40 percent of the Organization for Economic Cooperation and Development (OECD) plus Asian newly industrializing countries (NICs).[7] By 1985, this percentage had declined to slightly less than 30 percent, with the decline being shared by the United States, Japan, and the Asian NICs.[8] The 1970s and 1980s were a period of relative welfare decline for the countries of the EC.

In Europe, with its more rigid social structure and welfare programs and heavily regulated industrial sector, the rapidly changing world economy soon began putting heavy pressure on key sectors of the economy. But unlike the United States economy, particularly the labor sector, the European economies showed a noticeable lack of flexibility in adjusting. Evidence of this can be seen in figure 1–2. For some time, unemployment in the EC countries defied the downward trend evident elsewhere, most noticeably the United States. Although the unemployment rate in the United States was greater than the unemployment rate in the EC in the late 1970s, EC unemployment has been rising dramatically since then while United States unemployment has been declining.

Because of historical tendencies to protect jobs in sensitive sectors, European governments have relied to a great extent on the ability of the political sector to reduce the impact of strategic imports and protect the employment in and profitability of politically powerful industry groups. Such an expedient proved viable in the short term provided that the basic underlying structure of the economy was not changing. But, to make matters worse, the fundamental structure of the world economy was changing because the Japanese and U.S. economies were racing ahead in the key technologies that were becoming more and more essential to the everyday functioning of greater and greater numbers of components in the modern economy.

Many Euro-enthusiasts will remark that 1992 is just one more step in the evolution of closer European cooperation and that greater economic unification was not possible in the past because the economic system in Europe needed to mature further, pan-European institutions needed to be tested, and men of vision like

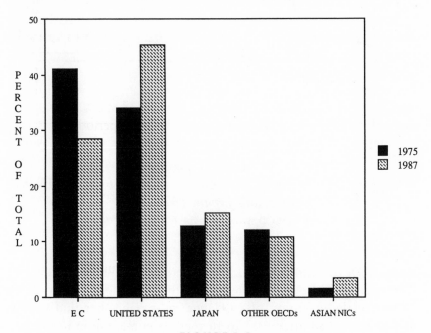

FIGURE 1–1

The Purchasing Power Equivalent Gross Domestic Product of the European Community, the United States, Japan, other OECDs, and the Asian NICs as a Percentage of the Total

Source: OECD, *Main Economic Indicators*, October 1986 and July 1989; IMF, *International Financial Statistics*, Annual Yearbook, December 1988; United Nations, *Statistical Yearbook*, 1985–86.

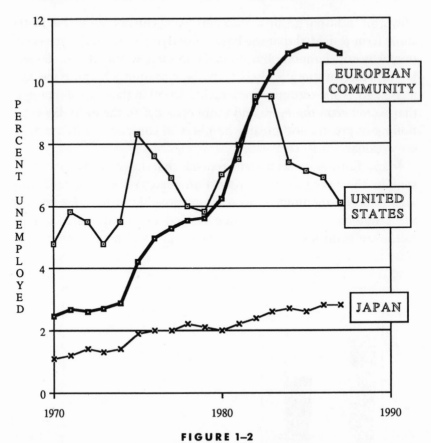

FIGURE 1–2

Unemployment Rates in the European Community, the United States, and Japan, 1970–1988

Source: OECD, *World Economic Outlook*, 1989.

Jacques Delors and Lord Cockfield were not available as catalysts. Although it is true that at the margin the role of past history plays a part in the evolution of 1992, we must remember that the EC bureaucracy had attempted to further economic union in the past only to find its aspirations dashed because of intercountry rivalry. In the thirty years of EC history, we have seen the unification game wax and wane. A program like 1992 was as feasible in 1969 or 1975 as it was in 1985. Indeed, when Lord Cockfield put his *White Paper* on the table in Brussels, public opinion was no more or less inclined to believe in a greater Europe (see chapter 4). While recognizing the importance of men and history in the details of 1992, the willingness of the member governments to back the vision of greater European integration is cold, calculated politics. In answer to our first question, why 1992 now, it should be acknowledged that *1992 is an outgrowth of European economic decline and a recognition that the root cause of that decline is similar across a major portion of the countries of the EC.* The 1992 program is, in the words of Carlo DiBenedetti, "a deadline not to be dead."[9]

But 1992 is more than just a knee-jerk reaction to the declining importance of the European market on the world scene. If the member states desired only to protect the principal sectors of the major economies and foster growth in certain key markets, many protectionist techniques exist that could solve the problem. Why choose a complicated process of economic unification that takes almost ten years to complete and requires many member states to alter the structure of their basic laws?

Why a Single Market?

As we previously remarked, the 1992 card is being played today because of the external pressure that stems from heightened competition on the world scene, but this alone does not imply that European countries need to remove barriers to trade across their own borders. Common external policies, or harmonized internal policies, could alone stem the flow of foreign goods. Indeed, 1992 has some aspect of this strategy in its structure, still, many heavily protected intracountry political interests have been sacrificed to promote "European unification." This policy implies that either individual member governments are willing to sacrifice internal political constituencies for external political benefits or that other internal interest groups are demanding that the government provide them with the opportunity to expand their "protected" market into other EC states. We argue for the latter.

Consider for a moment the EC report, *1992: The European Challenge,* by Paolo Cecchini and his associates. This report estimates that the economies of scale from a more integrated European market amount to approximately 4 to 7 percent of gross domestic product.[10] It is further shown that trucking and border restrictions cost European business approximately 15 billion European currency units (ECUs) ($13.6 billion and 3 percent of intra-Community trade).[11] If we believe that these economies of scale have not miraculously appeared in the last several years or that the value of the trucking restrictions has suddenly materialized, one is forced to ask the question, why did the restrictions exist in the first place and what has happened to cause governments to abandon them?

The answer should be clear. Banking restrictions that restrict the ability of banks to take advantage of existing economies of scale are meant to protect the banks and the banks' employees and perhaps to serve other political needs. Trucking restrictions are meant to protect the wages of the truckers and the profits of the trucking companies. If trucking restrictions are removed, as sensible as that may seem on the surface, it is because the trucking industry demands the change or because an alternative political coalition, more effective than the trucking industry, demands the change.

The structural aspect of 1992 is an outgrowth of the demand for change in the regulatory structure of Europe. The Single Europe Program is not regulation for the sake of some abstract "public interest," rather it is a reflection of a change in the demand for government regulation by specific powerful political and economic interests within the EC. Because this demand is pan-European the regulatory change demanded is pan-European.

Why would this demand for change in the regulatory structure exist? First, the changing structure of the world economy has neutralized the ability of many countries to protect sensitive industries. For example, the importance of computers in almost all aspects of business today makes it important that companies have access to state-of-the-art technology to be competitive on the world scene. If, because of weaknesses in its own computer industry, a country restricts the import of better computers from more efficient producers, the total economic cost may be too great. Although the restrictions may benefit the computer manufacturers within that country, the restrictions may hurt most every other sector of the economy, which would be forced to use substandard equipment or pay extremely high prices for quality equipment. All of a sudden, an attempt to protect the computer industry has caused banks, investment houses, and other industries relying on the availability of computer technology to fall behind foreign rivals who have better access to better technology. Such a scenario is more important today because of the growing importance of cross-border trade to the world's advanced economies and the inability to restrict efficiently many aspects of information technology.

Second, the technological changes of the 1970s and 1980s have caused many companies to outgrow the regulatory structure of their home countries. This trend is most evident in two areas: banking and investment, and product distribution. In banking and investment the role of technology has become of critical importance. In the space of ten years the flow of bank funds and trading activity has exploded because computers can handle transactions more quickly. This is most evident in the United States with the growth of superregional banks, although the structure of the banking industry has certainly been distorted by the haphazard nature of federal regulation.

In the capital markets, companies rely on their home markets for financing only if those markets are cheaper or if they are restricted by government policies. In retail product distribution, Europe can be a product manager's nightmare. The existing regulatory structures of the member states, erected as alternatives to the tariffs removed by the Treaty of Rome, make cross-border marketing tedious at best. Border delays, health restrictions with little to do with health, and the different company regulations on store hours and working conditions make pan-European operations difficult for many products.

Therefore, we can view the drive toward market unification as not so much a grand vision of a single Europe but as a reflection that the cost of doing business in twelve separate states with twelve regulatory structures has now become more costly than the market protection was worth. Note that we are not using the traditional EC line that there are Community-wide gains to be made by deregulating the Common Market. Those gains have existed for years and, although complaints existed, little was done to accommodate the inconvenienced. Given the changes in the underlying fundamental economics of doing business in the 1980s and beyond, demands for changes in regulation have arisen that could not be solved by any one country on its own. In the United States in the 1970s, the demand for regulatory change was being driven by the regulated, who found existing regulations more costly than a change in the regulatory structure even if the future brought greater competition from new entrants. The same is true in Europe today. *Nineteen ninety-two is a reflection of the fact that member state regulatory structures, which survived because of the benefits they provided for the regulated, are now more costly than a new regulatory structure. This new structure is pan-European because the root causes of the demand for this change, the external economic threat and the information technology revolution, are similar across the major European states.*

Is 1992 More than Just Reregulation?

It may appear that we are taking the Single Europe Program out of context by ignoring the fact that higher goals may be operating in its formulation and execution. The issues surrounding 1992 are certainly more complex than technology mixed with trade threats, yet these factors are the catalyst behind the program. Because the solution demands freer European trade, 1992 has, at least within the EC itself, a free trade dimension.

But 1992 has stronger global implications as well. The 1980s brought to the fore the relative economic decline of both the United States and Europe. But it is the decline of the relative power of the United States that has the more profound implications. Paul Kennedy notes in *The Rise and Fall of the Great Powers* that the relative decline of the United States is a reflection of a movement toward a more sustainable world economic equilibrium. It was simply inconceivable, says Kennedy, that with only 16 to 18 percent of the world's resources that the United States should hold 40 percent of the world's wealth.[12] Whether one agrees with Professor Kennedy's assertion that the United States' decline was inevitable and natural or whether one believes that collective human folly was the cause is not a matter of debate here. Whatever the reason, this relative decline has led to a power vacuum that the rising economic power, Japan, has shown itself either unwilling or unable to fill. The dollar is proving itself unsuitable for the role of major reserve currency and the United States' displeasure with its allies' economic and political behavior simply does not have the economic bite to match its bark.

One hears continuous mention of the power a single European market larger than either the United States or Japan could command. A market 320 million strong, if consistent in its policies to the rest of the world, would be a formidable voice, a voice that could conceivably be louder than both Japan and the United States. It is this opportunity to share world economic and political power that has the most appeal to outward-looking political leaders, because they want to change the rules of the world economic game to their liking. When the EC speaks of reciprocity and a single monetary union it is saying that it not only wants to play in the game but wants to write the rules as well.

The 1992 program is the EC's move in the process of filling the economic power vacuum left by the relative decline of the United States and the failure of Japan to fully assume the responsibilities of the number one economic power in the world.

A Brief Look at Post-1992 European Markets

What does the Single Market Program imply about the future of European markets? Generally speaking, European markets will take on more regional characteristics, much as in the United States, with the possibility of a heavy concentration occurring in specific sectors, such as banking and insurance. Non-European companies will be facing more, and increasing, pressure to invest directly in Europe rather than importing goods directly from non-Community production facilities.

It should be remembered that groups that can command strong political power within specific European countries will still have their voices heard. For example, the strength of the West German labor movement is not going to be attenuated because Spanish or newly liberated East European labor is cheaper. No German company would conceive of alienating itself from its workers by moving its production facilities to Spain. Yet should expansion be necessary, the company may consider Spain or Hungary an alternative. To this extent non-European multinational companies may have a comparative advantage in Eastern Europe and Spain since they carry less "national" baggage.

Because of high severance costs, European companies have great difficulty in downsizing. For this reason, the consolidation effect occurring in Europe will be scale enhancing. Restructuring in Europe will differ from that in America simply because it is so much more difficult to cut the fat out of an organization in Europe. This restructuring will prove interesting because on the one hand we hear continual discussion of the fragmented European market and how European companies cannot expand to the scale required to compete against the American and Japanese giants, but, on the other hand, the EC argues for a commitment to competition that may be inconsistent with allowing a smaller number of European champions to dominate EC markets. At what point does scale for external competition become monopoly at home? EC estimates of the gains resulting from integration implicitly assume that cost reductions will flow toward the consumer, but it is quite possible that the consolidation in specific industries could force prices up rather than down.

The key to understanding the structure of post-1992 European markets is recognizing that the primary financial, technological, and scientific industries will be the major beneficiaries of the Single Europe Program, because they are the catalysts behind the changes. Other industries that require the same types of regulations as these primary industries will see some spillover. For example, markets that are affected by distribution restrictions will also see some potential gains because the ability to centralize distribution will reduce the necessity of maintaining inefficient distribution centers. The major losers from 1992 will be the older industries that have lost their political power, such as steel, coal, and trucking, and those foreign corporations that will be forced to invest directly in certain European industries simply to satisfy regulatory restrictions that are meant to protect sensitive sectors Europe-wide.

Overall, post-1992 European markets will probably be no more or less competitive from the consumer's perspective. It is quite possible, indeed, that in specific sectors, consumers might find themselves facing pan-European or regional monopolists rather than their old national champions. In terms of world trade, 1992 will mark the completion of a tripolar economic world. This may not prove troublesome for the United States with its substantial and established European ties, but 1992 represents the threat of closing off potential trade for Japan and the Asian newly industrializing countries (NICs). Japan, with its substantial cash resources, could obviously play according to the new European rules and invest directly in Europe. For Japan, 1992 could be viewed as a strange sort of European tax, but for countries like Korea, Taiwan, and Brazil that are unable to directly invest in Europe and rely on their ability to undercut the competition through low wages, 1992 could prove devastating.

A Final Comment

The Single Europe Program is, first and foremost, a drive toward greater economic power on the part of the EC countries; as such, it must be recognized as a battle against the growing economic powers of the Far East. Nineteen ninety-two grew out of the economic malaise that affected Europe throughout the 1970s and early 1980s, which has grown critical in an ever more quickly evolving economic world. The pressure for political change in Eastern European countries was due, in large part, to the inability of their centrally planned industrial economies to compete with the world's emerging information and technological economies. Just as in Western Europe (although to a considerably greater degree), this growing disparity led to pressure for political change. The difference between the two cases is the source of the pressure for change. In Western Europe, it came from commercial interests; in Eastern Europe, it came directly from the populace.

Yet 1992 is also a uniquely European endeavor. It is interesting to compare 1992 to the experience in the United States over the last several years. The restructuring wave in the United States and its integration into a more open world economy was not easy and ultimately proceeded in spite of, rather than with the help of, the federal government. In Europe, because the role of government in the affairs of business is so much more pervasive, it is no wonder that restructuring requires "reciprocity" and "harmonization" put into operation through three hundred–odd directives. Nineteen ninety-two can be Europe's economic renaissance, but it will neither occur at the expense of national champions nor run counter to the social dimension that Europeans so strongly endorse. Nineteen ninety-two will leave Europe "different, but the same."

A History of the European Community and an Overview of Its Institutions

[It is desired to] . . . substitute for age-old rivalries the merger of their essential interests; to create, by establishing an economic Community, the basis for a broader and deeper community among peoples long divided by bloody conflicts; and to lay the foundations for institutions which will give direction to a destiny henceforward shared.

—*Preamble*, European Coal and Steel Community Treaty

To conclude that the present drive toward European economic and political integration exemplified by the Single Europe Program is solely a contemporary idea would be an error. Although modern mass communication and the increased importance of world trade, along with heightened global awareness, have brought the world closer together, thereby increasing the significance of recent European events to individuals in North and South America and Asia, 1992 is still only one of many historical attempts aimed at unifying Europe. Because the forces that have shaped the present developments have a historical background they cannot be ignored.

Earlier Historical Efforts toward a Unified Europe

For centuries, the quest for a greater Europe was nothing more than a drive for empire. As great rulers came and went, the momentum toward a more unified Europe rose and fell. From the early empires of Rome and Charlemagne, perhaps the most successful and sustaining instances of a single Europe, European unification was a reflection of realpolitik driven by the desire of the nobility to control the primary economic resources of the day, the land and the people. Because of the primitive nature of trade at this time, unification to expand the economic well-being of the state, independent of the ruling class, was of minor importance. Early European alliances did not reflect joint economic and trade interests but were primitive responses to threats to peace or power from outside invaders or alternative political alliances.

Although rulers recognized valid military reasons for unification, they were also aware of the purely economic justifications of increased factor mobility and more efficient tax collection and also desired to expand jurisdictional authority from a local to a national structure. For example, the fifteenth and sixteenth centuries saw French and English monarchs with mercantilistic inclinations attempting to modernize their parochial feudal fiefdoms into true nation-states. One of the major problems with the feudal structure was the multiple and haphazard tax system exemplified by the tolls that nobles and towns charged for the use of nearby roads and rivers. Monarchs attempted to eliminate these tolls and tariffs to foster freer trade within their domains and control the tax revenues derived from the tolls. They, in turn, placed highly protectionist policies at the national level and sold off monopoly rights to companies giving them control of lucrative trade routes.

France was not as successful in its elimination of internal tolls and trade restrictions as was Britain. It was not until the French Revolution that a successful break with the past system was accomplished, even though early attempts were made by Louis XIV and Colbert through economic unification and transport improvements. Because the change to an effective national jurisdiction was much more successful in England, it was the first nation in Europe to establish a nationwide market of relatively free trade.[1]

The greatest single factor in the ongoing development toward a more unified Europe was the spread of the Industrial Revolution. The division of labor and the creation of specialized production facilities created an interdependence among the European countries that continues today. Unlike culturally or politically driven unification efforts, economically driven endeavors like the Industrial Revolution were nation neutral.

The countries affected in succession by the Industrial Revolution did not industrialize independently, growing like plants in separate flower pots. Their transformation was a single process, the changes in each depending on the stages reached by the others, on the supplies, technologies and markets of its neighbors and the development of the world outside Europe. Though many experiences of industrialization recurred again and again in recognizable patterns, the whole process represented a unique phase in the history of the world.[2]

In the early stages of industrialization there was a growing interdependence among countries within Europe. The lure of exports on the horizon enticed industrially developing countries into new industries and also spread the knowledge of production methods and new product discoveries to other countries, which, in turn, fostered new industries in yet other countries. This process of spreading industrialization, beginning first in England and France, was the main force behind the transmission of knowledge and the economic power of industrialization from one country to neighboring regions and eventually overseas. The abundance of both natural and manmade seaports as well as the affordable cost of water transport created an economical means of product distribution throughout the world.

The three phases of the Industrial Revolution show a natural progression toward a more economically integrated Europe. From 1825 to the mid–nineteenth century, the dominant economic power was Britain. In the period 1816–22, continental Europe purchased almost 60 percent of Britain's total exports; in the period after 1829, it continued to absorb 51 percent of Britain's exports.[3]

As the industries of Britain expanded onto the continent, a number of industrial centers arose in those countries possessing the resources to provide the initial support for modern industry, and they, too, began to reap the benefits of Britain's success. These new industrial centers soon began to use their available technology, capital, and entrepreneurial and skilled labor to provide goods for less developed regions and even began to contest Britain in certain industrial areas.

Far from killing all native manufacture, therefore, Britain called forth a great deal of complementary industrial capacity, of the domestic type in the first instance, while also laying the solid foundations for later mechanization and at the same time encouraging the creation of vital social overhead capital, and of new markets in the east, as western Europe was being flooded by Britain. Continental industrialists [learned] to live with the new conditions, and to use them as springboards for the next stage. As long as the industrialized centre—in this early phase, Britain almost exclusively—was willing to permit imports to flow in and capital to flow out, the virtuous circle of mutual stimulation and economic growth could continue.[4]

From approximately 1850 until 1873 the second and probably the fastest period of European industrial expansion and investment took place. Britain altered its focus from the European continent toward overseas markets such as the United States, Australia, and India. During this period British exports to continental Europe fell from 50 percent in 1850 to 40 percent in 1870–74.[5] Even though there was a marked shift in British trade orientation toward the infant world market, it by no means meant that Britain was abandoning the European continent and the development of other industrial growth centers across the European continent.

In the period 1873 to 1914, developments of a different sort began to take shape. In addition to trade in manufactured goods, European countries began to export the capital equipment necessary to produce those goods. As more and more countries entered common arenas of production, economic centers throughout the continent and in the United States were beginning to compete directly with the dominant British industrial machine. The turn of the century brought greater competition between the budding industrial powers, but it also reflected a growing economic interdependence.

> Germany sent to Britain much semi-manufactured steel, and also many sophisticated machines, while Britain sent to Germany finished products. Germany sent electrical machinery to Britain, while importing British agricultural and textile machinery. Britain exported finer textiles, Germany coarser textiles, also cheap watches and clocks—while Switzerland exported expensive ones. More recently industrialized nations, like Italy and Spain, exported textiles; Sweden exported steel and timber. Not only did this trade in manufactures among the industrialized nations form a major component of world trade; it was also growing faster over much of the period than was the trade in food and raw materials, in spite of growing protectionism. By 1913 the commodity trade between the seven European industrialized countries—Britain, France, Germany, Belgium, Italy, Austria and

Switzerland—represented fully one-third of world commodity trade, and of their own exports 51 percent went to each other.[6]

The onset of World War I and the subsequent turbulent period between the wars effectively ended the economic symbiosis that the prior century had fostered, leaving Europe significantly less economically integrated than might have been predicted. As the world slipped into depression in the 1930s, free trade and economic interaction was forced aside by a wave of protectionism.

Establishment of the European Economic Community

The Postwar Move toward Greater Cooperation

Although we have seen that history is not without efforts to unify greater portions of Europe, it was not until the post-1945 period that forces converged to set the foundation stones for what is today the EC.

Europe was ravaged both economically and psychologically by World War II. The catastrophic losses in manpower and potential opportunities left both victor and vanquished exhausted. In the words of Dennis Swann, professor of economics at Loughborough University, the mood was one wherein "those who sought, and still seek, a united Europe, have always had at the forefront of their minds the desire to prevent any further outbreak of war in Europe."[7] To many, only further cooperation among the European states could resurrect the economies of Europe. Furthermore, the European continent was a living example of the post-1945 bipolar world. Because Europe was the potential battleground between the United States and the USSR, it was no wonder that Europeans felt the need for a collective voice. Only through unification could they rebuild Europe economically, create an interdependence that they hoped would prevent another war, and establish themselves as a voice among the other major powers.

On May 9, 1946, this desire for unification was verbalized by Sir Winston Churchill in a speech before the States General of the Netherlands.

I see no reason why, under the guardianship of the world organization, there should not ultimately arise the United States of Europe, both those of the East and those of the West which will unify this Continent in a manner never known since the fall of the Roman Empire, and within which all its peoples may dwell together in prosperity, in justice and in peace.[8]

Although the postwar mood was one of cooperation, the United States provided an additional incentive for mutual economic cooperation through the auspices of the Marshall Plan. Originally, the United States hoped that the Economic Commission for Europe (ECE) could play a role in channeling Marshall Plan funds.[9] The possibility of ECE Marshall fund management ended when Eastern bloc countries objected to the idea for fear that such aid would allow Western influence into their fledgling Communist states. This division led to the establishment of the Organization for European Economic Cooperation (OEEC), which also satisfied the American requirement that those countries receiving aid establish a cooperative organization to manage the resources and develop a common economic policy.[10]

In September of 1950, Robert Schuman, the French minister of foreign affairs, proposed the establishment of a European organization to pool and centralize the production and consumption of coal and steel. The European Coal and Steel Community (ECSC) would be open to all European countries but was initially established to coordinate French and German steel and coal production. Formally established by the Treaty of Paris (also known as the ECSC Treaty) on April 18, 1951, by France, Germany, Italy, Belgium, the Netherlands, and Luxembourg, the ECSC was, in actuality, more than simply an industrial protection package with rosy language about a greater Europe. The ECSC's four decision-making bodies, the High Authority, the Council of Ministers, the Court of Justice, and the Parliamentary Assembly, would ultimately provide the institutional structure for the future European Economic Community.

The increasing East-West tensions of the early postwar period heightened the perceived need for closer political and military cooperation in Western Europe, leading to the formulation of the European Defense Community (EDC) and the European Political Community (EPC). The purpose of the EDC was to integrate the armed forces of Europe and strengthen the Atlantic alliance. The

EPC, a logical outgrowth of the EDC, was designed to complement military integration through political integration and envisioned a democratically controlled European army. The EDC Treaty was a massive integration effort and was intended to merge the ECSC, the EDC, and the EPC to form a new organization containing a parliament, a council of ministers, and a court of justice. But this level of integration was not to be seen. Although five national parliaments accepted the treaty, the French government, the initial proposer of the union, found itself unable to generate support within the National Assembly and the treaty died.[11]

With the demise of the EDC and the general frustrations surrounding the OEEC, it became clear that the political sentiment at the time would not permit the complete military, political, and economic union that many statesmen would have liked to see. For European unification to proceed, the steps would have to be small, with specialized agreements substituting for grand plans. Despite rhetoric to the contrary, European leaders remained particularly committed to the well-being of their own nations regardless of the implications for greater European unity. The Treaty of Rome would be a reflection of this more refined and pragmatic approach.[12]

The Treaty of Rome and the Establishment of the European Community

In June 1955, the foreign ministers of France, Germany, Italy, Belgium, the Netherlands, and Luxembourg met at Messina, Italy, to try to continue their efforts to establish closer European cooperation. Because of the negative response to the EDC, the union would be established on economic terms. An intergovernmental committee was established under the chairmanship of the Belgian statesman Paul-Henri Spaak to investigate the feasibility of a European union in nuclear energy development and the prospects for a broader economic union between the six ECSC nations. The Spaak Report was later approved by the six nations, and they began to iron out the details for the formation of a European Common Market.

The Messina conference was both a reflection of the desire for greater European cooperation and an unveiling of the divisions over how far that cooperation should go. Britain, expressing its preferences for a free-trade area over a pan-European cooperative organization, was noticeably absent from the conference. Along with Sweden, Switzerland, Denmark, Norway, Portugal, and Austria, Britain would put its view of European cooperation into operation with the founding of the European Free Trade Association (EFTA) in 1960.

The ultimate outgrowth of the Messina conference was the signing of the Treaty of Rome on March 25, 1957, by the six signatories of the Treaty of Paris. The Treaty of Rome altered the institutions of the ECSC and established the European Economic Community (EEC) and the European Atomic Energy Community (EURATOM). The purpose of the Treaty of Rome was the expansion of the expressed ideals of the ECSC treaty, which consisted of

- the dissolution of barriers dividing Europe,
- the improvement and equalization of living and working standards,
- the abolition of restrictions on international trade,
- the removal of obstacles to concerted action among governments, and
- strengthening the cause of peace and liberty through closer relations between states.

Initially the Community narrowly pursued a common commercial policy that would place foreign and domestic policy at the control of the sovereign states. But, the language of the treaty was sufficiently vague to allow the EEC to evolve into a body that could address noneconomic social and political issues, should the member states consider such cooperation beneficial in the future.

The immediate objectives of the Common Market were

- to provide uniform customs duties for goods that enter any member state from outside the Community (part 2, title 1);
- to eliminate quota restrictions, customs duties, and equivalent taxes on inter-EEC, cross-border goods (part 2, title 1);
- to abolish restrictions on the free movement of community citizens, services, and capital (part 2, title 3);
- to permit any firm to operate in any member state in the community subject to equivalent laws and taxes (part 2, title 2, chapter 2);

- to prevent governments from giving advantages to their home businesses over and above the advantages given to non–home country businesses (part 3, title 1, chapter 1); and
- to establish common transport and agricultural policies.[13]

The Treaty of Rome further specified that the Community form systems to enhance competition and coordinate member state economic policies, expressed a hope for further approximation of member state laws, and established the European Social Fund (ESF) and the European Investment Bank (EIB).

The 1960s saw the expansion of the power of the EEC bureaucracy as it slowly instituted the regulations stipulated by the Treaty of Rome. In 1962, the Common Agricultural Policy (CAP) was born. Based on the expressed principles of the "establishment of a single market and consequently of common prices for most agricultural products; the assurance that those working in agriculture will enjoy a standard of living comparable to that enjoyed by workers in other sectors; preference for Community produce; financial solidarity through a European Agricultural Guidance and Guarantee Fund (EAGGF),"[14] the CAP was, and remains, nothing more than a subsidy program. Perhaps unbeknownst to the initial signatories of the Treaty or the Brussels bureaucrats who developed the program, agriculture commitments would soon grow to 75 percent of the budget of the EEC. By 1968, the common external tariff was established and the last vestiges of intra-EEC tariff restrictions were removed, thus completing the primary initial goal of the EEC to remove tariffs between member states.

Changes within the European Community

Since its inception, the Common Market has undergone a number of important changes, the most notable of which has been its expansion. In 1962, just two years after the formation of its brainchild the EFTA, Great Britain applied to join the EEC, only to be rebuffed through the efforts of French president de Gaulle.

De Gaulle's opposition, although expressed in terms of the need to complete the formative stages of economic consolidation between the EC-6 (the original six EC countries), was primarily based on the fear that France would lose dominance within the Community. Britain tried for membership again in 1967, once more to no avail. Only in 1970, in conjunction with applications from Norway, Denmark, and Ireland, was Britain's application accepted for full consideration. Charles de Gaulle had stepped down from the French presidency in April 1969, and the primary barrier to Britain's ascension was gone. Negotiations were lengthy, but in January of 1973, Britain, Ireland, and Denmark became members. A referendum was held in Norway to determine the fate of its application to the EEC. To the consternation of the Norwegian government, membership was rejected by slightly more than 53 percent of the voting population. The EC-9 (the EC-6 plus Britain, Ireland, and Denmark) was expanded again in 1980 with the admission of Greece and ultimately reached its current total of twelve with the admission of Portugal and Spain in 1986. Recently, Austria and Turkey applied for admission, but their applications have been rejected as untimely given the Community's preoccupation with the Single Europe Program.

In 1969, amendments to the various treaties established more formally the present-day structure and authority of the EC by merging the three existing communities—ECSC, EEC, and EURATOM—into one, and the post-1969 structure is very similar to the ECSC structure. It consists of a council of ministers, a commission of country-appointed representatives, a parliament, and a court of justice. The 1969 reforms simply served to consolidate a decision-making process that had become needlessly duplicated.

The path and momentum toward the Community's present structure and statement of purpose changed substantially as underlying motivations or advantages to a new structure came into play. In the formative years, memories of recent war provided a lubricant to enable many ends to be accomplished. France's leadership role, although put to the test on several occasions in the 1960s, was uncontested within the Community during this period. The 1970s brought Britain into the Community and the beginning of the end of French dominance. The British were satisfied to be in the EC at last but were unsatisfied from the beginning about the conditions of their entrance, that is, the high budgetary commitment required of them. The German economy raced ahead of its Community neighbors and soon became the dominant economy of the Community. To make matters worse, the 1970s saw a resurgence of protectionist measures aimed at replacing the tariffs removed in the late 1960s. Intracountry political circumstances caused the EC to stagnate in the 1970s and early 1980s as the British complained about the EC budget, the Germans urged Community governments to follow more conservative economic policies, and everyone complained about quotas, voluntary export restraints, country-specific product standards, and agriculture subsidies. Only with the resurgence of the world economy and the recognition of the failure of the socialist experiment in many European countries was the EC able to begin again its attempt to achieve greater European economic union.

EC Institutions—Structure and Operation

The EC has four primary institutions with several secondary agencies or committees attached. The *European Council* is the principal decision-making body of the Community. It is administratively assisted by the Council of Permanent Representatives (COREPER). The *European Commission* is responsible for formulating the specific policies of the EC, and its recommendations must ultimately be decided upon by the Council. The *European Parliament* is the sitting assembly of representatives from the member states. Unlike traditional legislatures, its decision-making powers are extremely limited. The *European Court of Justice* is responsible for adjudicating disagreements between parties and determining whether the member state laws are in compliance with EC law.

Two subsidiary organizations are worthy of mention. The *Economic and Social Committee (ESC)* is an advisory body of representatives from interest groups—employers, workers, consumers, and academics—within the member states. Composed of 189 representatives,[15] the ESC is required to submit an opinion on all matters that the Commission is putting forward to the Council. The *Court of Auditors* has responsibility for auditing the Community budget and providing opinions on the financial impact of legislation. Its investigative powers extend to any member state or to any country receiving Community aid. The workings of the primary institutions of the EC are shown in figure 2–1.

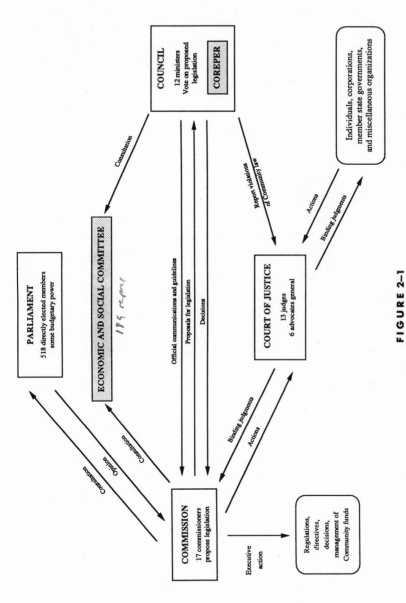

FIGURE 2-1

Institutions and Operations of the European Community

Source: Adapted from Drew, J., *Doing Business in the EEC* (Boston: Butterworths, 1979).

The European Commission

The European Commission is the primary operating body of the EC. It is responsible for the day-to-day operations of the EC bureaucracy and holds the sole right to propose legislation. Composed of seventeen commissioners, each nominated by his or her national government subject to approval of the Council, the Commission is responsible for

- ensuring that the provisions of the Treaty of Rome are adhered to,
- formulating recommendations and delivering opinions on matters dealing with the treaties,
- formulating decisions on and participating in the shaping of measures taken by the Council and by the Parliament, and
- exercising the powers conferred on it by the Council for implementing the rules laid down by the Council.[16]

Although nominated by their home governments, the commissioners are expected to act as independent individuals and not national representatives. The number of commissioners from each country is weakly based on population. France, Germany, Italy, Spain, and the United Kingdom each have two commissioners, and all other countries have one.

The Commission is headed by a president who is selected by the Council nominees. By law the president serves a term of two years, although it is most common for the term to be extended to four years so that it remains parallel with the term of the Commission as a whole. The president of the Commission bears the task of dividing responsibilities among the commissioners based on qualifications and political considerations. Each commissioner receives specific responsibilities and is effectively the EC minister for those areas, interacting directly with one or more of the Commission's twenty-two directorate generals. The Commission directorate generals are shown in table 2–1.

All binding EC decisions initially come from the Commission. The Council of Ministers, or European Council, can act only on formal proposals submitted to it from the Commission. What proposals to make and when to submit them is entirely up to the Commission. The Commission also carries out certain other activities by

TABLE 2-1

Directorates of the European Commission

Directorate Number (DG)	Directorate Responsibility
I	External relations
II	Economic and financial affairs
III	Internal market and industrial affairs
IV	Competition
V	Employment, social affairs, and education
VI	Agriculture
VII	Transport
VIII	Development
IX	Personnel and administration
X	Information, communication, and culture
XI	Environment, consumer protection, and nuclear safety
XII	Science, research and development
XIII	Telecommunications, information industries, and innovation
XIV	Fisheries
XV	Financial institutions and company law
XVI	Regional policy
XVII	Energy
XVIII	Credit and investments
XIX	Budgets
XX	Financial control
XXI	Customs union and indirect taxation
XXII	Coordination of structural instruments

the authority of the Council or provisions within the EC treaties.[17] Most recently, the Single European Act has assigned to the Commission primary executive powers including the issuance of directives and regulations that implement treaty and Council guidelines (see chapter 3).

The Commission has the responsibility of administering Community funds. The four major Community funds are the European Social Fund (ESF), aimed at improving employment opportunities within the EC, the European Agricultural Guidance and Guarantee Fund (EAGGF), the agriculture subsidy and price support system, the European Regional Development Fund (ERDF), which is responsible for providing infrastructure funds to less developed areas of the Community, and the European Development Fund (EDF), which is the foreign aid arm of the EC.

The Commission is the principal watchdog of the EC, ensuring that the terms of the treaties and measures agreed upon are carried out through EC institutions and by member states. When a transgression of EC law is at issue, based either on Commission concerns or because of evidence brought to their attention by a member state, corporation, or private individual, the Commission can initiate an investigation. If some party has indeed committed an infringement of EC law, the Commission will ask that party's home country to submit comments on the practice in question. If the Commission cannot be persuaded that the practice does not violate the common treaties or subsequent agreements, then it will issue a reasoned opinion. If the member state does not comply or force the party in question to comply within a deadline specified in the opinion, the Court of Justice will be asked to rule on the matter. The subsequent ruling has binding power on all parties involved. According to EC statistics, "In 1987 . . . the Commission instituted infringement proceedings in 572 cases, issued 197 reasoned opinions and referred 61 cases to the Court [of Justice]. . . . [Fifteen percent] of [the] cases involve[d] infringements of the rules either on the free movement of agriculture and industrial products or, to a lesser extent, on Community arrangements for farm products."[18] Over 70 percent of the infringements have been based on incorrect incorporation of Community directives or the failure to incorporate at all.[19]

To ensure a close relationship with the governments of member states, the Commission must solicit the opinions of three independent committees composed of home government representatives. These committees allow close consultation with member state governments and provide a means whereby member state lobbying can occur.

The first and least influential type of committee is an *advisory committee*. The opinions of an advisory committee are not binding, but the Commission is obligated to take notice of the views expressed. Advisory committees are primarily used in decisions involving the management of funds and in matters addressing the completion of the internal market.

Management committees are slightly more influential than advisory committees and were established to deal with issues relating to agriculture. Different management committees are formed to handle different issues before the Commission. Each management committee conveys its opinion on its assigned issue by a formal vote using a qualified majority procedure. Although the Commission is not compelled to act in a manner consistent with the committee's opinion, it is strongly obligated to take note of the opinion. If, by chance, the Commission's measure goes counter to the majority vote of the committee, then the measure must be referred to the Council. The Council can either reverse or agree with the Commission's original proposal either by a positive vote or by not acting on the measure within a month.

The *regulatory committees* are responsible for issues related to the management of the Common Customs Tariff and the adoption of common Community standards on items such as veterinary and plant health regulations. These committees are similar in influence and powers to management committees but have greater powers of appeal to the Council.

The Council of Ministers

The European Council is made up of the government ministers of member states and serves as the chief decision-making body of the EC. Although the primary representative of a government to the Council is the foreign minister, which minister is present at a specific Council meeting is a function of the topic currently being debated. For example, if the issue on the table were coordination of monetary policy, all the finance ministers would be present; if it were agricultural subsidies, the agriculture ministers would be present; and if it were air transport, the transportation ministers would be present.

Today Council matters are determined by a qualified majority vote (see chapter 3). In the past, voting was on either a simple majority basis or a unanimity basis. The Treaty of Rome specified that Council voting would require unanimity on almost all issues over a transition period ending in 1966. After the transition period, voting would be almost exclusively on a simple majority basis. This precipitated a crisis in the Community when the French refused to permit a majority vote it disliked to be binding on itself. The member governments reached an agreement known as the Luxembourg Compromise, which specified that a state could retain veto power when it felt that its national interests were at issue.

The Council is headed by a chair, or president, which rotates every six months, the order of the rotation being determined by the alphabetical order of the countries in their own language. During those six months, that representative is the de facto leader of the EC, speaking on its behalf and determining the agenda of the Commission and the Council.

In general, the Commission seeks to uphold the matters of concern to the Community, while the Council is responsible for voicing the individual member states' point of view. The Commission is responsible for drafting a proposal, which is then submitted to the Council for discussion. The Council can only deliberate on the proposal as given, and the Commission has the power to remove a proposal from consideration. The Council has two choices: it can adopt the Commission's proposal as written by a qualified majority, or it can reject or modify the Commission's proposal by unanimity. The most the Council can accomplish by majority vote is acceptance of the proposal as originally written by the Commission.

The Commission and the Council deliberate and pass several different types of legislation, and the importance and strength of that legislation is dictated by the treaty under which they are operating. Within the confines of the Treaty of Paris, the Commission can make "decisions," which are the strongest form of judgment, "recommendations," which are the next strongest, and "opinions," which have the least impact. Under the Treaty of Rome, the Council and Commission create "regulations," which are very general but binding on the member states, "directives," which are narrower in scope in that they identify the required accomplishment but do not generally dictate the method to achieve the end, and "decisions," which are in reference to a particular member state, organization, or individual.

The European Parliament

The Treaty of Rome originally established the Assembly, which was later renamed the *European Parliament*. Until 1979, the parliamentary representatives were determined by the member state parliaments from a list submitted by the government. After that date, European MPs were determined by direct election using each state's national electoral system. The European Parliament consists today of 518 Euro-MPs who are presided over by a president and fourteen vice presidents. The distribution of seats by country is shown in table 2–2.

The European Parliament does not consist of national groups but of Community-level political groups. The major political alliances (from "left" to "right") are the Communist and Allies group (7.9 percent of the 1990 Parliament), the Socialist group (40 percent), the Rainbow group (7.5 percent), the group of the European People's Party (a Christian Democratic group, 5.2 percent), the group of the European Democratic Alliance (1.3 percent), the Liberal and Democratic Reform group (5.2 percent), the European Democratic

TABLE 2-2

Country Representation in the European Parliament

	Euro-MPs
Belgium	4
Denmark	16
Germany	81
France	81
Greece	24
Ireland	15
Italy	81
Luxembourg	6
Netherlands	25
Portugal	24
Spain	60
United Kingdom	81

group (6.6 percent), and the group of the European Right (4.2 percent). These individual groups generally do not represent any one government and arise primarily to gain access to EC political funds.

The Parliament's principal responsibilities are to oversee the European Commission and to vote on the EC budget. In monitoring the Commission the Parliament attempts to ensure that its specific constituencies' interests are upheld and that lobbying interests of individual governments do not dominate Commission decisions. Most of the oversight activity is handled by the eighteen standing committees that prepare the work for the plenary sessions. The decisions of the Commission are communicated to the committees through a member of the Commission or a Commission representative. The committees bear the responsibility of writing the Parliament's opinions on Commission proposals.

Parliament has both direct and indirect influence over the Community's budget. It can propose modifications to the budget submitted by the Commission and on rare occasions has vetoed the budget altogether, which occurred in 1979 and 1985 with respect to the entire budget, in 1980 with a draft budget, and in 1982 with a supplementary budget. The Parliament cannot increase Community expenditures and has direct control over only the portion that is not a consequence of EC legislation. Its budgetary discretion is generally limited to the 20 to 30 percent of the budget related to matters such as administrative and operational costs.

As we will discuss in the next chapter, the Single European Act increased the balance of power between the Parliament and the Council by conferring the "power of assent" on the Parliament, thereby giving it more of a joint decision-making role. The act also established a procedure of cooperation in qualified majority decisions dealing with social policy, the internal market, economic and social cohesion, and research. Under the new procedures, the Commission continues in its chief role as drafter of legislation, but the Parliament now has more direct influence over decisions with the understanding that the ultimate decision still rests with the Council.

The European Court of Justice

The European Court of Justice consists of thirteen judges assisted by six advocates general. Each judge is appointed to a renewable six-year term, and the terms are staggered to ensure a partial replacement of the Court every three years. From among their members, the judges select a president who is responsible for directing the Court's work much like the chief justice of the Supreme Court in the United States. The advocates general provide reasoned submissions on cases that are heard by the Court.

There are four types of proceedings that the Court of Justice hears: "proceedings against a Member State for failure to fulfill an obligation, proceedings for annulment, proceedings against an institution for failure to act, proceedings to establish liability and references for a preliminary ruling."[20] In addition, member governments and national courts can request a preliminary ruling to determine whether their laws or regulations are consistent with Community law or to clarify or interpret some specific aspect of that law.

When a member state fails to fulfill an obligation it is beholden on the Commission, as guardian of the treaties, to act on the issue, but member states, corporations, and private citizens have the right to bring these violations to the attention of the Commission. The Commission requests the member state to submit its comments regarding the violation and then, in turn, issues a reasoned opinion. If the member state in question does not act on the opinion within a reasonable period of time, the issue may be taken to the Court of Justice for further action.

If the Court, after hearing the case, determines that the case is well founded, the member state authorities are required to take necessary actions to comply with the Court's decision. If the matter involves the member state's domestic laws, those authorities responsible for the legislation are expected to amend the member state's laws to conform with the Community's laws. The member state's court has an obligation to see that the judgment is observed.

Conclusion

The history of the EC has been a slow political recognition of the natural drive toward commercial cooperation between the states of Europe. This historical progression, although recognizable in early attempts at papal dominance and military conquest, accelerated in the nineteenth century with the onset of the Industrial Revolution.

Since that time, natural economies have served to drive the economies of Europe closer together.

But, in spite of this tendency, the European states represent unique and separate political, cultural, and social organisms. The nature of present-day EC institutions is itself a reflection of this fact. The European Parliament is weak because a strong pan-European Parliament would compete with national assemblies to satisfy the needs of local interest groups. The Commission, although theoretically independent of the political leanings of the home governments, is a reflection of their viewpoints. Therefore, it is expected that EC proposals will generally be in line with the collective philosophy of the governments of the member states. This does not mean, of course, that individual member state governments may not disagree with the collective philosophy of the Community, as appears to be the case with the current British administration. The ultimate decision-making authority of the Council serves to solidify the ability of the member state governments to direct EC policy. Perhaps the one wild card in the EC bureaucracy is the Court of Justice. As the most independent body with substantive influence, it has the potential to force EC and member state policy to match the letter of the law. As we will see in the next chapter, it is this aspect of the Court that makes it, at times, much more of a free-trade advocate than the EC in general.

3

The Single European Act and the Single Market Program

[We] are determined to improve the economic and social situation by extending common policies and pursuing new objectives, and to ensure a smoother functioning of the Communities by enabling the institutions to exercise their power under conditions most in keeping with Community interests.

—*Preamble,* Single European Act

Before the Single European Act

Since its inception, the EC had always failed to satisfy those wanting to see more comprehensive European integration. After the removal of internal tariffs in 1968, the EC went through something of an identity crisis; becoming more consumed in minor internal disputes over budgetary and agriculture issues and institutional reforms, it watched while European economic performance fell behind its primary rivals. This period of Euro-sclerosis and Euro-pessimism led many to conclude that the European Community was, if not dead, as good as dead. Yet even during this period of internal dispute and economic malaise, some European statesmen still held out the vision of a greater Europe.

As early as 1961, a draft treaty for a European union was an issue of discussion before the European Parliament. The Fouchet Committee's recommendation for forming a European confederation, although approved by the Parliament, was recognized by most as an attempt by de Gaulle to increase French political power in Europe, and the proposal died quietly in April 1962.[1]

The 1970s saw several further attempts at more complete European market integration. The Werner Plan of 1970 called for greater harmonization of economic, fiscal, and monetary policies between the member states and ultimately led to the formation of the European currency unit (ECU) and the European monetary system (EMS) (see chapter 5). The Vedel Report of 1972 proposed an increase in the authority of the European Parliament and Tindeman's Report of 1976 called for a European union within four years. Both reports proposed that the Parliament be granted authority over legislation, and Tindeman's proposal went so far as to argue for a common foreign policy and pan-European social and industrial policies. The value of the Tindeman's Report was its recognition that greater European union required a rethinking of the EC and its institutions as opposed to the fragmentary historical evolution that had been seen in the 1960s and 1970s.[2] Both reports were discussed by the Council but never formally acted upon. Finally, in 1979, the report of the "Three Wise Men" discussed the impact of the expansion of the EC to include the Mediterranean states on the operations of the existing EC institutions.

In spite of the obvious good intentions involved, these initiatives led to very little substantive change within the Community and obvious frustration from those looking for Community reform. On July 9, 1980, Altiero Spinelli held a meeting with eight other members of the European Parliament, known as the "crocodile group," to discuss the development of a plan for European union. By July 1981, the group had the power to convince the European Parliament to pass a resolution forming a committee with the expressed task of drafting proposed modifications to the existing treaties with the aim of furthering European union.

The outcome of this endeavor, "The Draft Treaty on European Union," was a comprehensive document that attempted to alleviate the piecemeal historical aspects of the institutions of the EC. The committee achieved this end by going beyond its original charge of looking only at amendments to existing treaties and starting from scratch. The Draft Treaty on European Union's major contribution was its proposal to alter the decision-making authority of the various EC institutions. As might be expected from a parliamentary product, this treaty increased the power of the European Parliament over legislative and budgetary matters. Although the Commission would lose some power to Parliament, it would obtain some additional authority at the expense of the Council, most notably the ability to adopt subordinate legislation without Council approval. The European Union Treaty would also increase the power of the Community relative to the member states by giving the Community greater control over such areas as economic policy, cultural and social affairs, and international relations. The primary driving philosophy of the treaty, the principle of "subsidiarity," would allow the EC to address those questions where a supranational authority would be more effective than the national governments. In this respect, the treaty represented a true European constitution of confederation, with a supranational authority making pan-European decisions and the national governments concerning themselves primarily with state matters. The treaty was adopted by Parliament on February 14, 1984, by a vote of 237 for and 31 against.[3] Although discussed in depth by the Council, the treaty was never officially voted on, and has never become Community law.

The European Union Treaty had clearly taken the initiative toward furthering European integration away from individual member country statesmen, their governments, and most particularly the European Council and put it squarely in the hands of the European Parliament. This state of affairs proved uncomfortable for the Council, which began its own European union study, the Genscher-Colombo initiative. This plan argued for increased political cooperation and a rebalancing of the roles of EC institutions through a strengthening of the European Parliament, more reliance on majority voting in the Council, and more frequent meetings at the ministerial level. The Genscher-Colombo plan led directly to the Solemn Declaration of European Union, signed in Stuttgart on June 19, 1983. At the same time, the Council also called for a "relaunching of the European Communities to tackle the most pressing problems facing the Community so as to provide a solid basis for the further dynamic development of the Community."[4]

The 1980s saw a plethora of calls for reform within the EC. In May 1984, French president François Mitterrand called for greater European cooperation in electronics, space, transport, and communications. A month later, British foreign secretary Geoffrey Howe called for practical rather than theoretical approaches to improving the institutional workings of the EC. At the Fontainebleau summit of June 25–26, 1984, the Council, finally achieving a solution to the EC budgetary impasse with Britain, called for the establishment of ad hoc committees to investigate greater European cooperation (the Dooge Committee) and the development of a "people's Europe" (the Adonnino Committee). Other moves were occurring simultaneously within the EC hierarchy. The Commission, based on calls for a more comprehensive internal market in Europe by the Council in Copenhagen (1982), Fontainebleau (1984), and Dublin (1984), was developing its own program under the guidance of Lord Cockfield. The Council, in March of 1985, called for the establishment of a "single large market by 1992." In December of that same year, the Intergovernmental Conference was held and ultimately led to the adoption of the Single European Act early in the following year. At almost the same time, the foreign ministers were, with minor reservations coming from the Italians, Danes, and British, giving their stamp of approval to the proposals put forth in the European Commission's *White Paper on Completing the Internal Market.*

The Single European Act

The first major step in achieving the success of the Single Europe Program outlined in the Commission's *White Paper* was the passage of the Single European Act. Although not specifically mentioning the Commission's internal market program, it provided a clear statement that the goals of the *White Paper* were to have the force of the Community behind them: "The Community shall adopt measures with the aim of progressively establishing the internal market over a period expiring on 31 December 1992. . . . The internal market shall comprise an area without internal frontiers in which the free movement of goods, persons, services and capital is ensured."[5]

The Single European Act represented a compromise of sorts, between those governments desiring more control of the EC by the sovereign states and those wanting to see a greater level of European cooperation as envisioned in the European Union Treaty of 1984. Although the European Union Treaty presented a grand vision of a more powerful EC and a more cooperative Europe, the Single European Act represented "a unity of purpose but no unity of means and no identical perception of the Community."[6]

Passed by the European Parliament on January 16, 1986, and adopted by all the member states and going into effect in February 1987, the Single European Act amended the EC treaties on a number of dimensions, the most important of which was the removal of the right of veto within the European Council that had been established by the 1966 Luxembourg Compromise. A system of qualified majority voting was instituted within the Council, and unanimity was retained for cases regarding taxation, professional qualifications, and the "rights and interest of employees." Henceforth, passage of EC directives would only require an approximate 70 percent majority (54 of 76 possible votes)—Britain, France, Germany, and Italy each receive ten votes; Spain gets eight votes; Belgium, Greece, the Netherlands, and Portugal each receive five votes; Denmark and Ireland each receive three votes; and Luxembourg gets two votes. The qualified majority voting system ensures that no large country or pair of states is sufficient to block a directive, and at least two large countries are necessary for passage.

The Commission was also granted the power to investigate and determine which national laws fail to meet the provisions set forth in measures passed by the Council and the European Parliament. Once it had determined which national laws failed to comply, the Commission would have the right to ask the member state governments to bring their laws into line with EC law. Because such power meant that member states abdicated their right to develop totally EC-independent laws, this provision required a referendum in Denmark, and Greece and Ireland refused to sign the document on February 17, 1986.[7]

The European Parliament found its powers enhanced through the expansion of its approval authority in matters of trade, applications for EC membership, and other agreements with non-EC countries (chapter 2, section 1). All proposals from the Commission that are either amended or rejected by the European Parliament could now only become law through the unanimous vote of the Council.

Finally, the act was responsible for making more explicit the European Community's objective of "strengthening . . . its economic and social cohesion" (title 2, section 2, subsection 4); determining a policy for the "strengthen[ing] [of] the scientific and technological basis of European industry" (chapter 2, section 2, subsection 5); outlining the objectives of the Community with regard to the environment (chapter 2, section 2, subsection 4); and restating its commitment toward the further development of the European monetary system (chapter 2, section 2, subsection 2).[8]

The Single European Act actually represented a minor legal alteration in the institutional operations of the EC. It provided for an internal institutional reform of the European Parliament, Commission, and Council aimed at speeding up the passage of legislation that was generally regarded as necessary by most governments and EC officials. Indeed, strong pro-unionists looked on the act as little more than window dressing. The true impact of the act is in its requirement that member states bring their laws into accordance with EC law. This provision, in conjunction with the expected changes in EC law envisioned by the *White Paper,* implied a substantial abdication of home government sovereignty to EC institutions.

The *White Paper on Completing the Internal Market*

The European Commission's *White Paper on Completing the Internal Market* outlines the calendar for the 1992 Single Europe Program. The *White Paper* was not intended to be an all-encompassing document to cover every issue related to the integration of the member states, but its inherent goal is the complete elimination of "nonessential" barriers to trade between those states. As such, it represents a strategic plan and an operational timetable for the expressed goal of a more comprehensive economic union of the EC states. As originally presented, the *White Paper* outlined 300 directives aimed at eliminating the major barriers to trade and integration. Since its initial publication, that number has been reduced to 282.

The Philosophy of the White Paper

The philosophy expressed in the *White Paper* is a simple one. Barriers to trade between states exist either to restrain trade for the benefit of some party or parties, or because such restraint is necessary as a matter of national policy. The *White Paper* breaks such restraints into three categories: *physical, technical,* and *fiscal.*

PHYSICAL BARRIERS. Physical barriers are most clearly represented by border delays and paperwork. Some obstacles, like customs posts, are the most visible forms of such barriers. Others, such as restrictions on the movement of individuals because of certification procedures, tax formalities, plant and animal health controls, road transport controls, waste transport controls, and statistical information gathering, are less visible but more economically costly to businesses and individuals.

The stated objective behind the removal of these physical barriers is "not merely to simplify existing procedures, but to do away with internal frontier controls in their entirety."[9] This ostensibly will be achieved by removing the underlying causes that are responsible for the need for controls. If removing the need for controls proves impossible, the Community will find other means than the use of border patrols to achieve the same effect.

In other words, the *White Paper* acknowledges that physical restrictions to trade have their origin in the need to protect differential national taxation rates, to support immigration policies, to aid in national security and police matters, and to protect sensitive industries. Nevertheless, it argues for the need to find alternative means of dealing with these issues that would eventually eliminate the need for physical constraints on trade. This, in and of itself is not necessarily conducive to a complete opening of markets in a laissez-faire sense. The *White Paper* notes specifically that "the reason for getting rid entirely of physical controls between Member States is not one of theology or appearance, but the hard practical fact that the maintenance of any internal frontier controls will perpetuate the costs and disadvantages of a divided market."[10] It is further stated that "any import restrictions would have to be applied on a Community-wide basis."[11] The possibility of erecting European quotas, voluntary export restraints (VERs), and Community-wide standards, in lieu of individual country restrictions, has led to the fear of a "fortress Europe."

That the elimination of physical barriers is economically important to the Common Market is hardly an understatement. One study indicates that customs procedures alone cost firms approximately 7.5 billion ECU ($6.8 billion) in administrative costs and between 415 and 830 million ECU ($377 and $755 million) in delay costs, not to mention an opportunity cost of anywhere from 4.5 billion ECU to 15 billion ECU ($4.1 to $13.6 billion) in forgone business.[12]

In addition to recognizing that frontier barriers are an effect and not a cause of trade restrictions, the *White Paper* also proposed that border documents be standardized. The Single Administrative Document was introduced in January 1988 and serves as a replacement for the seventy-odd customs forms previously used throughout the Community. At the same time, the Community also instituted the Harmonized Coding System, which serves as the descriptor and coding system for trade. In the future the EC hopes to institute a computerized customs clearance system, known as CADDIA (Cooperation in the Automation of Data and Documentation for Imports, Exports, and Agriculture), that will eventually replace the Single Administrative Document.

If the Community hopes that 1992 will see the ceremonial burning of border posts, it is probably a faint hope. Currently, the EC has yet to resolve problems surrounding the role of frontier posts in security and police matters, the control of tax evasion, and statistical information gathering.

TECHNICAL BARRIERS. Technical barriers refer primarily to the differential technical specifications among EC countries. Although some technical restrictions are permitted under the Treaty of Rome (see article 36), their use as a means of "arbitrary discrimination" is technically unlawful. Yet the illegality of using some technical restrictions inappropriately has not stopped member states from propagating their own technical standards as barriers to importation, particularly given the Treaty of Rome restriction on the use of tariffs and quotas.

The impact of technical barriers and their inconsistency with past and current EC law became evident in a number of European Court cases wherein such restrictions were declared illegal under the Treaty of Rome. The most famous of these cases was the *Cassis de Dijon* case. The European Court ruled that the German law that restricted the importation of a liqueur from France because it contained too little alcohol (!) represented a violation of the Treaty of Rome right of every member state's business to operate freely throughout the Community. In subsequent cases, the Court has shown its activism in this matter by declaring unlawful the centuries-old German beer purity laws *(reinheitsgebot)* and the restrictions on the import of pasta into Italy. The former case revolved around the German restriction that only products containing hops, malted barley, yeast, and water could be designated *beer*. The Court ruled that the German law was not based on "essential requirements" because the additives that German law did not permit in beer, which were common to many non-German beers, were in fact allowed in other drink products sold in Germany.[13] The latter case centered on Italian restrictions against the import of anything but 100 percent durum wheat pasta. The Italian government's defense, based on the harmful effects of additives to human health and other consumer protection concerns, was considered invalid by the Court. There was no conclusive evidence of health problems arising from the use of additives and colorants, and the Court viewed the banning of a product to protect consumers as clearly inferior to alternatives like requiring adequate labeling of the durum wheat content.[14]

Besides addressing the issue of general technical restrictions, the *White Paper* also addresses the need for

1. opening up public procurement within the Community;
2. the free movement of goods by the approximation of laws regarding
   a. motor vehicle and agricultural machine specifications;
   b. food labeling, inspection, and content specifications;
   c. pharmaceutical tests and marketing;
   d. chemical use, content, and labeling;
   e. construction and construction products;
3. a Common Market for services including banking, insurance, security transactions, transportation, and new technologies;
4. the free movement of labor and the acceptance of professional qualifications throughout the member states;
5. the protection of intellectual and industrial property; and
6. the removal of tax obstacles between enterprises in different member states.

FISCAL BARRIERS. The *White Paper* calls for the "eliminat[ion of] intra-Community *fiscal* frontiers" and the "sufficient" approximation of value-added tax (VAT) and excise tax rates. Interestingly, there are no proposals calling for the harmonization of individual or corporate income taxes, despite the considerable variation from country to country (see figure 3–1).

The need to remove fiscal barriers to trade is predicated on the belief that many trade distortions and physical barriers exist because of differences in tax rates and welfare systems. For example, for two countries with radically different excise and VAT rates to open their borders to trade in physical goods would create obvious arbitrage opportunities. Individuals in the high tax country would either travel to purchase in the low tax country or simply purchase large quantities in the low tax country and smuggle them into the high tax country. Such logic holds with respect to individuals as well. States providing large welfare benefits would find people immigrating simply to take advantage of the more beneficial system.

The primary fiscal barriers to EC trade are the differential VAT and excise tax rates among the countries. Figure 3–2 shows the different VAT levels of the EC countries and the European levels initially proposed in July 1987. VAT rates range from the zero percent reduced rates in Denmark and the United Kingdom, to a high rate of 38 percent in Italy. Six countries, Belgium, France, Greece, Italy, Portugal, and Spain, use an above-standard VAT rate—above 30 percent. Some countries, such as Denmark and the United Kingdom, rely on only one standard rate, while others have more than the traditional three rates—Belgium has six rates, and France and Italy have four rates each.

The Commission initially proposed two bands of VAT rates: a standard rate of between 14 and 20 percent and a reduced rate of between 4 and 9 percent applied to selective products, for example, food, energy, pharmaceuticals, and books. Several countries, most notably Britain and Ireland, complained about the reduced rates because they provide a zero rate for social essentials such as children's clothing. Most other countries were concerned about their ability to cope with a system that would provide no high rate but a European standard rate above their national standard rate. Finally, countries like Luxembourg and Spain were unhappy about having to increase their standard rates to meet the new proposals. Officials in Luxembourg estimated that the increase in their standard VAT rate could lead to a 7.5 percent price increase, which would put 6

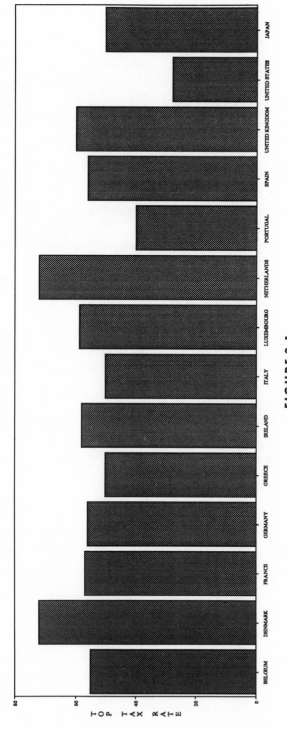

FIGURE 3–1

Top Income Tax Rates by Country

Source: Bartlett, B., "The World-Wide Tax Revolution," *Wall Street Journal*, 29 August 1989.

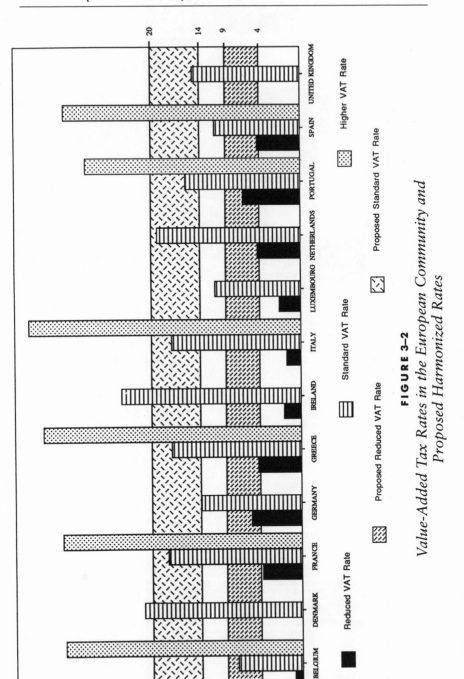

FIGURE 3-2

*Value-Added Tax Rates in the European Community and
Proposed Harmonized Rates*

percent of retailers out of business and leave 7 percent of the population unemployed.[15] These conflicts were resolved by a revised proposal developed by Christiane Scrivener, EC commissioner for taxation. Under the current guidelines, countries like Britain get to keep their special exemption rate and there is no maximum standard rate. Instead, the maximum is determined by local market forces as is seen in the United States with local and regional sales taxes.

Excise tax rates are also quite variable across the Community countries. The Commission has proposed harmonizing excise taxes on spirits, wine, beer, tobacco, and oil products. Figure 3–3 presents the existing excise rates on a selection of these commodities by country and the Commission's proposed rates. To equalize their excise taxes countries like Denmark and Ireland would have to decrease almost all their rates on the selected commodities, while Belgium, Luxembourg, Germany, Portugal, and Spain would be increasing their rates. The remaining countries would have to raise some rates while lowering others. The overall effect is expected to be neutral since the proposed European rates are an unweighted average of the existing rates.

The second set of fiscal barriers are restrictions on the movement of capital between member states. Current plans call for the complete removal of capital movement restrictions in eight Community countries by July 1990 and in Greece, Italy, Portugal, and Spain by 1992. The current proposals extend directives dating back to the early 1960s in which trade in direct investment, commercial credit, and personal capital was liberalized. Remaining restrictions on security transactions, deposit accounts, and most all financing transactions will be removed. In addition, the use of safeguard clauses, which allow countries to suspend the application of EC law and neutralize the earlier directives in this area, will be strictly limited.

Expecting that the proposals would lead individuals to hold deposits outside their home country to avoid taxes on bank interest and securities transactions, France, Italy, and Denmark were very concerned about the impact of capital movements on their tax revenues. France and Denmark ultimately backed down from their insistence that the directives include provisions on reducing tax evasion. Instead, the Community attempted, very briefly, to institute an investment income withholding tax. After the debacle in Germany,

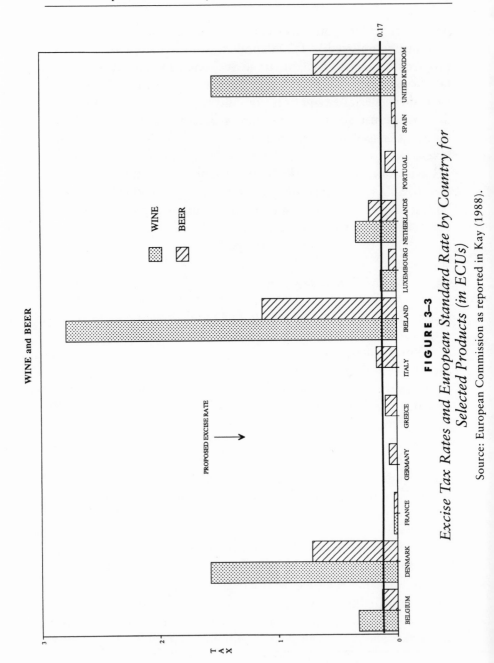

FIGURE 3–3
Excise Tax Rates and European Standard Rate by Country for Selected Products (in ECUs)

Source: European Commission as reported in Kay (1988).

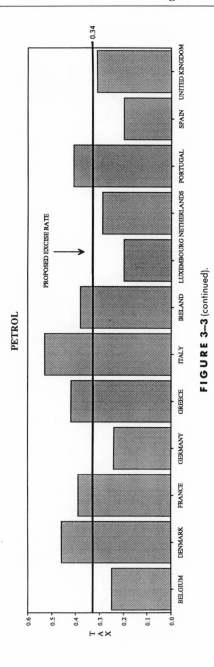

FIGURE 3–3 (continued).

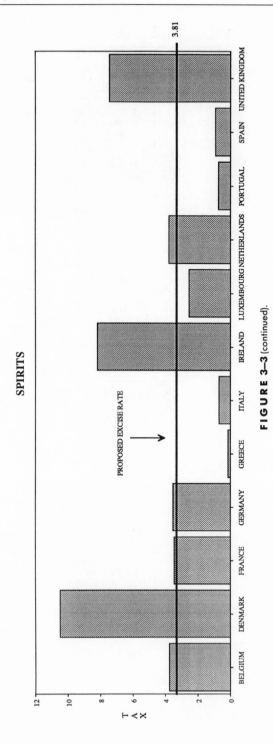

FIGURE 3–3 (continued).

where the tax was adopted, rocked the bank and bond markets, and was quickly removed, the EC dropped the proposal. Currently, the issue of how the Community will address the issue of tax avoidance and disparate income tax levels is open.

The 1992 Strategy

The Single Europe Program is correct in recognizing that barriers are not a cause of trade restrictions but that the desire for trade restrictions leads to the necessity of barriers. The radical differences in the structure, services, costs, and pricing of goods and services in the countries of the EC are based on nothing more than a combination of old-fashioned market protection devices mixed with a desire to control the commercial sector for monetary, fiscal, and social welfare policy purposes. As a reaction to this, the program intends to remove the need for the barriers and make them superfluous. The 1992 strategy is a three-pronged advance based on

- mutual recognition,
- selected harmonization based on the criterion of reciprocity, and
- mutual information procedures.

Mutual recognition ensures that business exercises its right to trade within the EC. Although member states may restrict goods on the basis of health, safety, or environmental concerns, the European Court has upheld the position that EC law does not merely prohibit barriers to trade but requires that one country accept the goods of another provided that the "essential requirements"—health, safety, and environmental concerns—are met. The right of mutual recognition is, in fact, guaranteed by the Treaty of Rome, but it was only with the precedent set by the *Cassis de Dijon* decision of the European Court that a broad definition of the "right to conduct business throughout the Community" was brought into play.

Selective harmonization recognizes that products can only be restricted in inter-European trade for health, safety, or environmental reasons. Harmonization does not imply that the EC requires all member state laws to look alike; instead restrictions based on the three essential requirements must be the same for all member states.

Buried within the principle of harmonization is the criterion of *reciprocity*. In its narrowest interpretation, reciprocity requires that before the EC will allow extra-EC companies and individuals to have full rights under the EC treaties, extra-EC countries must permit EC businesses and individuals to act under laws that guarantee rights identical to those in the EC. This means that before lawyers in the United States could conduct business in France, U.S. laws and institutional rules on the legal profession would have to be brought into "harmony" with EC law and practice. Although reciprocity does not require that the laws be identical, it does require that the effects of the laws be the same as in the EC.

Under a broader definition of reciprocity known as "national treatment" the EC would require only that foreign countries treat EC companies and individuals in a manner consistent with the treatment similar businesses and individuals receive in the home country. This broader definition has been most recently applied in the field of banking where the EC backed down from its stance on the Second Banking Directive requiring the United States and Japan to alter their banking laws before it would grant banking licenses to foreign banks. The rule applied to this case stipulates only that foreign countries treat Community banks on an equal basis with home country banks.

Which definition of reciprocity will ultimately come to dominate is uncertain. The softening of the banking directive was in direct response to the urging of Germany and the United Kingdom, both with substantial interests in the United States and Japan. Should reciprocity rear its ugly head in a case where internal EC lobbying is unaffected by direct external pressures like those in the banking case, it is likely that the narrower definition will dominate.

Mutual information procedures are based on a 1983 EC directive that requires a member government to notify the Commission of regulatory and legislative developments in advance of their enactment. This provides the Commission with the opportunity to react to the changes in advance and notify the member government of its opinion about the law or regulation's consistency with EC law.

The Impact of Trade Barriers

In a recent survey conducted for the European Commission[16] businesses ranked the following as the major barriers faced in inter-European trade:

1. administrative customs barriers (physical),
2. national standards and regulation (technical),
3. frontier delays (physical),
4. EC law,
5. capital market restrictions (fiscal),
6. regulation of freight transport (technical/physical), and
7. VAT differences (fiscal).

Clearly, physical barriers dominate business thinking in trans-European trade, but, as noted earlier, the physical barriers are nothing more than necessities driven by technical and fiscal barriers. Border delays, for example, are required to ensure that VAT and excise taxes are paid, that the products meet the receiving country's technical specifications, that the trucker is not violating transport regulations, that the goods being imported or exported are not banned or subsidized, and so on. Such differences lead to products being imported into Italy at five times the cost of importing the same products into Belgium.

When we look at the barriers to trade by industry we find some interesting breakdowns. Table 3–1 lists the most troublesome barriers to trade in selected industries. Although almost every industry feels it is affected by border delays, they are most prevalent in the

TABLE 3-1

The Most Important Barriers to European Trade by Industry

Industry	Most Highly Rated Barriers
Consumer goods	National standards, frontier formalities
Food, drink, and tobacco	Frontier delays, national standards
Oil, mining, and processing	Frontier delays, transport restrictions
Chemicals	National standards, frontier delays
Engineering	National standards
Office and data processing machines	Capital market restrictions, frontier delays
Motor vehicles	VAT and excise taxes, national standards

Source: Nerb, Gernot. *The Completion of the Internal Market: A Survey of European Industry's Perception of the Likely Effects,* (Luxembourg: Office of Official Publications of the European Communities, 1988).

traditional manufacturing sector. Technical standards dominate in the more complex manufacturing fields—chemicals, engineering, and automobiles. VAT differences in automobiles are known to lead to price differences between countries on the order of 200 percent and are clearly recognized as critical for the automobile industry. Finally, capital market restrictions are considered most important by the data processing industry, even more so than technical standards.

THE IMPACT OF FRONTIER FORMALITIES AND TRANSPORT RESTRICTIONS. We noted earlier that customs delays and formalities cost European businesses an estimated $20 billion annually. Perhaps more than any other trade restriction in Europe, national frontiers and transport restrictions are blamed for the fragmentation of European markets.

Yet, the border delay problem is more complex than it appears on the surface. Industries that are protected by their governments obviously are not concerned that others might have to deal with some administrative hassles to guarantee the same protection. Protected industries may even accept the fact that other countries may follow the same protectionist policies; for example, Japanese and American automakers both appear very satisfied with the present system of VERs even though administratively it must be a nuisance for both countries. The border problem raises the ire of businesses for two other reasons. First, the border delays associated with the protection of any one industry impose costs on all other protected industries. The fact that automobiles must be checked to make sure that they meet safety requirements imposes delays on those importing food that must be checked for health standards, and vice versa. Food producers may accept that there are delays for food inspection, but they would prefer to have the checking of automobiles removed to speed up the process. Second, the imposition of border controls to check for compliance with regulations in regulated industries imposes costs on the legitimate import of nonregulated products since those products must be checked as well or simply waste extra time waiting at the border. Only in this latter case is the benefit from removing the barriers clear.

Examples of border restrictions and delays abound. For example, health inspections in Spain are estimated to add delays of three to five weeks, and the Greeks require an 80 percent deposit on the import value of goods as minor as biscuits.[17] In Italy, the hours of customs inspection are split for imports and exports; one shift is in the morning, the other in the afternoon. Pelkmans and Winters, in their paper on Europe's domestic market, note that many important border stations are not even open twenty-four hours a day.[18]

The value of these restrictions varies by country and type of firm. It is fairly clear that small firms suffer disproportionately. Ernst & Whinney estimates that the cost per consignment for importers is approximately $42 for firms with under 250 employees but only $25 for firms with more than 250 employees.[19] Import and export costs also vary considerably from country to country. The cost of an agent for trade between Italy and France is approximately $96 per consignment, but between France or Italy and Belgium the cost is only about $23 per consignment.[20] Figure 3–4 provides the agents' costs of handling consignments between a sample of EC countries.

Road haulage restrictions are of two primary types. First, the European quota system requires haulers to apply for restricted permits to move goods either to, from, or through member states. If the permits for the shipment of some commodity between two states are used up, the shipper must transship the merchandise through a third country where the permit quota has not been exhausted. Second, *cabotage* prohibits nonresident haulers to move goods within the boundaries of a member state. Therefore, although U.K. truckers could deliver merchandise between Lyon and Birmingham, they could not transport goods between Lyon and Paris. Interestingly, the major cost of empty loads (trucks traveling to destinations empty) was found to be related to cabotage in 13 percent of those questioned and permit restrictions in only 5 percent. Haulers questioned specified that the major cause of empty loads was awareness of business opportunities, that is, knowing of customers requiring shipment, and *not* regulation.[21]

The foregoing information indicates that trucking companies are themselves obviously annoyed at border delays but are not necessarily unhappy with the national regulations, particularly cabotage, which provides them with a protected market. Less cumbersome border formalities would certainly increase the market for haulage in total, thus making all trucking more lucrative, but there is no inherent need for truckers to seek reduced trucking regulation.

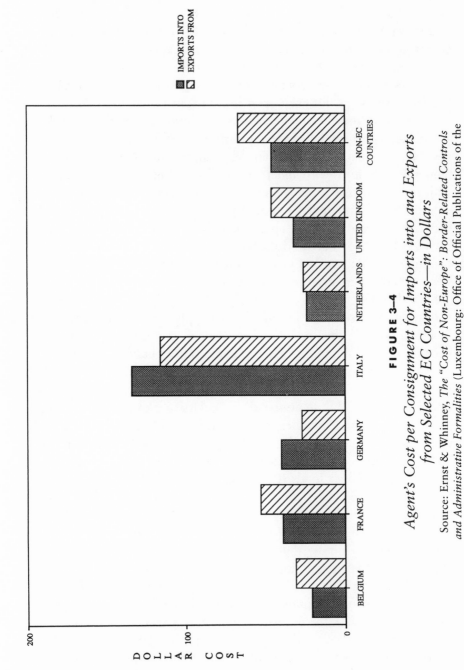

FIGURE 3–4

*Agent's Cost per Consignment for Imports into and Exports
from Selected EC Countries—in Dollars*

Source: Ernst & Whinney, The "Cost of Non-Europe": Border-Related Controls
and Administrative Formalities (Luxembourg: Office of Official Publications of the
European Communities, 1988).

THE IMPACT OF TECHNICAL BARRIERS. When we look at individual technical barriers we see how individual market protectionism led to the "fragmentation" of commerce across Europe. As we noted earlier, technical standards are most important in complex manufacturing and high technology fields, nevertheless the cost of technical requirements is perhaps the most pervasive barrier to trade, affecting almost all industries to a varying degree. Also, since border delays are themselves partially a function of the need to check that the technical specifications of products being imported meet the regulations of the importing country, much of the consternation about frontier formalities is really a complaint about technical standards.

The costs of technical standards are primarily twofold. First, meeting the technical standard incurs a cost over and above the cost of producing the good under some alternative lower standard. The second cost is the elusive cost of forgone business: the forgone profitability of not entering a market, the higher price being paid by consumers because of the lack of alternatives, or the lost opportunities for developing nonstandard products despite an existing demand. All combined, the costs of technical restrictions in the EC are estimated to be in the billions of dollars. Table 3–2 provides a listing of the costs of the technical standards in ten industries. The Commission has estimated these costs to range from $145 million in the pharmaceutical industry to a possible high of $20 billion in the financial services industry. These numbers are really only the Commission's guesses, and may be high because of overoptimism on the Commission's part, or underestimated, because the figures are based only on a set of sampled industries and do not include estimates for many other industries operating under different countries' regulatory standards.

One could clearly write an entire treatise of case studies of technical and product standards in Europe. We will focus on four short cases for illustrative purposes only—tractors, automobiles, telecommunications equipment, and foodstuffs.

Tractors. A classic case of technical barriers to trade is pictured in figure 3–5. Selling a tractor in Europe requires meeting specifications for more than thirteen different components of the tractor. Specific regulations exist with respect to mudguards (almost all

TABLE 3-2

Estimated Costs of Various European Community Technical Standards by Industry (millions of dollars)

	Estimated cost
Telecommunications equipment	17,500 ECU ($15,909)
Financial services	11,000 to 22,000 ECU ($10,000 to $20,000)
Public procurement	8,000 to 19,000 ECU ($7,270 to $17,270)
Business services	6,600 ECU ($6,000)
Motor vehicles	2,600 ECU ($2,360)
Telecommunications services	4,000 ECU per year (3,636 per year)
Building materials	2,520 ECU ($2,291)
Foodstuffs	500 to 1,000 ECU per year ($460 to $910 per year)
Transportation	415 to 830 ECU ($380 to $750)
Pharmaceuticals	160 to 258 ECU ($145 to $236)

Source: Commission of the European Communities, *Research on the "Cost of Non-Europe": Basic Findings,* compiled from various volumes (Luxembourg: Office of Official Publications of the European Communities, 1988).

countries), steering systems (Germany), passenger seats (banned in the United Kingdom), windshields (all countries with Belgium being the strictest), tires (all countries), and the stamping of mufflers (Italy), to mention only a few. The development of European standards has shown the depths to which standard seeking can fall. As noted in the *Financial Times,* directives dating back to 1974 have yet to be implemented.[22] It has been argued that the existence of these disparate standards, combined with the small size of the European tractor market (approximately 200,000 units per year), has led to a heavily fragmented market containing over fifty manufacturers, with the three largest (Fiat, Massey-Ferguson, and Case) controlling approximately 39 percent of the market. But the European market compares favorably with the United States market. As a point of comparison, the United States, with annual sales in tractors of approximately 50,000 units (down from 200,000 units in 1977) supports fewer manufacturers, nonetheless the top six are comparable to the European top six and account for approximately

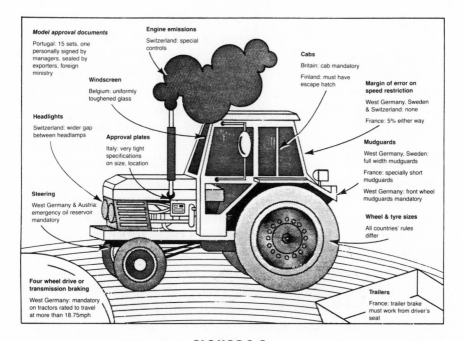

FIGURE 3–5

Tractor Regulations in European Countries

Source: "Ploughing a Furrow to 1992," *Financial Times*, 6 June 1988.

the same percentage of the market (60 percent for the American top six and 62 percent for the European top six).

Nineteen ninety-two is important to the tractor manufacturers. "We want it to happen," says Dick Seagrave of JI Case. But the difficulty of achieving what might appear to outsiders to be a matter of some simple give-and-take with national regulatory authorities makes a harmonized tractor market a vision of the future. Notes Mr. Seagrave, "opening up the tractor market in 1992? . . . Hell, we know it's going to take longer than that."[23]

Automobiles. Automobile technical standards are pervasive throughout the EC. In addition to disparate emission standards and safety approval procedures, European automobile manufacturers and importers must meet a host of annoying specific technical standards. These vary from items as minor as stamping the engine block with the manufacturer's name for importation into Italy, to moving the steering mechanism to the right side for import into the United

Kingdom. The EC is currently proposing the harmonization of pollution emissions and safety certification (whole vehicle type approval) standards.

Although no direct cost is attributed to the technical barriers to the automobile industry as a whole, an EC survey determined the costs for some technical barriers in three automobile companies. Figure 3–6 provides a listing of the technical standards mentioned in the survey and the estimated cost of meeting each standard for Volkswagen, Rover, and General Motors. For these three companies, the estimated cost of meeting the mentioned standards is approximately $107 per car for Volkswagen, $96 per car for Rover, and $18 per car for GM. These numbers underestimate the costs of technical restrictions because they measure the incremental cost of small technical standards. For example, all three manufacturers did not give a cost estimate of producing right-hand side drive cars because they already produce those types of automobiles. In addition, although there was no direct measure of the cost of meeting the disparate safety and emissions standards, all three automakers indicated that there would probably be no staff reductions as a result of the harmonization of these standards. Using the estimates given in figure 3–6 and adjusting for the size of the market, a guess is that the cost of the technical standards throughout Europe could be on the order of $900 million to $1 billion. As noted earlier, the EC estimates the total cost of automobile technical specifications, including the lost gains to specialization, to be on the order of over $2 billion (see table 3–2).

Telecommunications Equipment. Telecommunications is estimated to be one of the most rapidly expanding markets into the 1990s. As of 1986, the United States and Japan accounted for approximately 46 percent of the world telecommunications market with the EC possessing about 20 percent. Although the Community as a whole has more than twice the market share of Japan, no one EC member state accounts for more than one-half the Japanese market and one-eighth of the American market. The largest players, France, the United Kingdom, and Germany, each had between 4 and 5 percent of the world market as of 1986. Most interestingly, there is little intra-Community trade in telecommunications equipment, and

| | | ESTIMATED COST TO | | |
TECHNICAL RESTRICTION	COUNTRY	VOLKSWAGEN	ROVER	GM-EUROPE
Dim/dip lighting	U.K.	DM 55 ($29)	£10 ($16)	£8 ($13)
Side repeater flashers	U.K. and Italy	DM 59 ($31)	£10 ($16)	£3 ($5)
Right-side steering	U.K.	already produced	already produced	already produced
Third brake light (rear center)	U.K. (Proposed)	DM 60 ($32)	£15 ($24)	N.A.
Yellow headlamps	France	DM 28 ($15)	marginal	N.A.
Minimum ground clearance	Italy	N.A.	N.A.	N.A.
Labeling the engine block	Italy	N.A.	N.A.	N.A.
Laminated windscreens	Ireland, Italy and Denmark	N.A.	£25 ($40)	N.A.
Tail lamp fusing	Germany	already produced	N.A.	already produced
Total Production (1987)		2,129,000	465,000	1,393,000
Total Cost of Modifications (in local currency)		DM481,154,000	£27,900,000	£15,323,000
Total Cost of Modifications (in dollars)		$253,239,000	$44,640,000	$24,517,000

N.A. = no answer

FIGURE 3-6

*Country-Specific Automobile Technical Specifications and the
Cost of Meeting Selected Requirements by
Three European Manufacturers*

Source: Ludvigsen Associates, Ltd., *The EC 92 Automobile Sector*, (Luxembourg:
Office of Official Publications of the European Communities, 1988).

more than 50 percent of imports into EC member states come from the United States and Japan.

According to Jürgen Müller of INSEAD, the fragmentation of the European market is a function of three factors: "selective procurement and certification procedures, incompatible standards, and input specificity."[24] This fragmentation has led to small and highly specialized national markets where, although the gains to specialization might be enormous, sufficient scale cannot be achieved to take full advantage of these potential gains. In addition, any attempt to harmonize national standards would present enormous costs for the countries whose standards were discarded.

Figure 3–7 provides a graphical description of the price differentials of several EC countries relative to the world average. On average, the prices of European telecommunication equipment and services range from 37.5 percent above competitive world levels for transmission and switching equipment to 65 percent above world levels for central office equipment. Office premise equipment is an intermediate 51 percent more expensive than world levels. When we total the effects of these price differentials, as is done in table 3–3, we see that price increases from local market protection cost approximately $3 billion or almost $10 per European inhabitant. The costs are borne differentially across countries. Belgians appear to be paying $20 per inhabitant too much, while Italians are paying only about $6 too much per person.

The EC proposal for a pan-European telecommunications market presented in the *Green Paper on the Development of the Common Market for Telecommunication Services and Equipment*,[25] is aimed at reducing the influence of national public postal and telecommunications (PTT) bureaucracies on the certification of national standards and control of national telecommunication systems. It is apparent to almost all Europeans that the high costs of equipment and service and the disparate equipment standards that have fragmented the European market have been maintained solely for the preservation of the national PTT monopolies. Although they may be able to maintain their national monopolies over some aspects of the national telecommunication markets, such as in basic voice transmission services, the PTTs are expected to separate their operational and regulatory functions. They must publish their connectivity specifications and adhere to the standards of the European Telecom-

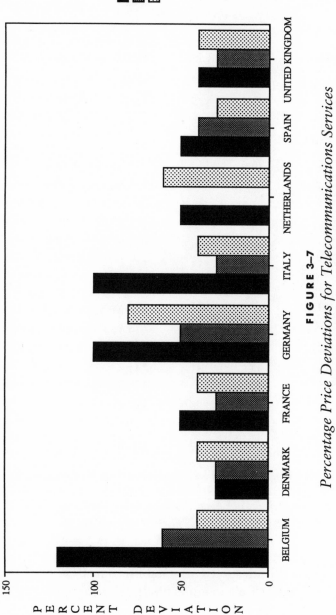

FIGURE 3–7

Percentage Price Deviations for Telecommunications Services and Equipment by Country—1985

Source: Jürgen Müller, *The Benefits of Completing the Internal Market for Telecommunication Equipment/Services in the Community* (Luxembourg: Office of Official Publications of the European Communities, 1988). Note: COE = Central Office Equipment; TRN = Transmission/Switching; and CPE = Customer Premise Equipment.

TABLE 3-3

*Estimated Value of Maximum Price Reductions in the
Telecommunications Market—1985 (in millions of
ECUs and dollars)*

COUNTRY	COE	TRN	CPE	OTHER	TOTAL	PER CAPITA
Belgium	120.0	46.0	27.6	27.6	221.2	22.4
	$109.1	$41.8	$25.1	$25.1	$201.1	$20.4
Denmark	12.0	9.2	13.8	13.8	48.8	9.5
	$10.9	$8.4	$12.5	$12.5	$44.4	$8.7
France	252.0	96.6	144.9	144.9	638.4	11.6
	$229.1	$87.8	$131.7	$131.7	$580.4	$10.5
Germany	432.0	165.6	248.4	207.0	1,053.0	17.3
	$392.7	$150.5	$225.8	$188.2	$957.3	$15.7
Italy	204.0	39.1	58.7	58.7	360.4	6.3
	$185.5	$35.5	$53.4	$53.4	$327.6	$5.7
Netherlands	36.0	N.A.	34.5	20.7	N.A.	N.A.
	$32.7	—	$31.4	$18.8	—	—
Spain	96.0	55.2	36.8	73.6	261.6	6.8
	$87.3	$50.2	$33.5	$66.9	$237.8	$6.2
United Kingdom	184.5	94.3	141.5	141.5	561.7	9.9
	$167.7	$85.7	$128.6	$128.6	$510.6	$9.0
Total of the eight	1,336.5	506.0	706.2	687.8	3,145.1	10.6
	$1,215.0	$460.0	$642.0	$625.3	$2,859.2	$9.6
EC Total	1,378.5	539.9	727.0	708.0	3,356.1	10.4
	$1,250.7	$490.9	$660.9	$643.7	$3,051.0	$9.5

Source: Müller, Jürgen, *The Benefits of Completing the Internal Market for Telecommunication Equipment/Services* (Luxembourg: Office of Official Publications of the European Communities, 1988).

munications Standard Institute (ETSI), established in 1988, thereby opening their markets to all manufacturers who meet the ETSI standards.

Foodstuffs. Perhaps the most serious effort has been put into the erection of product-specific trade barriers in the foodstuffs industry.

Historically, both the EC countries and the EC itself have provided substantial support for agriculture. This includes not only the 60 to 70 percent of the EC budget that goes into agricultural support mechanisms but also the literally thousands of product-specific regulations that serve to restrict both world and intra-Community trade in foodstuffs. In ten foodstuffs sectors alone there are 218 nontariff barriers to trade. Of these barriers, 29 percent are ingredient restrictions, 31 percent are labeling restrictions, 6 percent represent tax discrimination, 18 percent are content restrictions, and 29 percent are simple importing restrictions. Extrapolating these totals to the entire $342 billion European foodstuffs industry, we estimate that approximately 1,200 to 1,300 country-specific technical requirements exist in the twelve EC countries. The estimated savings from removing these restrictions are on the order of $460 to $910 million per year.

Examples of the specific restrictions on foodstuffs make for entertaining reading.[26] Ingredient restrictions are aimed at increasing the cost of importing specific commodities by forcing importers to meet a standard different from that required to sell the good in their domestic market. Examples of these restrictions include

- the banning of artificial sweeteners in soft drinks in France;
- the pasta purity laws in Italy, France, and Greece (Pasta that cannot be sold in these countries can, of course, be produced and exported to unknowledgeable foreigners);
- Spain requires whiskeys to be aged for three years before being sold, and alcohol content must be between 40 and 58 proof; and
- the use of certain artificial sweeteners in chocolates and confectionery items, permitted in the Benelux countries, are not permitted in Germany.

Content and denomination restrictions are directed at preventing the use of a generic name and serve, like ingredient restrictions, to increase the cost to importers. Some examples include Germany's beer purity law, which restricts the use of the term *beer* to only those products meeting the specifications of the law; Italy, France, and Spain require the use of a minimum amount of fruit juice in soft drinks (France—10 percent, Spain—8 percent), and in Italy the drink must contain 12 percent fruit juice before the name of the fruit can be used; a producer of biscuits in Germany cannot label the biscuits *"biscuit a la cuiller"* unless the egg content is at least 0.25 grams per biscuit, whereas in France, the requirement is a minimum of 0.24 grams per biscuit.

Labeling and packaging laws are a particular nuisance across the EC countries. Some restrictions simply specify what must be on the package, but others require that importers comply with recycling laws and transport restrictions. The most classic example of a packaging restriction is the Danish recycling law. Denmark requires that soft drinks and beer be sold only in refillable containers. Since this requirement differentially increases the cost of distribution to importers, because they must send the product into the country packaged and then ship the empties out, imports of soft drinks and beer collapsed when the law took effect (see figure 3–8). The EC has taken the Danes to the European Court on two occasions over this matter. When the law was first passed in 1977, the Court ruled that it violated article 30 of the Treaty of Rome. The Danes responded by passing a law that was, on paper, slightly less stringent. In 1982,

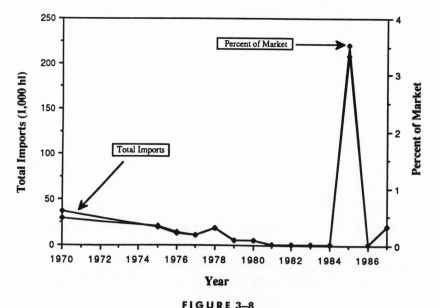

FIGURE 3–8

Beer Imports into Denmark and Market Share
of Non-Danish Beers

Source: Combined Statistics, *Common Market Brewer's Association/EFTA Brewing Industry Council,* 1983 and 1987.

the Commission began another investigation. This time the Danes reacted by allowing nonrefillable containers in limited volumes but requiring that the importers institute a mandatory deposit and return system for the bottles. Other countries have similar restrictions:

- Spain requires eleven different sets of items to appear on packages, and these range from the ingredients and net weight to conservation instructions and a health registration number;
- Spring water cannot be transported in bulk in any EC country except the Netherlands and the United Kingdom;
- Spain does not allow beer or soft drinks to be transported in bulk containers and bottled locally, and anything over three liters is defined as bulk transport; and
- Italy requires all packages to have labels in Italian that are at least as large as the largest labels in another language.

Although tariffs between the member states are technically unlawful, many member states have ingeniously developed differential tax allowances that effectively tax imports. The taxation of Dom rum in France does not even hide the fact that discrimination is occurring. French rum is taxed at Fr 4, 405/hl and Spanish and West Indian rum at Fr 7, 655/hl. Perhaps the most sophisticated system is the Wort tax method used for beer. In six EC countries (Belgium, Ireland, Italy, Luxembourg, the Netherlands, and the United Kingdom) the tax on beer is assessed prior to fermentation, less a wastage allowance, but for imports the tax is levied on the final product with no wastage allowance. By controlling their wastage and taking advantage of the allowance, domestic brewers face a lower tax. This tax savings varies from 6 percent in Ireland and the United Kingdom to 10 percent in all other enforcing countries.

Many specific importing restrictions involve border delays and not technical requirements. For example, Spain requires imported spirits to go through a one- to two-week process of tax and health inspections. The cargo must be sealed until health inspection is performed even though a certification is required for the health authorities of the exporting nation. Other restrictions are of a more technical nature and may include the banning of some or all irradiated products from Belgium, France, Germany, Italy, the Netherlands, and Spain and the requirement of veterinary certification for meat imported into the United Kingdom.

THE IMPACT OF FISCAL BARRIERS. The tax harmonization necessary for the removal of fiscal barriers to European trade is one of the most troublesome issues and has been and will continue to be one of the most vociferously fought areas of European integration. We noted earlier that the initial EC proposals were modified to allow for the very high VAT rates of several countries. The internal political reality of many of these countries was such that they simply could not adjust their fiscal and internal political policies to accommodate the lower rates.

Table 3–4 provides estimates of the effects of the Community's initial VAT tax proposal. In two countries with very high VAT rates, Denmark and Ireland, the tax consequences are quite devastating. Lee, Pearson, and Smith estimate that these countries would lose, respectively, 9.5 percent and 4.4 percent of their total tax receipts. France would lose approximately 1.7 percent of its revenues, while countries like Germany and the Netherlands would see substantial increases in their receipts.[27] If Denmark were to totally harmonize

TABLE 3-4

Revenue Consequences of Fiscal Harmonization Assuming Unchanged Spending Patterns

	Changes in Revenues from Excise Duties and VAT	
	As Percent of Indirect Tax Receipts	As Percent of Total Tax Receipts
Belgium	+ 3.0	+ 0.7
Denmark	− 27.0	− 9.5
France	− 6.0	− 1.7
West Germany	+ 6.0	+ 1.6
Ireland	− 10.0	− 4.4
Italy	− 3.0	− 0.8
Netherlands	+ 6.0	+ 1.4
United Kingdom	+ 2.0	+ 0.6

Source: Lee, Pearson, and Smith, *Fiscal Harmonization: An Analysis of the European Commission's Proposals* (1988) as reported in Kay, J., "Europe without Fiscal Frontiers," *European Management Journal* (1988).

its VAT rates, it is estimated that it would need to raise personal income taxes by 13 percentage points to compensate for the lost revenue, giving it a top marginal rate of 81 percent.[28]

The results reported in Table 3–4 are predicated on the assumption that consumption patterns do not change. Yet with the opening of borders to intra-Community trade, we should expect not only potential consumption changes, but also potential tax-induced consumption changes, particularly in the case of high-priced goods such as automobiles. The likelihood that the allowable higher rates can be sustained will be a direct function of the market's ability to adjust to the differential rates. Denmark, with an open border with Germany, may find maintaining and enforcing a VAT difference of more than 8 percentage points extremely difficult, just as Ireland would have difficulty maintaining a 10-percentage point differential with Northern Ireland. This is already in evidence as the Danes and Irish have attempted to restrict "duty-free" allowances, and now face European Court sanctions. Greece, on the other hand, could drop its 35 percent high VAT rate and raise its standard VAT rate of 16 percent without much difficulty because of its moderately isolated position.

One rather interesting possibility that may arise from the new VAT proposals is that the average level of VAT paid by Europeans could rise. This follows simply from the fact that countries with low VAT rates will be forced to raise their rates to meet the harmonized standards while the countries initially required to reduce their rates may not have to do so. The result is that while the VAT rates will be slightly closer together than before 1992, the average indirect tax burden of European companies and consumers may be increased.

The European tax system has different effects in different industries. A classic example of the impact of tax-induced price distortions is seen in the automobile industry. Automobile taxes vary by as much as fifteen times across the EC countries. Tax rates in Germany are the lowest at 14 percent. Taxes on automobiles in Belgium, France, Luxembourg, and Britain range from 20 percent to almost 40 percent and in the Netherlands and Ireland from 50 percent to almost 80 percent. Nothing, however, compares to the astronomical rates of 160 percent in Greece and 200 percent in Denmark. These tax distortions have led to higher prices and lower profit margins in the high tax countries. For example, the pretax price of a car in Denmark is 30 percent below that of a car sold in Germany, yet the after-tax price is 88 percent higher.[29]

Figure 3–9 provides evidence of the impact of differential taxation on the prices of automobiles across EC countries. Using a price index (EC average = 100) for three types of automobiles based on engine power, we see that all types of automobiles are relatively inexpensive in Belgium and Luxembourg with Germany running a close third. Automobiles are also relatively inexpensive compared to average in France, Italy, and the Netherlands. Small cars are differentially expensive relative to large cars in the United Kingdom, although the opposite is true in Spain and Portugal. Denmark, Ireland, and Greece are uniformly the most expensive for all sizes of automobile.

The Overall Effect

The EC expects 1992 to create a burst of economic energy throughout the Community. According to Paolo Cecchini, author of *1992: The European Challenge,* "Its attainment means not just the simple elimination of constraints sapping effective business performance, but above all a new and pervasive competitive climate. One in which the players of the European economy . . . can exploit new opportunities and better use available resources."[30]

This effect is expected to occur because of the lowering of costs, the increase in competition, and the growth in investment that will serve to increase national income and purchasing. The cycle would then be self-perpetuating and cause greater long-term growth in the Community. In the long term, the Commission believes that consumer prices could fall 4 to 6 percent and GDP could grow by 4 to 7 percent. Estimates of employment growth vary from almost two million to as many as six million new jobs. Short-term expectations see approximately the same level of price reductions and GDP growth as predicted in the long term but only about one to two million new jobs.[31]

The numbers from the Cecchini Report should, of course, be viewed somewhat skeptically. Estimates made in conjunction with earlier attempts to reduce trade barriers have found that the cumulative effect of reducing tariffs by 7 percent led to increases in

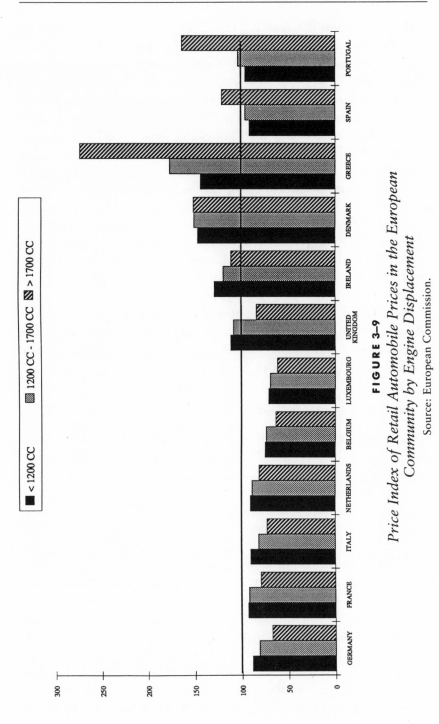

FIGURE 3-9

*Price Index of Retail Automobile Prices in the European
Community by Engine Displacement*

Source: European Commission.

GDP of between 0.5 and 1.5 percent.[32] Stephan Magee estimates that the cost of all the trade barriers affecting the United States' trade, both inside and outside the country, amounts to only 2 percent of GNP.[33]

The EC estimates are predicated on the assumption, first, that the gains to greater European integration are everyone's for the taking—all that is necessary is relinquishing those "bad" barriers that are stopping Europeans from truly taking advantage of all those economies of scale. Yet there is little or no discussion of the extent to which concentration in European markets will undoubtedly increase after 1992. This concentration will put not downward but upward pressures on prices. There is no concern about what, if anything, will stop individual governments, or groups of governments, from creating future obstacles to European business. A second problem with the EC's estimates is that almost 50 percent of the estimated gains in GDP and employment are because of "supply-side" effects caused by the releasing of new opportunities into the market. If we ignore this intangible, we can provide a more realistic estimate of perhaps an increase in EC GDP by 2 to 3 percent and a comparable percentage decrease in prices.

European Progress to Date

Talking about what should and can be achieved by Europeans is one thing, for the EC member states actually to act on those problems requiring a solution is another. Figure 3–10 provides summary information on EC progress in achieving workable Single Market laws in the member states as of March 1990. Of the 282 directives specified for implementation, 151 have been adopted by the Council as of July 1, 1990, and 120 of these are currently effective, that is, either implemented or waiting to be implemented by the member states. Of the approximately 109 directives passed by March 1990 for which information is available, only 12 have been incorporated into member state law by all twelve EC countries. Figure 3–10 also shows that there is a distinctly northern European propensity to implement EC directives. France, the Netherlands, Denmark, Germany, the United Kingdom, and Ireland have implemented at least 70 percent of the directives that apply to them. Greece, Spain, Italy, and Portugal, however, have implemented less than half of the di-

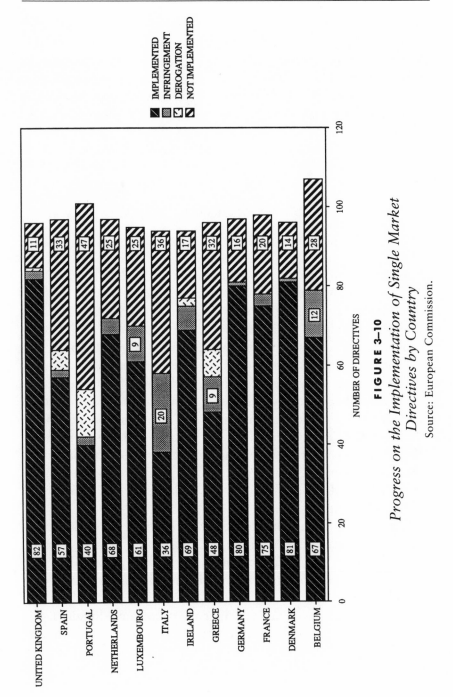

FIGURE 3-10

*Progress on the Implementation of Single Market
Directives by Country*

Source: European Commission.

rectives, although Spain has shown remarkable improvement in this dimension, and Italy and Greece alone are responsible for 30 percent of the cases in which European Court rulings have been ignored (infringements). What is perhaps most interesting about these figures is that the United Kingdom, typically viewed as the country least enamored with 1992, has by far the best implementation record of all of the EC countries.

Appendix B provides a listing of all of the Commission directives and their status to date.

Conclusion

The single market program of the European Community is the outcome of a long process of continuing economic, social, and political integration set off by the initial formation of the EEC in 1957. The 1960s and 1970s saw the limitations that national political realities imposed on attempts at continental unification. Pan-European statesmen attempted to circumvent what they considered to be parochial national interests through their actions in the European Parliament. The fruit of their efforts was the European Union Treaty. The ultimate compromise between the Parliament, the Commission, and the member state governments was the Single European Act. It was neither a complete act of union nor a complete abdication of the European ideal to national sovereignty. Instead, it is a pragmatic "let's work on what we can, and not what we can't" document aimed at altering the European regulatory balance and bringing it more in line with the economic reality of the late twentieth and early twenty-first century.

Putting this program into operation by concentrating on alleviating the supposed causes of intra-Community trade restrictions rather than dealing with the symptoms is clearly the correct approach. Also, the chosen multilateral approach has advantages over product-by-product or even industry-by-industry approaches. Getting governments to commit to the package of three hundred–odd directives makes it considerably less likely that any one country would attempt to block progress in the key sectors of the program. This multilateral approach is strengthened by the move to qualified majority voting in the Council. Countries are much more likely to compromise on an issue that they know they cannot block with a veto, and because member states know that they could be outvoted, they have a considerable incentive to compromise in an attempt to salvage the best outcome possible for their country.

In the next chapter we will discuss the single market program, which is heavily driven by the desires and needs of European business. European integration will always be a schizophrenic sort of process wherein one group's desire for open markets is attenuated by another's desire for protection. Noel Malcolm, in the September 1989 issue of *Spectator,* considers the European ideal of unification a reflection of "corporatism"—a philosophy that appeals to those "managerially-minded" individuals who are "offended by the [apparent] inefficiency of adversarial politics" and those "men of good will [so] distressed by the disunity and hostility produced by any system in which representatives of one interest-group can fight against those of any other."[34] The growth in the power of this European corporatism is at the heart of much of the development and success of the Internal Market initiative.

1992: European Challenge or European Reaction?

The idea is simple, case for it unanswerable; and yet the practical difficulties at present seem insurmountable . . . [yet] our destiny lies . . . with Europe.

—Michael Heseltine, The Challenge of Europe: Can Britain Win?

Democratic governments, by their nature, are pressure-responders rather than problem anticipators.

—Walter Heller, "What's Right with Economics?" American Economic Review (1975)

Nineteen ninety-two is hardly the result of some singular grand vision of a greater European economic and political union. As we have shown in the prior chapter, the evolutionary process that has led to the single market program has been percolating over the last decade. Nineteen ninety-two stands as a curious compromise between individuals' and political groups' wanting to wrest components of political control from the member states and the member states wanting to keep their decision-making authority.

The single market program's political origins lie in the visions of left-leaning politicians like Altiero Spinelli and Jacques Delors, yet the surface reality-cum-propaganda is one of an unbridled free market. Indeed, the primary author of the *White Paper,* Lord Cockfield, is an English conservative aligned, to some degree, with Margaret Thatcher. This curious mix of players, along with the ever present conflicting statements made by the major participants, leaves most observers confused as periodic glimpses of left-leaning Euro-chauvinism appear through the cracks in the 1992 wall otherwise plastered with pro–free market posters.

As 1992 approaches, the wealth of discussions, teleconferences, and study groups expands. Yet, in spite of the wealth of discussion, 1992 pundits usually succumb to the same two major pitfalls. First, in attempting to predict the effects of 1992, they have a tendency to examine each of the program's components out of context, that is, as isolated instances of bureaucratic relaxation or tightening. Second, in a desire to understand the causes of the single market phenomenon, they make a futile search for the single political philosophy behind the program.

With regard to the first point, in attempting to get an adequate forecast of what 1992 will bring and, therefore, be prepared for the future, one should not examine each of the recommendations and directives of the EC in isolation. To truly understand what is occurring in Europe today, it is necessary, first, to examine the whole, and only then can one investigate how the individual parts contribute to that whole. Although most companies and individuals are correctly concerned about how 1992 will specifically affect them and their industries, we are implying that one cannot simply look at the Commission's directives and understand the implications for one group or industry.

As regards the second point, it is necessary to recognize that the EC political game is not all that much different from the intracountry political games seen in the United States and Western Europe. For this reason the Community is taking a multilateral approach that provides strong incentives for deal making between countries for support of those programs of most importance to home country political coalitions. For example, French acquiescence in the case involving the import of British-built Japanese cars into France may be coming at the expense of British acquiescence on an issue of particular importance to the French such as the regulations defining the minimum European-produced programming required on EC television broadcasts.

This chapter will provide an alternative way of viewing 1992 and will allow the reader to get beyond the rhetoric that portrays the single market program as either the laissez-faire renaissance of Europe discussed by European businessmen or the one-sided protectionism feared by American trade officials. Nineteen ninety-two is a product of recent European economic and political history and a reflection of the demands of political and commercial interests for a substantive change in the political organization of the European commercial sector. Perhaps the most concise way of expressing what the single market program represents is with the oxymoron coined by Noel Malcolm to describe the "new" Labour party: "supply-side socialism."[1] The program represents the desire, not to unleash the market, but to allow a controlled chain reaction for "European" society's benefit.

A Framework for Understanding 1992

The 1992 single market program is more a political event with economic consequences than an economic event with political consequences. That is not to say that economic factors have not influenced the political transformation that is occurring in Europe today but rather that 1992 is a manifestation of changes in the European "political marketplace." The simplest way to see this is to make a cursory comparison between 1992 and the wave of "deregulation" or "reregulation" in the United States during the late 1970s and early 1980s. But before proceeding directly with the comparison, let us briefly outline a theory that will prove useful to our examination.

The economic theory of regulation, developed primarily by economists of the Chicago School—George Stigler, Mancur Olson, Sam Peltzman, Richard Posner, and others—views government intervention in the marketplace as fundamentally amoral and nondoctrinaire.[2] Regulation, including elements such as taxation, commercial regulation and deregulation, social and environmental policy, and trade policy (rather than satisfying any need for the public "good" or solving problems related to the public good) are the equilibrium solution to the joint satisfaction of competing politicians' welfare and the welfare of competing constituencies. Political coalitions form to pass laws that benefit one section of the society at the expense of another section of the same society or another society altogether. When necessary, the politicians balance the demands of competing interest groups through the mixing of economic and social regulation, such as is seen when monopolies are sanctioned by the government but are forced to provide "below cost" services to influential sections of the population, such as the elderly.

What is important about this theory is not its commonsense beginning but its conception of politics as an economic marketplace where regulatory change is the output.[3] This theory also clearly states what regulatory winners and losers will look like. Regulatory winners tend to be groups that are small in size, hence mitigating what is known as the free-rider problem.[4] These groups are also relatively homogeneous, thereby alleviating conflicts over goals, and otherwise possess characteristics that foster group cohesion, such as physical location, the structure of political representation in the society, and so on. The regulatory losers fail to possess these characteristics and tend to be large, nonhomogeneous, and diffusely located.

The classic regulatory winner most of the world over is agriculture. The portion of the population devoted to agriculture production is generally small (typically less than 5 percent of the population of industrial countries), stable, homogeneous, and geographically concentrated. The agricultural lobby receives monetary support, which is large relative to the group's income, through the imposition of minor price increases on millions of consumers. None of the consumers have the incentive to fight the price rise, since to do so imposes an enormous cost on the individual consumer lobbyist who can at best gain only marginally for him/herself.

Additional examples of interest-group regulation include tariffs and trade restrictions that traditionally benefit specific industry groups, as well as their workers, while taxing foreign firms and domestic consumers. Consumers are too diffuse and disorganized to react to the price increases, while the only reaction for foreigners (who, incidentally, do not vote) is to retaliate in another sector of the economy. As long as their retaliation does not involve a "politically" sensitive area, the restrictions usually withstand the test of time. Witness the recent United States/EC beef hormone battle. This was particularly rancorous because each side attacked the other's agriculture industry.

A slightly more relevant example is automobile VERs, which restrict the number of automobiles that may be imported, thereby increasing the price of both domestically produced and imported automobiles. In the United States, this practice affords protection for vehicle manufacturers and workers. The importing companies gain on two dimensions: they can increase the price of their products and are able to divide the market legally between importing manufacturers. The domestic producers reduce the competitive pressures created by the imports, and the importers relieve themselves of the necessity of competing against each other for market share. The losers are, of course, the purchasers of automobiles.

An immediate reaction to this type of restriction is that it takes a very cynical view of the political process. Are politicians not sensitive, caring individuals driven by a desire for the greater good as defined by their political doctrine? Of course they are. And there is no reason to doubt that under the right circumstances, politicians might pursue policies based on some vaguely defined general welfare. Yet because it is so costly for individual voters to express their preferences on the minute details of laws and because the gains from doing so are so small to each person individually, the tendency in parliamentary democracies is for representatives to react to the problems most immediately pressing to those most able to influence the political process. As Ambrose Bierce notes, "politics [is] the conduct of public affairs for private advantage."[5]

1992 as "New and Improved" Regulation

What does this thinking imply about the single market program? One of the implications of the Chicago School's theory is that changes in the regulatory structure will only occur when there are fundamental changes in the coalitions that win or lose as a result of the regulation. A simpler way of expressing this is to say that changes in regulation will occur only because of changes in the demand for regulation or changes in the state's ability to supply regulation. Since the ability to supply regulation rarely changes, it is more traditional to concentrate on changes in the demand for regulation.[6] With 1992, however, there is both a demand for change in the regulatory structure and a change in the supplier of that regulation.

Returning to the topic of regulation in the United States, we have experienced two major episodes of regulatory change that bear a remarkable resemblance to 1992. Beginning with the New Deal legislation of the 1930s and the social and environmental regulation of the 1960s, America saw a rapid expansion of federal power in the area of roads, welfare, environmental protection, and consumer rights, to name a few, with most state regulation being superseded by federal regulation. Much of this change was driven by business, which found it more convenient to operate under the protection of one regulatory structure. Then, in the late 1970s and early 1980s, the United States went through a radical process of deregulating many of those selfsame industries on which so much time and effort had been spent regulating "for the public interest."

To our knowledge, no one has yet asked the question, Why did this deregulation occur when it did? Why increase federal power in the 1960s and early 1970s only to quickly relinquish that power? The answer we wish to venture is twofold and has little to do with U.S. businesses experiencing a doctrinaire dissatisfaction with regulation per se. The United States deregulated specific industries because of two fundamental factors: the oil shocks of the 1970s and the growing dominance of foreign competition, most notably, Japanese competition. The deregulation of such things as airlines, oil and gas, trucking, the environment, and so on, were *demanded* by the industries themselves because owing to external circumstances and economic fundamentals the old regulatory structure was no longer beneficial to the industry. The same story can be told in relation to the recent deregulation of banking and telecommunications, where the rapid evolution of information technology altered the fundamental nature of the business, and the old regulatory structure became economically antiquated in a dynamic world. For example, the breakup of AT&T was as much AT&T's choice— based on rapidly changing technology and the ability to profit from new opportunities—as it was a government decision based on concerns about the power of AT&T's monopoly position in local communications services.

The U.S. experience with deregulation exhibits how underlying structural economic changes lead to demands for regulatory change. Although this demand for deregulation was couched in doctrinaire terms, it had little to do with political philosophy. In addition, although consumers on the whole benefited from deregulation, they had little to do with its initiation or ultimate success.

Let us now translate this experience to the current European situation. What has occurred since the 1960s, 1970s, and early 1980s that would lead to such a radical reaction by European governments and politicians? At its simplest, the problem may be approached on three dimensions: the sociopolitical environment, the fundamental "internal" economic environment, and the "external" economic environment.

The Role of the Sociopolitical Environment

Many think the sociopolitical environment is a strong factor leading to 1992, and it, indeed, serves as a very obvious reflection of the changes being seen in Europe. There is no doubt that the negative economic experiences of the 1970s, the failed socialist experiment, and labor strife were responsible for the more conservative political attitude of Europeans and their move toward more economically conservative governments. Also, it is clear that the increasingly positive relations between France and Germany (remembering that 1992 is an initiative heavily influenced by the French), the resolution of EC/British budgetary disagreements, and the easing of tensions between the Eastern and Western European powers have played their part. But in spite of these influences, we argue that there is nothing substantively changing the basis for why political coalitions would suddenly become more "European" or why Europeans are now prepared to scrap organized European social democracy for messy laissez-faire capitalist anarchy. The sociopolitical changes seen in Europe in the last decade ensure only that the Euro-rhetoric is correct and the horizon is less clouded by doctrinaire differences.

Evidence for this fact can be seen in the voting patterns and opinions of Europeans. Figure 4–1 shows the popular vote for left-of-center noncommunist parties in national European Community member state elections since 1970.[7] Although these figures clearly ignore the fact that the Social Democratic and Labour parties of the 1980s are considerably less strident than they were in the 1970s, they point out clearly that left-of-center parties are not the political dinosaurs that many people have surmised. Since 1970, these parties have on average generated between 30 and 40 percent of the popular vote in their respective countries, and no pattern of decline is evident. So why then do the left-of-centers get the death knell?

The years 1987 and 1989 were two of the worst for left-of-center parties in the last twenty years. Also, two previously powerful so-

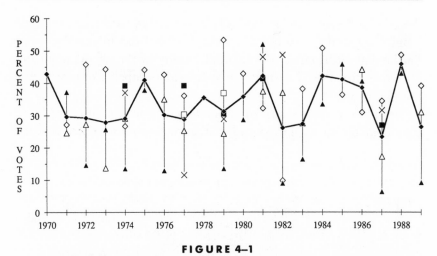

FIGURE 4-1

Vote Shares of Left-leaning Political Parties in European Community Member State National Elections, 1970–1989

Source: Cook, C., and J. Paxton, *European Political Facts, 1918–84* (New York: Facts on File Publications, 1986); Arms, T., and E. Riley, eds., *World Elections on File* (New York: Facts on File Publications, 1989). Note: Each point represents a national election that occurred during that year. The bold line is the population-weighted mean for all the elections that occurred during that year.

cialist parties have fallen on hard times in the 1980s, the British Labour party and the West German Social Democratic party. The 1988 elections in France and Denmark, however, point out clearly that the left is not dead. In France alone, all left-of-center parties (including the communists) polled almost 50 percent of the popular vote, higher than almost any previous election in the last twenty years. In Denmark, although the main Social Democratic party lost 8 percentage points from the previous election, left-of-center parties still polled over 43 percent of the vote (down from about 50 percent in 1984).

What does this evidence indicate? Although left-of-center parties are certainly less socialistically oriented economically, they have not been abandoned by the voters for right-of-center parties. In the early 1970s and early 1980s, these parties performed about as poorly in national elections as they have in the late 1980s. There is no substantive information, except in isolated instances, indicating that European voters have changed their attitude toward their countries' political parties. Based on voting behavior, there is little evidence that Europeans are socially more conservative or that they would not move to socialist parties, as they did in the European Parliament elections in 1989, should many of the left-wing parties currently down on the ropes generate leaders capable of motivating the electorate.

What about Europeans' opinions toward the Community? Have they changed in the last decades? Figure 4–2 presents the historic

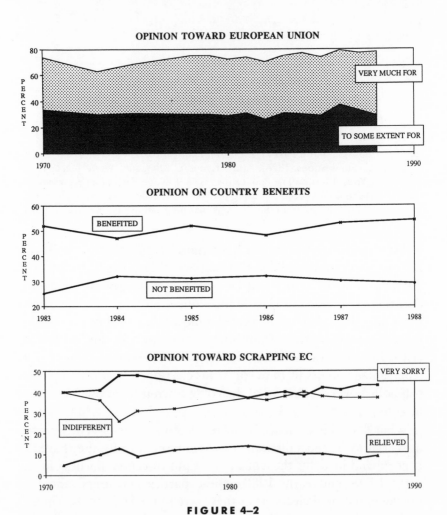

FIGURE 4–2

European Public Opinion Regarding the European Community

Source: European Commission, *Eurobarometer* (Brussels: Directorate-General Information, Communication, Culture, Surveys, Research, Analyses, December 1988).

pattern of European public opinion regarding the EC. All three graphs show that the population at large has not changed its opinion of the EC much over the last twenty years. In 1970, 34 percent of those surveyed were "very much for" European union with another 40 percent "to some extent for" it. In 1988, these percentages were 29 percent and 49 percent respectively. Indeed, the highest percentage of individuals saying they were "very much for" European unification occurred in 1962 (not shown).[8] Looking at the third graph, we see that the percentage of people who are indifferent to scrapping the EC is approximately the same as the percentage who would be "very sorry" (about 40 percent). This percentage has also remained relatively constant for almost twenty years.

These figures are not meant to imply that EC citizens do not value the EC. The second graph in figure 4–2 shows that 50 percent of those surveyed think that their country has benefited from the EC and over 70 percent are positively inclined toward the Community. The general evidence, however, does not point to a ground swell of public support behind 1992. Nineteen ninety-two is not a popular revolt for a free market. It is neither predicated on public opinion, nor does it appear to have substantively altered the opinions of those individuals surveyed.

Changes in the Fundamental Economic Environment

On the fundamental economic level, we find that 1992 is driven by what are primarily supply-side changes. Just as the single market program did not arise because of populist support, the single market program is not fundamentally a proconsumer movement. This is most obviously reflected in the EC's need to launch a rather extensive advertising campaign to educate the general European population about 1992. Even the Commission, through its study of the potential implications of 1992 entitled "The Cost of Non-Europe Research Program," puts its emphasis not on gains to European consumers but on European business. The assumption is that European consumers must gain because of the increased efficiency and competition that will be unleashed by the program. This leads to a curious question: If consumers are the primary gainers and the gains to companies are mixed, some winning, some losing, why were the consumers not breaking down the door of the EC bureaucracy and local parliaments demanding freer markets? Also, these consumers obviously have been suffering from the fragmented European markets for centuries. Why should they need change now? The answer is that some gains to consumers no doubt exist from the single market program, just as they did for users of airlines, trucking companies, and phone services in the United States from deregulation. But these gains would have continued to be ignored, as they have been in the past, if more concentrated gains had not existed for the important political coalitions of the EC countries. The downward pressure on prices that are predicted are not the reason for 1992. They are one aspect of the political quid pro quo demanded as the price for the change in the regulatory structure.

If the European consumer is not the driving force behind 1992, where do we look for the pressure for change? A major place to look is at the fundamental way that business is conducted. The European business community is being woken up by its inability to meet the technological challenge of the last two decades of the twentieth century. The fundamental economic factor driving 1992 is *technological change* and specifically, changes in *information* and *production technology.*

According to OECD statistics on high-technology trade, the EC, indeed Europe in general, has fallen further and further behind the United States and Japan in the technology race. Figure 4–3 shows

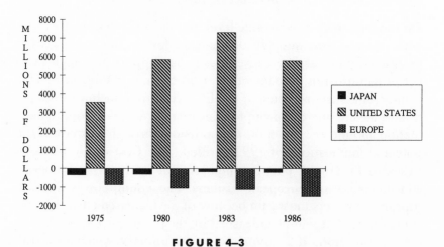

FIGURE 4–3

Trade Balance in the Technological Sector in Millions of Dollars

Source: OECD.

the technological balance of payments of Japan, the United States, and Europe, which includes the four most technologically advanced EC countries, Germany, France, Italy, and the United Kingdom. Over the eleven-year period spanning 1975–86, the four major EC countries have maintained an approximate $1 to $2 billion technological trade deficit with the world. According to Ian Mackintosh, a European information technology consultant, "the first, most obvious aspect of Europe's general deficiency is the extraordinary delay in appreciating the overwhelming revolutionary nature of silicon technology . . . European firms have generally ignored the potential of microelectronics."[9]

The lag in technological innovation can also be seen in the historic European commitment to research and development (R & D). Figure 4–4 highlights the R & D gap. Both the United States and Japan have spent approximately 3 percent of GDP on R & D during the 1980s while the EC countries have spent slightly less than 2 percent. The EC deficiency is concentrated in eight countries, with France, Germany, and the Netherlands being the exception. The counterargument to the R & D weakness of countries like Greece is that less developed countries need to invest in capital equipment first. Figure 4–5, however, shows that this argument, although partially valid, is weak. EC fixed investment is approximately 20 percent of GDP. Although the lower technology countries initially had high capital investment rates, by 1988 they had dropped to the Community average, and the high- and medium-technology countries were indistinguishable. The Japanese and Asian NICs had their typical high investment rates (almost 30 percent), and the United States had its pitiful 15 percent.

Nor is the European R & D gap caused by government-sponsored investment in the United States and Japan. In the United States, almost 49 percent of R & D is done privately. In Japan, it is much higher at 65 percent, reflecting a much lower defense-related orientation. In the Community, however, the level of private R & D is slightly but insignificantly lower than America's at 46 percent.

The picture that one gets from these figures is consistent with the Euro-sclerosis that plagued the Community in the late 1970s—the symptoms being slow growth, low investment spending, and as we shall discuss shortly, high unemployment. As Robert Lawrence and Charles Schultze point out in their 1987 study, "the European econ-

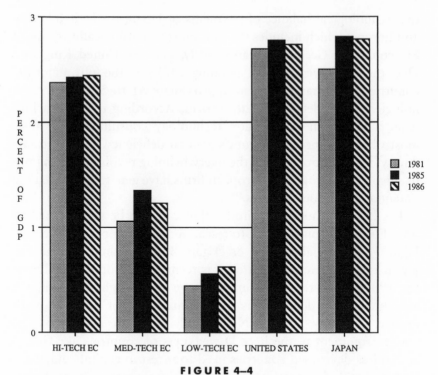

FIGURE 4-4

Research and Development Expenditure as a Percentage of
Gross Domestic Product

Source: OECD STIID Database. Note: Hi-Tech EC: France, Germany, the
Netherlands, and the United Kingdom; Med-Tech EC: Belgium-Luxembourg,
Denmark, and Italy; and Low-Tech EC: Greece, Ireland, Portugal, and Spain.

omies have exhausted the benefits of relative backwardness, and
they are now experiencing problems in graduating from a catch-up
economy to one on the frontier of technology."[10] The rapid pace of
technological innovation today makes achieving that goal even
more difficult.

Although the Community's technological lag pervades almost all
industries, we will focus on four main areas that have the greatest
importance to 1992: computer and electronic technology, telecommunications, financial markets and institutions, and production
management (process technology). In all four areas, the European
Community has found itself lagging significantly behind its United
States and Japanese rivals.

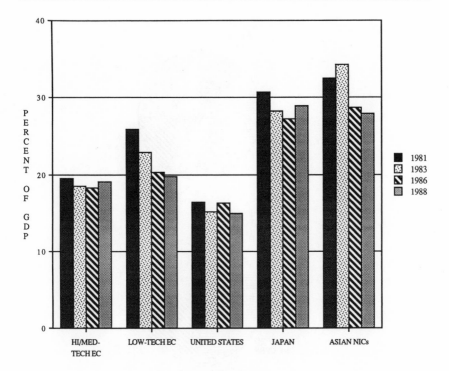

FIGURE 4–5

Gross Fixed Investment as a Percentage of Gross Domestic Product, 1981–1988

Source: IMF, *International Financial Statistics* (Washington: International Monetary Fund, 1989).

COMPUTER AND ELECTRONIC TECHNOLOGY. Europe's position in computer and electronic technology has suffered over the last decade. This is evidenced in the electronics industry in general[11] and within critical sectors of the computer and data processing industry. Figure 4–6 shows the growing dominance of the Japanese in the field of electronics. In 1980, the United States was clearly the major player in the field of electronics, with over 45 percent of the world market. Europe's position was second with a 26 percent market share.[12] By 1988, the American position had eroded significantly with Europe also feeling the pinch of the Japanese electronics wave. Although the Japanese expanded rapidly into the United States market, their predominant success was in consumer electronics. In the

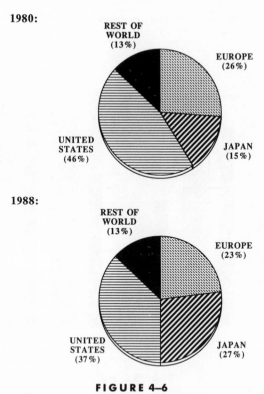

FIGURE 4–6

Share of World Electronics Market, 1980 and 1988

Source: EIC, *Electronics in the World* (New York: EIC, 1988).

field of computer technology, the American position, although erod-
ing slightly, was still dominant (see figure 4–7).

Were one to examine the individual sectors of the electronics industry, Europe would prove dominant in only one, telecommunications equipment. Japan is dominant in consumer electronics,
semiconductors, and connectors. America is dominant in all other
areas including data processing equipment and software, measure-
ment equipment, and automation. As we will show shortly, even
the European dominance in telecommunications is suspect.

Figure 4–8 shows that, in real terms, Europe's trade balance in
electronic technology has fallen dramatically in the last eight years.
In 1979, Europe had a very minor trade deficit in the entire electronics sector, active components (which include semiconductors),
and data processing (which includes computers). By 1987, the Eu-

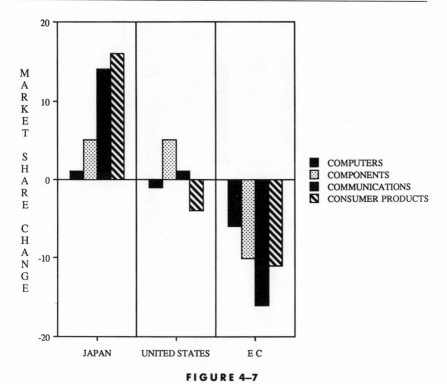

FIGURE 4–7

Change in World Market Shares in Electronics, 1980–1985

Source: OECD, *STI Review* (Washington: OECD, April 1989).

ropean deficit in electronics was over $15 billion with a deficit of almost $10 billion in data processing equipment alone. It proves most interesting that, although the total European trade imbalance is about evenly split between the United States and Japan, the major source of Europe's imbalance in high-technology equipment is with the United States.[13]

According to the standard 1992 line, we would expect that a major portion of the problem in the European electronics industry stems from fragmentation, but there is no indication that the existing European system is responsible for restraining European electronics companies. The major European electronics companies, each holding at least 2 percent of the market, are IBM, Siemens, CGE, Olivetti, Philips, and Thomson. The top five companies operating in Europe together hold 25 percent of the market, and the next five hold another 9 percent. In the United States, only four

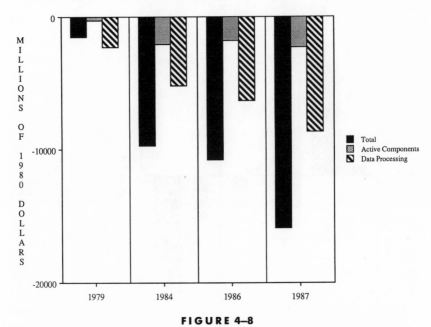

FIGURE 4–8

European Electronics Industry Trade Balance, 1979–1987

Source: EIC, *Electronics in the World* (New York: EIC, 1988).

companies are able to generate more than 2 percent market share; IBM, AT&T, Digital Equipment Corporation, and GM. Together, the top five companies operating in the United States hold only 20 percent of the market and the next five only 10 percent. In the individual market sectors of the electronics industry, the same pattern appears.[14] Europe is more significantly dominated by large firms than the United States, although less so than Japan. Where the European firms fall short is in the world market. Of the top eighteen electronics companies, eight are American, seven are Japanese, and only three are European. European firms control European markets, yet little else.

TELECOMMUNICATIONS TECHNOLOGY. On the surface, the competitive position of European companies in telecommunications technology appears quite strong. If we examine the Community's position in the world market, it appears that it is one of the dominant players. Examining OECD export and import trade in telecommunications, we see that, in 1984, the EC controlled approximately 32 percent of the total trade market. In comparison, the United States controlled 33 percent and Japan only 18 percent. But these figures mask two problems in European telecommunications.

First, the European share of OECD trade has been falling. In 1978, the EC share was almost 48 percent, whereas the American share was only 24 percent and the Japanese share 13 percent.[15] The negative time trend of European telecommunications market development is consistent with the earlier evidence for electronic technology in general.

Second, much of the dominance of the Community companies is, as with the case of electronics, driven by the captive European market. This is particularly true because of the importance of PTTs in the determination of national standards and the purchasing of infrastructure equipment. In public switching equipment alone, several examples highlight this dilemma. Siemens controls more than 50 percent of the business in Germany and Portugal; in Belgium and Spain, ITT dominates with over 60 percent of the market; and in Italy, ITALTEL dominates with a 65 percent market share. These figures are understatements since consortia of the large firms including the above plus CIT-ALCATEL, Ericsson, Plessey, and Philips dominate virtually every other country.[16]

The dominance of these large firms has increased the dependence of European companies on European markets, while the European goods have found less of a market outside of Europe. In the entire decade of the 1980s, the EC has maintained a negative balance of trade with both the United States and Japan in telecommunications equipment (see figure 4–9).[17] Unlike electronics, however, this trade imbalance is relatively stable but is expected to continue its slow decline in the 1990s.

The single market program in telecommunications is aimed at aiding the telecommunications industry in two ways. First, the program seeks greater cooperation and rationalization in European production and product development so that the individual country national champions can become joint European champions. This aim is predicated on the belief that greater economies of scale and experience and learning effects will allow the new European champions to compete on a large scale. The dominance of the twelve largest European companies in EC projects such as BRITE, ESPRIT, and RACE is evidence of the EC aim.[18] In conjunction with its de-

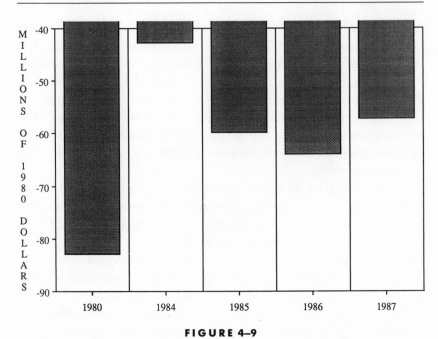

FIGURE 4–9

Net Trade Balance of the European Community with the
United States in Telecommunications Equipment

Source: CBEMA, *The Information Technology Industry Data Book* (Washington:
CBEMA, 1989).

sire to increase the scale of European companies, the EC believes
that open procurement will relieve Community countries of the
need to sustain their telecommunications champions. Although
some companies may find themselves swallowed by the new European champions, open procurement is meant to relieve the telecommunications industry's need to depend on preferential treatment
from individual governments.

EUROPEAN FINANCIAL MARKETS AND INSTITUTIONS. If there
is an area that has suffered because of the existence of national frontiers, it is the financial services industry, including banking and financial markets. Indeed, perhaps the major driving force behind
1992 is the necessity of competing against the increasingly domi-
nating financial markets and institutions of the United States and
Japan. In financial services, two areas are critical: financial mar-

kets—stock, futures, and options exchanges, and bond markets—
and financial institutions—banks, other financial intermediaries,
and insurance companies.

Financial Markets. In financial markets, Europe has suffered in two
ways. First, limited financial markets constrain companies' abilities
to raise investment funds in the cheapest and quickest manner possible. Second, financial markets serve to price and distribute risk
efficiently throughout the economy. The inefficient trading systems
and lack of derivative securities markets (futures and options, for
example) in many EC countries force an inadequate distribution of
financial claims on their economic systems. In this respect, firms
seeking more efficient means of raising capital and financial firms
wanting an opportunity to take advantage of the explosion of services seen in the markets of the United States and London both need
1992. Yet there is also an external threat inherent in the demand
for changes in the financial markets. Because firms are allowed to
list themselves and trade over the counter on any exchange, to float
bonds in almost any currency in many markets, and to conduct
private financial business anywhere in the world, European financial markets, with the possible exception of the City of London, face
the real possibility of having their national exchanges relegated to
positions similar to the regional exchanges in the United States,
which trade low-volume, local stocks, with relatively high risk and
limited access to capital.

The need for a pan-European trading system is clearly evidenced
by the low level of market capitalization of European firms. In
1980, the United States and Japanese stock markets had levels of
capitalization of 82 percent and 135 percent of GNP, respectively,
whereas in Europe the level was only 20 percent of GNP (see figure
4–10).[19] By 1987, the European situation had improved but it still
shows some weakness. Market capitalization per dollar of GNP
was still approximately 10 percent below that of the United States
even though firms of similar size appeared on the exchanges (market value per firm was $154 million in the EC and $151 million in
the United States). When we examine market capitalization relative
to savings, we see that Europeans are less likely to move their savings into equity, unlike Americans and Japanese. Although both the
United States and Japan have market value to savings (MV/SAV-

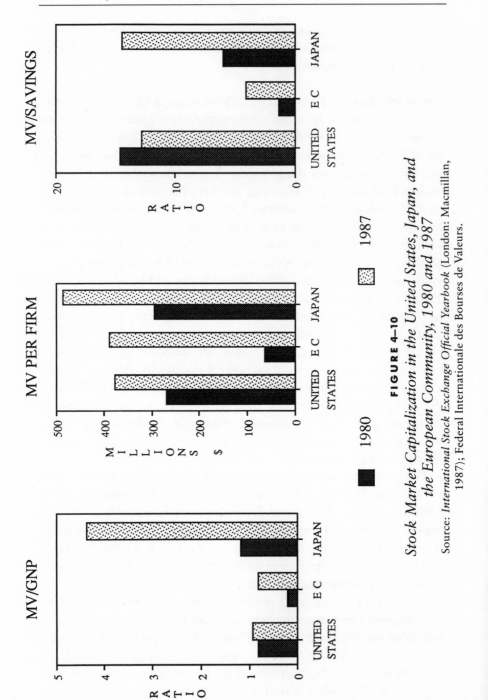

FIGURE 4–10

Stock Market Capitalization in the United States, Japan, and the European Community, 1980 and 1987

Source: *International Stock Exchange Official Yearbook* (London: Macmillan, 1987); Federal Internationale des Bourses de Valeurs.

INGS) rates of the same order of magnitude—ratios of approximately 15:1—the EC has a ratio only one-third as large.

We also see that transactions on the European exchanges are dominated by trading in the equity of very few firms. Gabriel Hawawani, in his study on European equity markets, has shown that even though the market value of the top ten domestic firms on the New York and Tokyo stock exchanges account for between 15 and 20 percent of the total market capitalization, these figures are on the order of 50 percent for the European exchanges. The Paris exchange is the lowest with a concentration of 24 percent, and Amsterdam is the highest with over 80 percent of the capital in the top ten firms. In Germany, Belgium, Spain, and Italy the top ten domestic firms account for over 50 percent of the market.[20] Since there is no indication that Europe contains fewer firms than the United States and Japan, the conclusion must be that the expense of raising capital on the European bourses is simply too high for intermediate-sized corporations.

A recent survey by Arthur Andersen & Co. highlights corporate Europe's demand for better capital market access.[21] Europe-wide, the demand for capital was given as the number one reason for listing on a foreign exchange. Interestingly, those companies located in the European countries with the most developed markets—France, Germany, Belgium, Luxembourg, and the United Kingdom—typically ranked some other reason as more important. This ranking no doubt reflects the ability of their home market to satisfy their capital needs. In addition, the survey clearly indicated that the major problems with almost all European exchanges, again London being the most notable exception, consisted of (1) the lack of automated clearing systems, (2) slow clearance and settlement, (3) the lack of derivative markets, and (4) the lack of cross-trading between exchanges. In all cases, complaints center on the failure of European exchanges to permit the technical quality of services found in the markets in New York, London, and Tokyo. And, again, these services primarily involve information technology innovations we have seen arise in the financial markets because of the commercial growth of computer technology.

Financial Institutions. Financial institution services in the EC vary considerably based on the nature of national regulation. In terms of international standing, the largest EC banks prove to be relatively dominant players on the world scene. Table 4–1 presents figures on the distribution of banking assets of the major banks in the United States, Japan, and the EC relative to the world market. In addition to revealing the obvious growth of the Japanese superbanks, the figures show the ability of the Community banks to hold their own against this onslaught. While the major American banks watched their world market share fall by almost one-half in a seven-year period, the major EC banks saw their position erode by only 14 percent. More important, while the major American banks' asset size fell in real terms by $100 billion, the major European banks saw their asset size increase by $1 trillion. The effective cause of this change was the large number of United States banks that fell below the $40 billion asset cutoff used to define a major bank. The Japanese banks grew by almost $3 trillion during the same period.

Although much of the decline of the United States banks and the rise of the European banks is driven by exchange-rate changes,

TABLE 4-1
World Distribution of Major Bank Assets
(in 1987 dollars)

	1980	1987
United States		
Total major bank assets	978,376	878,313
Average per bank	54,354	73,193
Percent of world market	16.35	8.62
European Community		
Total major bank assets	2,672,661	3,906,261
Average per bank	55,680	79,720
Percent of world market	44.68	38.33
Japan		
Total major bank assets	1,432,278	4,097,128
Average per bank	59,678	132,165
Percent of world market	23.84	40.20

Source: Authors' estimates.
Note: A major bank is defined as one possessing more than $40 billion in assets.

other aspects of the changes are due to more obvious banking fundamentals. First, the United States banks were seriously constrained by the debt burden of the less developed countries (LDCs) and the low American savings rate. Second, the regulatory structure of the United States obviously constrained bank expansion. Whatever gains to expansion existed were concentrated in the smaller scale retail sector of the industry and led to the development of the highly profitable and rapidly growing superregional banks. In spite of this fact, the largest American banks were comparable to the largest European banks, but there were simply fewer of them in the late 1980s. The Japanese banks grew most predominantly because of exchange-rate changes and the favorable balance of payments position of the Japanese economy.

From a world perspective, there is little reason to argue that 1992 represents an attempt of European banks to meet foreign competition. Their loss of market share is due solely to their inability to meet the more than 100 percent rise in the average size of Japanese banks, a feat no one would ever expect any country to achieve in such a short period of time. It is likely that the Community was willing to back down on its initial reciprocity stance regarding the Second Banking Directive because it saw little threat to European banks from foreign banks. The reciprocity card was viewed as unnecessary given the strength of the European banking system. Where, then, might we find the desire to alter the regulatory structure of European banking?

As in the case of a demand for regulatory change in the financial markets sector, the answer lies in the opportunities for expanding efficient banking systems into inefficient banking markets. More specifically, 1992 represents a unique opportunity for the stronger banking nations—Germany, France, and the United Kingdom—to provide expanding services into "underbanked" areas of the Community. In this respect, 1992 represents a trend almost identical to that followed in the United States in the last ten years. The EC banking initiative is primarily driven by the desire to rationalize production through the expansion of financial services into both underbanked areas of the Community—most notably, Italy, Spain, and Portugal—and underbanked areas of the commercial sector—most notably midsize corporations known in the United States as the middle market. As such, a fair portion of the pressure behind

TABLE 4-2

Cost of Selected Financial Services in Eight EEC Countries Relative to the Average Cost in the Four Lowest Cost Countries (in percentage deviations)

SERVICE	COUNTRY							
	Belgium	Germany	Spain	France	Italy	Luxembourg	Netherlands	United Kingdom
Consumer Services:								
Term loan (annual cost)	41	136	39	n.a.	121	−26	31	121
Credit card (annual cost)	79	60	26	−30	89	−12	43	16
Mortgage (annual cost)	31	57	118	78	−4	n.a.	−6	−20
Traveler's check	35	−7	30	39	22	−7	33	−7
Private stock purchase	36	7	65	−13	−3	7	114	123
Private government bond purchase	14	90	217	21	−63	27	116	36

Commercial Services:								
Letter of credit (three months)	22	−10	59	−7	9	27	17	8
Foreign exchange draft	6	31	196	56	23	33	−46	16
Term loan (annual cost)	4	6	19	−7	9	6	43	46
Institutional stock purchase	26	69	153	−5	47	68	26	−47
Institutional government bond purchase	284	−4	60	57	92	−36	21	n.a.
Expected reduction in prices from 1992 initiative	11%	10%	21%	12%	14%	8%	4%	7%
Expected customer savings (In millions of dollars)	$987	$6,486	$4,512	$5,217	$5,640	$141	$423	$7,191

Note: All costs expressed in the percentage deviation from the average cost in the four lowest countries except for expected price reductions.

Source: P. Cecchini, *1992: The European Challenge* (Brookfield, Vt: Gower, 1988).

this initiative arises from the unwillingness of corporations to continue to be forced to deal with national banking systems.

The opportunities that exist are seen most readily in table 4–2. In terms of the price of banking services the most expensive countries in which to bank are Spain, Italy, Belgium, and France, but in terms of commercial services, which we argue are the most important, Spain and Italy are clearly the most expensive. Although the EC estimates enormous savings for individual consumers, which will no doubt come about, the desire to change the regulatory structure is aimed first and foremost at consolidating the banking system for the banking system's benefit. It is inconceivable that because consumer term loans are expensive in Germany, German banks would consider it to their advantage to undo their German monopoly position. The price differentials among EC countries exist, not because of inefficiencies in the banking system (no one would expect any bank to do anything but be as efficient as it could under its existing regulatory system), but because of the desire to hold prices as high as possible in the captive national market. With banking deregulations in the United States, increased consumer services was the price banks paid for the right to expand across state lines. The prices of German term loans should fall because the Germans would hardly be granted access to Belgian markets were the Belgians excluded from the opportunity to market their services in Germany. In the United States, the end result of the expansion was the replacement of local monopolies by superregionals, which brought a higher level of services with greater profitability because of the gains to rationalized production from economies of scale and scope. The same should be expected in Europe.

That the changes in European banking for the commercial customer are overstated can be seen in a study by Greenwich Associates.[22] Currently, European companies deal with almost twenty banks on average and consider approximately two of these their lead banks. Europeans view domestic banks as primarily oriented toward long-term relationship banking, whereas they are much more likely to view foreign concerns as transaction oriented. Overall, European corporations are relatively satisfied with the level of services and are found to prefer to deal mostly with domestic banks except in cases of cross-border activities requiring the services of merchant banks.

PROCESS TECHNOLOGY. Process technology is directly related to the computer and advanced electronics areas, and the evidence cited earlier regarding European weaknesses on these fronts is confirmed when we examine the advance of the technological revolution to the office and the factory.

In figure 4–11 we see that the European trade balance in office automation and automation equipment has steadily declined in the 1980s. By 1987, both office automation and automation and data processing equipment reached a combined deficit of $3 billion. In spite of this deficit, some EC countries have managed to bring the factory of the future into operation. Figure 4–12 shows that although in 1981 and 1982 the average EC usage of robots was approximately one-half that of the United States, by 1983 average robot usage in seven EC countries was on par with America. Both, however, had one-tenth the average usage of the Japanese. Yet, the average for the EC hides wide divergences across EC countries. By 1988, Germany, France, Belgium, and Italy had over 100 robots per 100,000 manufacturing workers. Unfortunately, Spain, the Neth-

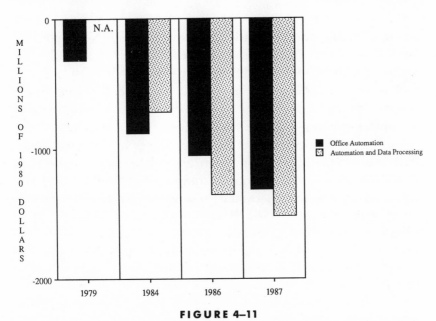

FIGURE 4–11

European Automation Equipment Trade Balance, 1979–1987

Source: EIC, *Electronics in the World* (New York: EIC, 1988).

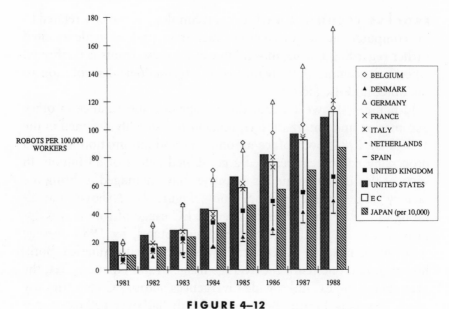

FIGURE 4–12

Usage of Industrial Robots in Selected Countries

Source: International Federation of Robotics.

erlands, Britain, and Denmark had fewer than 60. No doubt, Ireland, Greece, and Portugal have proved even less successful in integrating high technology into their factories.

European manufacturers, facing a limited and therefore expensive market for factory technology and confronted with the inability to replace expensive workers with more efficient automated systems, have failed to integrate high technology into the workplace with the same relish as their American and Japanese competitors. *The Economist* accuses European companies of "looking on factories of the future as intellectual curiosities best left to researchers to study with taxpayers' cash."[23] The application of new industrial technology is more than simply capital investment; it also requires the "willingness and ability of the labor force—at both management and shop floor level—to accept and adapt to the new technology."[24]

The Role of External Economic Forces

The third dimension of importance to understanding the causes of the single market program is the role of external economic forces.

We can subdivide the role of external economic pressures into four major influences: the rise of Japan as an economic power, the rise of the Asian NICs, the European unemployment problem, and the relative economic decline of the United States.

THE RISE OF JAPANESE ECONOMIC POWER. The first and perhaps major external factor behind the single market program is the rise of Japan as an economic power. Figure 4–13 shows the relative GDP growth of Japan, the United States, selected Asian NICs, and the EC. Since 1980, as is shown, the EC has been in relative economic decline, particularly with respect to Pacific rim countries. In addition, our earlier discussion has shown that there is a particularly wide gap in technologically sensitive industries, which are the industries that represent the major economic markets of the future. Even more interesting, this technology gap exists between the United States and Europe even though there is no substantive European growth gap relative to the United States in general.

That the Japanese have had trade relation difficulties with established economic powers is hardly news. The recent Omnibus Trading Act with its "super-301" provision, which allows the president to designate countries as unfair trade partners, reflects United States ambivalence on this matter. Nevertheless, the EC has had even greater difficulties adjusting to the Japanese trade juggernaut. To sections of Britain, Japan represents a source of jobs and external investment, but to France, Japan represents unfair competition. William Pfaff put it most concisely when he noted in an *International Herald Tribune* article that "Europe believes in managed trade. . . . Japan believes in managed trade much more than do the Europeans."[25]

In certain respects, Europe desires to compete and win against Japan; however, there is no clear consensus as to how this war could be won. The single market program has characteristics that can satisfy those wanting to go directly against the Japanese and those wanting the Japanese to begin to play by European rules. On the one hand, the reciprocity card could simply force other countries to negotiate an agreement bilaterally with the EC. In the words of Michael Heseltine, "This is good old-fashioned politics . . . I have always been curious about how free-traders expect to penetrate the real fortress—Japan, for example—if they deny themselves the only battering ram [reciprocity] available."[26] Given this philosophy, it is

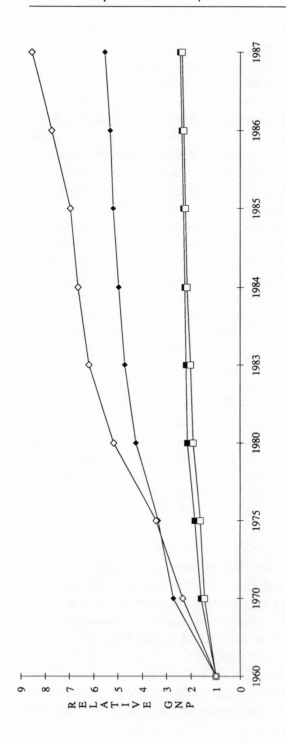

FIGURE 4–13

*Relative Gross Domestic Product of the European Community,
the United States, Japan, and Selected Asian NICs
(1960 = 1.00)*

Source: International Monetary Fund, *International Financial Statistics,* Annual
Yearbook, December 1988 (Washington: International Monetary Fund).

understandable why the EC would want one large club aimed in one direction rather than twelve odd-sized clubs.

On the other hand, 1992 can also serve to force Japanese firms to invest directly in Europe rather than importing finished or semi-finished products from their home production facilities. Given the likelihood that the "battering ram" philosophy will fail (it has never succeeded without military force), 1992 will probably prove most effective through this second route. Indeed, Japanese firms are currently rushing to invest directly in Europe to avoid being shut out by 1992. Figure 4–14 shows the increasing movement of Japanese direct investment into the Community. Figure 4–15 indicates that most of that investment is concentrated in the United Kingdom, with a moderate amount being invested in France and Belgium. Whether Japanese firms will be able to continue their turnkey strategy, such as with the Nissan Bluebird factory in England, or will be

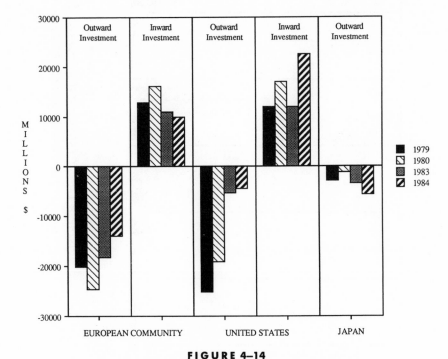

FIGURE 4–14

Cross-Border Investment Flows by Source

Source: Dunning, J., and J. Cantwell, *IRM Directory of Statistics of International Investment and Production* (Basingstoke, England: Macmillan, 1987).

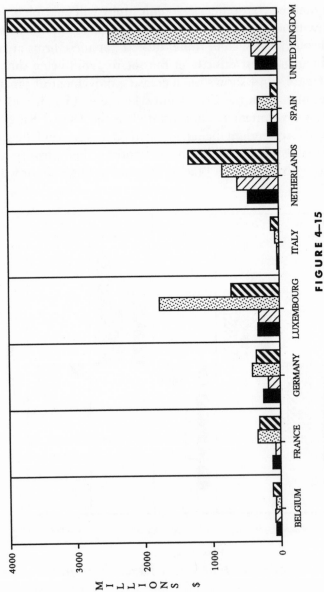

FIGURE 4-15

Japanese Direct Investment in Europe by Country, 1984–1988

Source: "Japan's Community Chest," *Corporate Finance* (May 1989).

ultimately forced to produce almost all of their components in Europe remains to be seen.

THE RISE OF THE NEWLY INDUSTRIALIZING COUNTRIES. A second external factor contributing to European unease is the rise of the economic power of the newly industrialized countries (NICs). As Paul Kennedy has shown in his book *The Rise and Fall of the Great Powers,* the relative economic position of the Eastern Pacific rim NICs has improved substantially and is expected to continue to improve, because these countries possess the resources to dominate the major components of manufacturing into the twenty-first century.[27]

Figure 4–13 shows the strength of several of the Asian dragons who have followed export-oriented economic philosophies that most obviously have served to hurt mature economies like those of the European Community. In addition, as primary production sources for Japanese exports, the NICs are particularly vulnerable to 1992-induced losses. Industrializing countries like Korea, with high debt levels, must rely on low labor and currency values to generate the exports necessary to fund the interest and principal payments of this debt (debt, it should be noted, owed mostly to Western and Japanese banks). Their differential advantages lie in low wages (see figure 4–16) and long working days. While an average worker in Japan works 2,168 hours per year and Americans and Germans work 1,900 hours per year, Koreans work an average of 2,800 hours per year. In Belgium and Denmark a manufacturing worker works only 1,500 hours per year.[28]

Should Japan be forced to invest directly in the European Community countries, this investment would no doubt come at the expense of production facilities in countries such as Korea, Thailand, and the Philippines. Given the inability of these countries to invest directly in the Community themselves, because they are still under-industrialized at home, they will have permanently lost employment and GDP to the EC. In this respect, 1992 could rightfully be viewed as a transference of wealth from cheap wage and currency countries directly to the EC.

THE PROBLEM OF PERSISTENT UNEMPLOYMENT IN EUROPE. As we have noted before, European countries, like all countries, promulgate policies aimed at protecting employment in sensitive

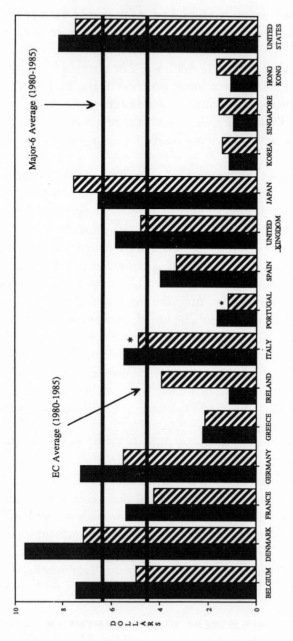

FIGURE 4–16

Average Manufacturing Wages in Selected Countries, 1980 and 1985

Source: United Nations, *Statistical Yearbook, 1985/86* (New York: United Nations, 1988).

sectors of the economy. Indeed, most of the protectionist measures employed in Europe after the abolition of tariffs in the late 1960s were specifically aimed at protecting employment from the economic malaise of the 1970s. For a period of time, these measures appeared to be working because European unemployment remained low in the early 1970s. Nevertheless, since that time, both the rate and the absolute magnitude of European unemployment have risen to staggering levels (see figure 1–2). What makes this trend even more amazing is that it continued to occur, and even accelerated, during an era of economic prosperity. One cannot underestimate the importance European governments place on solving the unemployment problem. Because European countries have been unable to solve the problem individually, 1992 represents a collective attempt at supply-side socialism.

The European problem is troublesome for three reasons. First, the EC has one of the world's lowest population growth rates: Community estimates put its population growth at 2 percent over the period 1985 to 2005. Expectations of population growth for the world during that period are on the order of 35 percent, and even the United States expects a growth rate of between 15 and 20 percent. The conclusion is simple. The EC economy has proved unable to create jobs even in good economic years. Given the dominant role that employment stability and job creation play in the European social democratic tradition, this state of affairs is particularly frightening to Western European leaders. The future bodes higher required social support to an aging population with a diminishing working tax base to support it.

The second problem facing Europe is the distribution of unemployment. During the 1980s, all of Spain and Ireland, northern England, southern Italy, plus major sections of western and southern France consistently had unemployment rates of more than 10 percent. In Ireland, unemployment has led directly to an emigration-driven population decline, even though the Irish have the highest birthrate in the Community. As might also be expected, the European unemployment problem has been heavily concentrated among the young (over 40 percent of the unemployed are less than twenty-five years of age) and female segments of the population (almost 50 percent of the unemployed are women). An even more frightening statistic is that unlike the unemployed in the United States, more than 50 percent of the unemployed in Europe have been jobless for more than a year, and more than 30 percent have gone without a job for more than two years.

The third major problem of European unemployment is the level of jobs in service industries. The young and female sections of the major industrialized nations find themselves increasingly employed in service positions, yet as figure 4–17 shows, the EC has failed to get on the services bandwagon. In the United States, the major area of employment growth is not in traditional manufacturing but in services, and much of the employment driven by the technological revolution is services employment. Although approximately the same percentage of the labor force was in services in the United States in 1975 as in 1985, the growth in service jobs during that period was on the order of 15 to 30 percent, which proves the robust ability of the American economy to create jobs. In the Community, although considerably more people are employed in service industries today than in the past, the growth of services employment is below that of both the United States and Japan. The implication is that European expansion in services would occur primarily

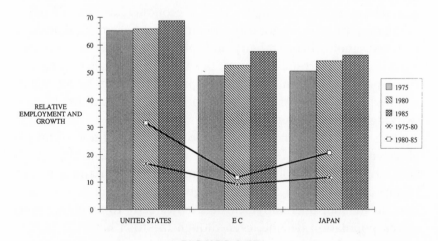

FIGURE 4–17

Employment in the Service Sector

Source: Eurostat, *Basic Statistics of the European Community* (Luxembourg: Office of Official Publications of the European Communities, various years). Note: The bar graphs represent the ratio of employees in the service sector to employees in the industrial sector. The bold lines represent the growth in services employment.

at the expense of employment in traditional industry and not be driven by the creation of new jobs. Since the EC has failed to advance in the primary technological markets of the late twentieth century, it is no wonder that its workers have not been able to take advantage of the economic benefits that follow with the growth of those markets.

THE RELATIVE DECLINE OF THE UNITED STATES' ECONOMIC POWER. Since the early 1970s, and in the 1980s in particular, there has been evidence of the persistent erosion of the relative world economic position of the United States. As Paul Kennedy notes, much of the United States' economic power was due to the void created by World War II. The relative economic changes seen today partially reflect the movement back to a more stable equilibrium, but this return to equilibrium has potential costs.[29]

First, this change creates an economic leadership void that the Japanese have failed to fill. The apparent ill ease that the Japanese have in inheriting the United States' mantle is truly complex and worthy of many treatises on its own. Several aspects of the problem are worth noting here. First, economic leaders must almost always be military leaders as well. Japan's constitution along with the general persona of its people have made Japan's assuming a world military role almost unthinkable. Japan's dithering over its role in the Persian Gulf crisis is a case in point. Second, the major economies of the world today still remain Western in orientation. Economic power also contains a curious streak of cultural chauvinism that must prove enticing to those outside the dominant economy. For Britain in the nineteenth century and the United States in the twentieth century, adopting the economic leadership role was relatively easy, since their major trading partners shared basic cultural antecedents. For Japan, this prospect has proved difficult since much of its culture is so totally foreign to westerners. Although one finds many westerners in Tokyo, it is difficult to find assimilated foreigners in cities like Osaka or Kobe. Finally, the Japanese political process is truly complex and it is not easy to understand how Japanese political leaders wield power. As Karel van Wolferen notes, westerners simply do not understand the nature of Japan's collective leadership that causes its leaders to rarely be able to grant concessions to foreign governments. Japanese elected officials are invariably unable to move the bureaucracy that they nominally head. Van Wolferen writes:

> [U]nless the relative lack of governmental responsibility in Japan . . . is recognized, relations with Japan are bound to deteriorate further. Statecraft in Japan is quite different from in Europe, the Americas and most of contemporary Asia. . . . All [political cliques] are components of what may be called the System. . . . No one is ultimately in charge. . . . If Japan seems to be in the world but not of it, this is because its prime minister and other power-holders are incapable of delivering on political promises they may make concerning commercial or other matters requiring important adjustments by one of the components of the System.[30]

Second, the decline of the United States dollar as the primary reserve currency and denominator for cross-border transactions has led to instability in the financial sector. The Japanese yen has failed to satisfy the reserve role, and, of the European currencies, only the deutsche mark commands the stability to serve as a truly international currency. Figure 4–18 shows the currency denomination of cross-border transactions from 1981 through 1988. There is a clear

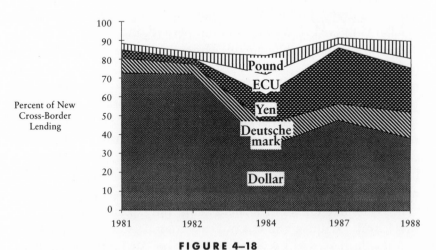

FIGURE 4–18

Currency Denomination of Cross-Border Transactions, 1981–1988

Source: Bank for International Settlements, *International Banking and Financial Market Developments.*

decline in the use of the dollar in these transactions and a rise in the usage of the yen and, to some degree, the mark. In 1981, 73 percent of all cross-border transactions were denominated in dollars, 8 percent in marks, and 5 percent in yen. By 1988, only 38 percent of these transactions were in dollars, 24 percent were in yen, and 14 percent in marks. The recent dramatic decline of the dollar versus the mark and the expected increase in East European trade implies that this trend will continue.

Today we have three overlapping currency zones. The dollar still plays a role on the world market but significantly less so than even ten years ago. The mark zone encompasses most of Western Europe and is rapidly expanding to include growing areas of Eastern Europe as well. The yen zone is quickly rising in the Pacific. The European Commission hopes that the european currency unit (ECU, see chapter 5), a basket of European currencies, will come to serve as the primary reserve currency in Europe, and perhaps beyond. Nevertheless, as figure 4–18 shows, there is little evidence that the ECU is the currency of choice for cross-national transactions.

Finally, since the United States is the major trade partner with both Japan and the EC, any change in its level of demand has radical repercussions on these economics. As we showed in figure 1–1, the United States still accounts for a significant proportion of world wealth, equaling approximately that of the EC and Japan combined. Although its per capita wealth has declined over the last decade, the United States has experienced population growth and an expansion of the work force that preserves the nation's ranking as the world's dominant economy in total value terms. The stability of the world economic system, although less dependent on the United States, still rolls as the United States rocks.

The 1992 Quid Pro Quo—The Social Dimension

The single market program not only involves altering the nature of national government involvement in the intra-Community commercial sector, it also calls for a commitment to the environment, workers, and less developed areas of the Community. The Single European Act states that

> Member States shall pay particular attention to encouring improvements, especially in the working environment. . . . The Commission

shall endeavor to develop dialogue between management and la-bour. . . . The Community shall aim at reducing disparities between various regions . . . [and it shall] preserve, protect and improve the quality of the environment.[31]

The social dimension, in which we would include not only the foregoing stipulations but the price decreases expected to be seen owing to the opening of the European commercial sector, represents the political quid pro quo for the expansion of intra-Community markets. As the *Financial Times* notes, "the 1992 programme is more than just a charter for capitalists. . . . For Mr. Jacques Delors, and others who think like him, the social dimension also has a wider political significance. It is seen as a symbol of the sort of society the Community should be attempting to create."[32]

Labor Policy

That European countries' labor policies have kept them at a com-petitive disadvantage with both the United States and Far East has long been recognized. The European Social Democratic tradition with its strong commitment to government-management-labor dia-logue is both itself a cause of the rigidity of the European labor system and a reflection of the pressures that have led to that rigidity. Much is made of the fact that 1992 will create a free market in labor, with firms having the opportunity to move production to countries with cheaper wages, such as Spain, Greece, and Portugal and workers having free access to jobs anywhere in the Community. Indeed, as figure 4–16 shows, there are substantial differences in the level of manufacturing wages across European Community coun-tries. Wages in Greece, Ireland, and Portugal are literally one-third of the wages in the major six economies (France, Germany, Italy, the United Kingdom, the United States, and Japan) and one-half the Community average. On the surface, these figures point to potential gains from the movement of labor-intensive production facilities to the low wage countries.

On the other hand, EC actions have consistently shown the Com-munity's commitment to maintaining a high level of corporate so-cialism such as is seen in Germany. Of course, free labor markets and a commitment to corporate socialism do not have to be mutually exclusive. A commitment to worker health and safety is not at odds with permitting firms to close plants in one country and to open others in countries with cheaper wages. The desire to see a freer European labor market does, however, ignore the specific structural and political characteristics of the European labor market.

Suppose, for the sake of argument, that conditions in Europe change sufficiently that firms could instantaneously shift production to low wage countries. The immediate effect would be an increase in the labor costs in countries such as Spain and Portugal and a decline in countries such as Germany and Denmark. We would also expect low skill jobs to concentrate in low wage/low education countries and high skill jobs to concentrate in high wage/high education countries.

Is this what will occur because of 1992? Of course not. Many examples exist that show the natural rigidity of European labor markets. In Germany today very few people work on Sunday, and there is movement toward a four-day workweek. The Danes' consternation over 1992 was directly related to the program's effect on Denmark's liberal social welfare system. Within the EC countries, certain factors will serve to mitigate the tendency of jobs to move to low wage countries.

First, as the skill needs of employers rise, the pressure to move jobs to low wage countries will prove weak. In the United States, for example, the dominant job creation areas are in places such as San Diego, Los Angeles, Cambridge, and San Jose, not Jackson, Mississippi, Wheeling, West Virginia, and Baton Rouge, Louisiana, in spite of their high unemployment and low wage levels.[33] Skilled jobs move to areas with high education levels and skilled jobs are the wave of the future. High technology jobs will remain in the high wage countries. Portugal, Ireland, Greece, and Spain have had consistently high unemployment rates over the last decade, in spite of the fact that they possessed even lower relative wages in the past.

Second, the strength of the unions in countries such as Germany and Belgium will simply not permit the kind of quick adjustment envisioned. One Belgian CEO was very cognizant that a recent merger between his company and another led to an enormous duplication of jobs. Nevertheless, because of the negative press he knew his company would receive by firing Belgians, while keeping on similar workers in another country, his decision was to allow slow attrition to replace more immediate changes.

Other examples serve to highlight this dimension. The German *mitbestimmung* system, which ensures worker representation on the boards of directors of companies, will severely limit the ability of German corporations to move employment, particularly in weak economic times. Lucrative union-negotiated or legally sanctioned severance agreements make removing workers extremely difficult in almost all European countries. In Belgium and Germany, a fifteen-year salaried employee could expect approximately eighteen months' salary for dismissal without cause. In the United Kingdom the same worker could expect about fourteen months' pay, and in France about twelve months' pay. The numbers are much smaller for hourly employees, varying between one month's pay in Belgium to eight months' in the United Kingdom. But, for an executive, the severance is more on the order of a half-year's salary.[34] For mass layoffs and plant closings, many countries, such as Germany and Belgium, require government approval and the development of a "social plan," which is normally developed in conjunction with a workers' council and is aimed at easing the burden on the workers and the community. The social plan is, in effect, a tax on plant closings and employee termination.

Third, the attempts to develop a European corporate charter, although certainly proper as a means of reducing the need of corporations to incorporate in several different countries simultaneously and of further harmonizing European company law, is also a reflection of the desire for a "fair" set of corporate rules for workers. Current plans would allow a company to choose one of three "European" options, the German *mitbestimmung,* the Franco-Belgian *comites d'entreprise,* and the British system of open negotiation. The German option, as we discussed previously, ensures workers representation on the board of directors of companies. The *comites d'entreprise* sets up a system of elected workers' councils. The British system is, of course, no system at all but rather a catchall for whatever comes out of the negotiations between the corporation and its workers. As might be expected, unions are concerned that the British model will come to dominate, so they have been lobbying hard with the EC bureaucracy to get preferential treatment for the German and Franco-Belgian models through devices such as tax incentives to corporations. German, Dutch, Belgian, and French corporations, invariably committed to their national style of corporate charter, are afraid of being priced out of markets because of uncompetitive labor costs.

The Environment

The development of a pan-European environment policy is also a case of political necessity mixing with fundamental logic. The tendency for separate but adjacent countries to force pollution and other social bads on their neighbors is a common occurrence. This is a particularly acute problem in Europe with its high population density, small land size, and diverse wealth levels. The Germans and Danish have well-developed environment codes, whereas the Greeks, Irish, Portuguese, and Spanish have the least developed policies. The result is the classic case of an economic externality—all countries overpollute thereby imposing larger than necessary costs on all Europeans. The problem is further exacerbated in Europe because local authorities are responsible for protecting the environment in many of the countries, and since the EC deals with national rather than local governments, an additional roadblock is set up between EC policy and its implementation.

Environmental concerns are not only the purvey of the "Greens." A recent conference board study found that environmental issues were one of the top five areas of greatest concern to companies.[35] This rating reflects not only what appears to be genuine concerns about the environment but also the obvious reality that environmental regulations pose enormous costs to corporations. In intercountry environment debates countries such as Denmark and the Netherlands, with no automobile manufacturers, support very stringent and quickly implemented automobile emission standards. Countries with automobile production facilities, such as Italy, Spain, France, and the United Kingdom, are pushing for lower standards and a wider implementation window.

A pan-European environmental policy would obviously aid in resolving the economic externality problem, but it would also serve to stop competition through environmental policy. With totally harmonized European standards, such competition would no doubt decline. Indeed, there are many who would argue that there should not be any competition for the least sustainable level of environmental regulation. Whatever the answer to that question, a pan-European environmental code, should one ever be developed, would force high standards on countries previously holding to lower standards and not force any maximum standard on any country. The end result will mean that tougher environmental codes will have to be met by corporate Europe.

Current plans include measures such as the reduction of automobile emissions by 70 percent and the development of water purity standards. Yet even with the added authority of the Single European Act and favorable European Court rulings, the likely success of the Community's programs is low. Since 1972, the EC has issued more than 120 directives regarding the environment, almost all of which have been ignored by at least one of the member states. Italy has refused to implement more than 40 environment directives, and Greece and Germany have ignored over 25 each.[36] Southern Europe is not as "Green" as the more affluent north, and this has been reflected in the debate within the Community. The concerns of the governments in the south is simple: many are afraid that the EC could price itself out of world markets by setting new environmental standards without regard to costs in terms of jobs and corporate profits.

Regional Policy

The third major social dimension of 1992 is the Community's recommitment to European regional policy, that is, the policy committing the wealthier regions of the EC to enhancing the economic climate of the poor and declining industrial regions. Per capita wealth varies across the Community with income in Greece, Portugal, and Ireland being approximately one-half that of Luxembourg, Denmark, and Germany. Income in southern Italy is approximately equal to that of Spain, even though the income of northern Italy is close to that of England and France. Historically, the EC has committed a relatively small amount of money to EC regional policy, yet 1992 has definitely increased the pressure on the Community to be more cognizant of the regional impact of EC policy. A reflection of this commitment is the steady increase in EC regional funds that have gone from 5 to 6 percent of the budget in the early

1980s, to 5.9 percent in 1985, to almost 10 percent in 1989.[37] The staff of the regional directorate (DG 16) has almost doubled since 1986. Total structural funds, which include regional policy funds in the European Regional Development Fund plus training programs under the European Social Fund, are estimated to reach 25 percent of the budget by 1992.[38] *The Economist* has gone so far as to question whether regional policy will be the "budget-buster of the 1990s."[39]

Price Decreases—Why 1992 Is Not Aimed at Consumers

The obvious selling point of 1992 to Europeans in general is that it will expand their range of product and job choices and increase their effective wealth through price decreases of an average of 7 percent. Yet, as we have noted earlier, one cannot look at the gains to single individuals to determine why 1992 is occurring. European consumers would no doubt have gained if the European airline cartel was dismantled anytime in the last twenty years, yet no substantive attempt was made to provide this most obvious benefit. This does not mean, however, that the development of the single market program was unaffected by the gains to consumers, since consumers must ultimately vote for politicians. Whether or not consumers gain from specific single market initiatives will be a function of whether or not the special interests affecting EC decisions can achieve their ends without having to pay in substantial price declines.

As one example of a set of circumstances wherein a changed regulatory structure triggers a decline in prices, consider the case of banking. Banking services prices are expected to fall anywhere from 5 to 50 percent, depending on the country and service. Why is this necessary? To permit German banks to expand into Belgian or Dutch markets without permitting Belgian and Dutch banks the opportunity to compete in Germany is simply impossible. Therefore, allowing substantially increased competition as part of the price for cross-national expansion of banking services becomes necessary. The alternative would be to sanction a set of European superbanks *a priori*, yet exactly which banks would receive this laurel makes it nearly impossible to achieve such an end.

On the other side of the coin, consider the standards for European television and automobiles. Because of the heavy lobbying of the French, European television standards limit the choices of Europeans for television programming. In effect, the reduced choice forced on the European viewing public is a hidden price increase. Similarly, there is no doubt that permitting European content requirements for automobiles is definitely inferior, from the consumers' standpoint, to allowing the import of foreign-produced Japanese autos. Although European automobile standards and tax harmonization may equalize the price of automobiles in general, external restrictions will still serve to limit consumer choice and keep automobile prices higher than would otherwise be the case were consumers to have access to a freer market.

Reflecting on the Facts

Let us spend a moment putting this all together into a coherent whole. We see in 1992 closer inter-European relations driven by similarities in the views of the leaders of European countries. Even Margaret Thatcher, at times appearing to play the Euro-curmudgeon, seemed to be simply playing a strategic intra-Community game. Yet this closer political cooperation is not a cause of 1992 but primarily a concurrent result of the pressures leading to the need for the single market reforms. Needless to say, the lack of such cooperation could be a detriment. Behind 1992 are the twin threats of *technological* obsolescence and *external threat*, conveniently a common goal and, excusing the language, a common enemy. Technological change has caused a fundamental alteration in business and has led to organizational and regulatory change. The Japanese/Asian threat has accentuated the need to react to that change. Alan Philip, in his 1988 *European Management Journal* article, states that

> the leading member states were clearly scared by the growing evidence of Western Europe's inability to stay competitive, especially in high-technology industries, and by the difficulty that highly regulated and protected parts of their economies were having in adapting to changing economic forces and in maintaining employment. The fragmentation of [EC] markets, bringing in its train duplication of R & D, uncompetitive products and small-scale "national champions" unable to match the weight of U.S. or Japanese multinationals, was seen as the single greatest obstacle to the future prosperity of all [EC] citizens.

Not for the first time were those who favored European integration able to play on the fears of national leaders to persuade them to take steps which are set to erode the sovereignty of the nation-states.[40]

In the United States, we have seen these factors bring about a radical change in regulation and then a radical corporate restructuring wave partially unleashed by this change in regulation. In Europe, the reaction is 1992, for specific structural reasons. First, many of the gains to be achieved by reorganization require a scale that goes beyond national boundaries. Second, the gains to rationalized production across EC borders are simply too great, relative to the benefits of specific groups from stopping such rationalization. Third, such gains necessitate a governmental organization beyond national boundaries to protect national interests. That is, although 1992 represents a transfer of sovereignty, that responsibility implies an implicit contract to protect certain basic European coalitions. For example, the current discussion of a pan-European corporate charter clearly holds an obligation to protect European unions, particularly in Germany.

Nineteen ninety-two is, therefore, the corporate renaissance of Europe. But, as Carlo DiBenedetti notes, it is a fight for European economic survival. The single market program is the European attempt to control its relative economic decline. Where necessary, and where the political coalitions allow it, surviving means opening markets through harmonization. Where the costs of more competitive markets outweigh the gains to specific political coalitions, harmonization will serve to restrict market access.

Nineteen ninety-two is the European reaction to a rapidly changing world. In the United States, Japan, and the Asian NICs, the technological revolution of the 1970s and 1980s has been met through traditional means. In the United States, the efficiency of the financial markets has allowed for a corporate restructuring never before seen and possibly never imagined. Although some regulatory changes were necessary, the extent of government involvement in business in America never approached that of Europe. Japan and the Asian NICs had a somewhat easier time adjusting to the rapid changes since their economies were still growing and developing with the technological revolution. In Europe, the regulatory structure was such that a regulatory solution was the only way out. Nineteen ninety-two is a bureaucratic solution to an existing regulatory structure that does not permit change when change must occur.

Much is made of the fact that the EC today represents a market containing approximately 320 million people and $2.7 trillion in gross domestic product, placing the Community's GDP second behind the United States' GDP of $4.5 trillion, and slightly ahead of Japan's $2.4 trillion GDP. But sheer size is really a pariah. On a per capita basis, the Community's $8,500 per person falls significantly behind Japan's $11,000 per person and the United States' $18,400 per person, although much of the difference is owing to the recent entrance of poorer countries into the Community. In terms of exports and imports, the EC dominates both the United States (imports of $490 billion, exports of $341 billion) and Japan (imports of $212.4 billion, exports of $302.9 billion). But much of the Community's trade dependence represents intra-Community trade. The last decade has seen the Community countries fall behind significantly in world trade in general and in high-technology production trade more specifically. Although the figures suggest that the Community's market potential approaches that of the two dominant economies in the world today, that market potential has proved elusive.

5

1992: The Monetary Dimension

We must now look afresh at the case for monetary union because there are new arguments, new needs, and new approaches to be assessed which go to the heart of our apparently intractable problems.
—Roy Jenkins, First Jean Monnet Lecture,
Florence Italy, October 27, 1977

Although they are part and parcel of the 1992 initiative, the proposals for economic and monetary union as set forth by the Delors Report "impl[y] far more than the Single Market programme," than the mere linkage of twelve separate European currencies.[1] Because the desire for greater monetary union, along with its sister the European Social Charter, reflects an idea either never or not fully laid out by the *White Paper,* we have chosen to deal with monetary union as a separate topic.

In one respect, the push toward the formation of a European monetary union (EMU) has the aspect of an afterthought to it, as if it were a last-minute recognition by specific EC governments that the free flow of capital, so readily embraced as a linchpin of the 1992 program, would, in effect, completely neutralize independent national monetary policy. The other side of the argument, represented most effectively by the early views of Margaret Thatcher, sees an economic and monetary union as backdoor federalism, an attempt to inextricably link the economies, and ultimately the societies, of Europe together while lowering former great states to the status of Euro-provinces. Although Mrs. Thatcher, bowing to domestic political pressures, moderated her views on this matter, the apparent quickening of the pace of European political union caused by the apparent consensus in the Community for monetary union lends credence to her thinking.[2]

EMU is also a reflection of the same forces that have shaped the 1992 program and, in certain respects, is a natural analog to the enterprise. Just as the Single European Act and 1992 are a compromise between the strong pro-Community forces and the more conservative community-of-sovereign-states lobby, the plan for economic and monetary union is a reformulation of earlier plans drawn up by the same pro-Community forces. This conservative group is obviously concerned about the question of policy sovereignty since EMU implies an abdication of independent fiscal and monetary policy initiative.

The pro-Community body is buttressed by two arguments. First many corporations desire to operate under one monetary regime, thereby reinforcing the pan-European regulatory structure they are working so hard to construct. A 1988 survey by the Association for the Monetary Union of Europe indicated that 86 percent of executives surveyed wanted to see a European currency created. Second, EC governments recognize the need to protect their fiscal and monetary policies, which are deemed necessary for internal economic considerations, against attack by fiscally stronger countries, for example, Germany, once the single market ideal is achieved.

The initiative that is today causing consternation in London and Frankfurt differs marginally from an earlier plan, known as the Werner Report, which was developed over twenty years ago. Yet unlike twenty years ago, the question is not monetary union or no monetary union, but when is the most appropriate time for such a union and how should it be implemented?

Discussing the European monetary system (EMS) initiative in 1977, *The Guardian* argued that "politics is the art of the possible and economic and monetary union in Europe are not now in that realm."[3] Twelve years' time has obviously changed that reality. During the Community's Madrid summit in June 1989, Italian prime minister Circiaco de Mita noted point-blank that the decision to endorse the Delors Report was not the result of "an economic but a political discussion. [It] was a political decision."[4] Just like the 1992 program itself, EMU is a political issue, even though the stakes are fundamentally economic.

The recognition that full monetary integration of the Community is inevitable is also seen in the statements of those less attracted to the prospect. Although they are not necessarily enamored with the implications of EMU for their country or central bank, even the Germans have voiced recognition of this reality. In a *Wall Street Journal* editorial, Karl Otto Pöhl, president of the Deutsche Bundesbank, stated, "EMU is a desirable political and economic goal. . . . It is up to governments and parliaments to decide whether further institutional progress toward monetary union is possible."[5] Yet the German central bank quietly sticks to its position that monetary union should be the crowning achievement of the single market program, a position not inconsistent with the view the Bundesbank voiced twenty years ago at the time of the Werner Report. Herr Pöhl, in remarks to the press in Frankfurt on December 14, 1989, notes that "The Bundesbank and I myself would have preferred to wait a few years [before discussing monetary integration] . . . . [I]n other words, if the European Monetary system had been completed and experience gathered with the liberalization of capital movements. . . . But the Heads of State or Government have decided otherwise."[6]

The battle of the EMU left former British prime minister Mrs. Thatcher as the singular voice crying that EMU is a socialist wolf in capitalist sheep's clothing. "The Delors Report," said Prime Minister Thatcher, "is not about economic and monetary cooperation; it is about getting federalism through the back door. I think quite a number of people in Europe know that if you took federalism at full toss people would say no."[7] But even in spite of this apparent negativism, Nigel Lawson, former British chancellor of the exchequer, speaking of the British position vis-à-vis EMS membership, stated publicly that he believes that "it [British membership] is not a question of whether, it's a question of when."[8] Most observers felt that it was likely that the United Kingdom would become a full member of the European monetary system by the end of 1990, if only owing to a fear of being left on the sidelines in any future deliberations. These beliefs were confirmed by the sudden entrance of the British pound into the EMS on October 8, 1990.

The History of European Monetary Integration

Since the Treaty of Rome, European monetary integration has been a vaguely and haphazardly approached objective of the European Community. As in most cases of concerted EC member state action, the pressure for closer monetary cooperation arose because of developments outside the Community. Jacques van Ypersele notes that the first moves toward further monetary cooperation were driven, not by some higher economic ideals, but by the reality of persistent balance of payments surpluses in the original EC-6 over the period 1958–61 and the subsequent revaluation of the mark and guilder in March of the latter year.[9] This minicrisis, along with the Community's "action plan" for the second stage of the development of the EEC, which focused on domestic and international monetary policy, exchange-rate coordination, and country-level budgetary initiatives, was responsible for the first Community initiative in 1964—the establishment of the Committee of Governors of the Central Banks (CGCB, subsequently changed to the Committee of Central Bank Governors, CCBG) and a Committee for Medium-Term Economic Policy (CMTEP).

The CMTEP is a consultative body responsible for coordinating various member state economic policies and developing five-year plans stating Community-wide goals and objectives. The purpose of the CCBG is to facilitate the exchange of information between Community members and to coordinate credit and exchange-rate policies. It has no binding authority but does work closely with the other Community committees in the technical areas of "monitoring and manag[ing] of EC exchange rates, the creation and administration of credit mechanisms, and the possible identification of common EC positions on international monetary issues."[10]

The global economic stability of the 1960s, mixed with the Community's preoccupation with what it considered the more fundamental questions of economic symbiosis, was responsible for the lack of development of further monetary initiatives on the part of the EC. The increasing monetary instability of the late 1960s created concern about the viability of the Common Market, most particularly the Common Agricultural Policy. This concern was made apparent, in early 1969, in two reports (known as the Barre Reports), which stressed the growing linkage between the EC country economies and the "danger that incompatibility between . . . policies and . . . strategies will become a threat to the existence of the customs union."[11]

If we look on the developments after the fact, the Barre plans were the intermediate stopgap between the Bretton Woods system of fixed exchange rates and the development of more coordinated exchange-rate policies within the Community as exemplified by the EMU and the EMS. The Barre plans called for the "setting up of machinery for monetary coordination" as an alternative to the international mechanisms that had "been unsuccessful at warding off crises."[12] Unlike the earlier initiatives, these plans called for setting up substantive short- and medium-term credit facilities that would go beyond the mere discussion of economic coordination because they would allow countries faced with short-term currency difficulties to call on other member states to aid them with the funds necessary to weather their difficulties. Should more long-term assistance be necessary, medium-term facilities would be available under specific conditions. The plans also recognized that unless economic policies were brought into better alignment through discussions prior to implementation, making the credit facilities available would be meaningless. According to the Barre report, "the most important step to be taken . . . is the tightening-up and the more effective application of consultation procedures prior to the adoption of economic measures by the Member States."[13]

The Development of the EMU and the Snake

At the Hague summit in December 1969, building on the discussions engendered by the Barre Reports, the leaders of the EC countries made a commitment to study the feasibility of closer European monetary policy cooperation. But differences of opinion between the various finance ministers led to the establishment of a study group, under the chairmanship of M. Pierre Werner, the prime minister of Luxembourg, that was charged with the responsibility of producing a concrete plan for achieving economic and monetary union. As noted by Dennis Swann, even though each state had its own national interests, all of the EC-6 stood to gain something from the establishment of a European monetary union. This was strongly true for France, whose concern about the EC agricultural subsidy system put its formidable weight squarely in the camp of those favoring fixed exchange rates.

The Werner Report, published in October 1970, subsequently became the primary blueprint for European monetary integration and, as we will see, the Delors Report of 1989 does not differ substantively from it. In fact, much of the 1992 program can be seen both explicitly and between the lines of the Werner Report with its call for free capital movements and the necessary harmonization of economic policy instruments. The Werner Committee recommendations specifically called for the development of a European currency unit (ECU), a centralized European credit policy, a unified capital market policy, a common policy on government budgetary finance, and the gradual narrowing of exchange-rate fluctuations to be slowly instituted through a two-stage plan. Stage one would take approximately three years and its hallmark would be the closer coordination of monetary, fiscal, and regulatory policies through the harmonization of laws and instruments of policy. The second stage would see the tightening of Community coordination ultimately leading to the complete elimination of fluctuating exchange rates.

The Werner Report represented a compromise between two moderately opposed economic viewpoints. Those dubbed the "economists," representing mostly the strong-currency Dutch and Germans, argued for coordinating economic policies before attempting to coordinate monetary policies. To them, monetary union is the crowning achievement of a true common market. In the other camp were the "monetarists," composed primarily of the French, Italians, Belgians, and Luxembourgians, who believed that monetary coordination would lead to greater convergence in the economic policies of the participating countries. To them, monetary coordination represented a means to further economic coordination. Even today, the philosophical dividing line is drawn between these same two groups, although there appears to be relatively more weight in the "monetarist" camp today than there was in 1970.

As with most early Community initiatives, the Werner plan was driven not by academic concerns about the benefits of closer monetary cooperation but by French worries about the maintenance of the subsidy component of the Common Agricultural Policy (CAP). As the franc declined in value, the French were finding that their EC agriculture subsidies were being eroded, and their ability to continue their government-driven economic growth program was undermined.

The French, looking always for a subsidy from the Community for their national development plans, wished to proceed by instituting a system for mutual support of fixed exchange rates. They argued that this would produce economic convergence, the essential requisite of a common economic policy. But the West Germans rejected that approach, as they believed that such a scheme would involve them in using their considerable foreign exchange reserves to support the currencies of states which were following irresponsibly lax and inflationary economic policies. For the Germans, the common economic policies had to come first, and of course they wished to insist that their own preference for monetary stability, rather than the growth-oriented policies of France, should be the basis of the common policies.[14]

The Werner Report was reviewed by the Council in February 1971. By March of that year, instead of implementing the Werner plan, the Council adopted a resolution aimed at coordinating short-term economic policies and established both a mechanism for providing medium-term financial assistance to governments facing exchange-rate difficulties and a procedure for promoting greater cooperation between central banks. As befitted the time, the grand program laid out by the Werner Committee was eschewed for the pragmatic nonsolution of nonauthoritative intergovernmental bodies of bureaucrats.

The monetary crises of the early 1970s that led to the rescinding of the gold convertibility of the dollar and the floating of the guilder and mark created pressure for forming the "tunnel," a sort of dampened floating currency zone, as an alternative to the decimated postwar Bretton Woods system of fixed exchange rates. The tunnel, which evolved from an agreement of the G-10 nations (the major economic powers) in December 1971 known as the Smithsonian Accords, permitted participating currencies to fluctuate within a ±2.25 percent band around a bilateral central exchange rate, and each currency had an established rate with every other currency in the agreement. If a participating country's currency moved outside the band, theoretically that country's central bank was responsible for unlimited intervention to bring the currency rate back within the band. EC countries concerned about the difficulties that a 4.5 percent band implied for the Common Agricultural Policy proposed a more limited exchange-rate mechanism, known as the "snake," which allowed a maximum total band of 2.25 percent.

The "snake within the tunnel" reflected concerns about the effect currency movements were having on the EC agriculture support system and the erroneous belief that the volatility of intra-European currency movements was due to dollar difficulties and reflected nothing inherent about European economic policies. The "snake" was implemented in April 1972 by the EC-6 and subsequently by the United Kingdom, Ireland, Denmark, and Norway. Because several countries were unable, or to some extent unwilling, to maintain their currencies in the snake bands, Britain, France, and Italy left the arrangement. The United Kingdom's departure was almost immediate, occurring within two months of its joining the scheme. Italy forsook the arrangement in February of 1973 and France in January of 1974. M. Giscard d'Estaing referred to the snake as *"un animal de la prèhistoire monétaire européene."*[15] In reality, the snake was not a prehistoric creature but a superfluous entity, constraining the currencies of countries that were least likely to violate its bands in the first place. France attempted to rejoin the arrangement in late 1975 only to once again be rudely reminded of the instability of its currency. The numerous realignments and proposals that followed simply highlighted the difficulty of merging currencies backed by radically different production systems and government policies.

The absence of a majority of the wealth of the European Community from the exchange-rate arrangement caused by the non-participation of Britain, France, and Italy created a gap in the development of a common market. Primarily, the failure of the experiments with monetary integration was a reflection of the inability of EC member states to commit themselves to the level of cooperation and economic fortitude that was necessary for such an enterprise to have even the remotest chance of success.

The Development of the European Monetary System

In October of 1977, Roy Jenkins, president of the Commission, called for a renewed effort at establishing an EMU. Even though Jenkins's call was uniformly criticized, behind-the-scenes support for exactly what he had in mind was growing independently between French president d'Estaing and German chancellor Schmidt. The subsequent discussion of the development of the European monetary system is meticulously outlined by Peter Ludlow in his book *The Making of the European Monetary System*, and the history of EMS presents a most interesting image of the politics of the European Community in the late 1970s. As is clearly elucidated by Ludlow, the EMS was not formed through grand consensus but through the strength of the French-German alliance, the fear that weaker currency nations would be left in a second-tier Europe, and the ability of countries, such as Ireland, to be bought into the arrangement with structural grants from the Community.[16]

The EMS is basically a supersnake that imposes less strict exchange-rate conditions on participating currencies. Since it is based on the ECU rather than on direct parity with currencies outside the EC system, most importantly the dollar, specific pressures from third currencies like the dollar or the yen are less likely to cause difficulties in maintaining parity within the EC so long as all the currencies move in roughly the same direction, which, of course, has not proven to be the case.

The makeup of the ECU, as originally structured and as it stands today, is shown in table 5–1. It is not true that the ECU is a pseudomark, although predominant weight is given to the German currency; nor is the ECU skewed to the strong EC currencies, e.g., the mark and the guilder. The lira accounts for virtually the same weight as the guilder, and the French franc and pound sterling together have the approximate weight of the mark. The result is a system that takes advantage of the improbability that any currency will move in the same direction against all other currencies and therefore ensures that exchange-rate fluctuations against a basket of currencies will be less than against any single currency.

The exchange-rate mechanism has two simple parts. First, should a currency deviate by more than ±2.25 percent (the range is ±6 percent for Italy) from its bilateral rate set against any other EC currency, the central banks of the countries involved are responsible for intervening to reestablish a rate within the bilateral rate parameters. (This would be done by selling the strong currency and buying the weak currency, swapping the currencies between the two central banks, or by buying and selling a third currency, such as the dollar.) Second, should the currency of any country move outside of this "divergence indicator," the country in question is expected to take remedial action to prevent further appreciation or depreciation. Such action is not, however, mandatorily required. The divergence indicator is set at 75 percent of the allowable divergence (±2.25

TABLE 5-1

Composition of the European Currency Unit (as percentage of ECU)

	March 13, 1979 through September 16, 1984	September 17, 1984 through September 18, 1989	Since September 19, 1989
Belgian and Luxembourg franc	9.7	8.5	7.9
Danish kroner	3.1	2.7	2.5
French franc	19.8	19.0	19.0
Deutsche mark	33.0	32.0	30.1
Irish pound	1.1	1.2	1.1
Italian lira	9.5	10.2	10.2
Dutch guilder	10.5	10.1	9.4
Pound sterling	13.3	15.0	13.0
Greek drachma	—	1.3	0.8
Spanish peseta	—	—	5.3
Portuguese escudo	—	—	0.8

Source: International Monetary Fund. Numbers may not total 100 percent because of rounding.

percent) against the ECU. So, for example, a heavily weighted currency, such as the mark, is permitted to fluctuate less—approximately ±1.1 percent—than a low weighted currency like the drachma, which can fluctuate approximately ±2.23 percent.

To provide the institutional mechanisms to support the EMS exchange-rate regime, the EC provides three levels of support to a country faced with exchange-rate pressures. First, through the European Monetary Cooperation Fund (EMCF) a country can borrow funds very short term (normally for less than three months). Under specific circumstances the terms of the loan can be extended for up to an additional three months, but the amount cannot exceed the limits prespecified for that country. Second, for countries facing more persistent balance of payments problems, there are short-term facilities that provide loans from participating central banks for periods of up to three months. As in the case of the very short term EMCF facility, these loans cannot exceed prespecified quotas and can be extended for an additional three months. Finally, if the balance of payments difficulties of a country are particularly severe, there are medium-term facilities that permit two- to five-year loans. As with the shorter term loans, there are explicit limits on these loans—approximately 14 billion ECU on all loans. Unlike the prior facilities, the medium-term facilities require the approval of the Council of Ministers and the fulfillment of specific fiscal and monetary requirements. As originally developed, these lending facilities were available only if a country's currency deviated outside the preset central rates, in which case intervention was obligatory under the EMS agreement. The Basle/Nyborg Accord of September 1987 made a very short-term financing facility available for intramarginal interventions, that is, as a preventive measure.

Perspectives on the European Monetary System

The EMS is generally viewed as a success within the Community. According to a recent EC publication, "after ten years the EMS has proved to be a convincing success. It has promoted lower inflation and brings more stable exchange rates, thereby fostering healthy economic growth."[17] Indeed, based on the measured volatility of the EC currencies both relative to one another and to outside currencies, there is no doubt that the post-1978 period reflects greater exchange-rate stability within the Community. Of course this should not be a surprise because saying that something that is constrained is less variable than something that is not constrained is nothing more than a tautology. The real question is whether the Community has performed better on key economic dimensions than otherwise would have been the case, which is a virtually impossible hypothesis to prove or disprove to the degree required to sway political discussion. Yet three factors show that we cannot automatically conclude that the EMS is an unqualified success.

First, the EMS has had eleven realignments since its inception (see table 5–2). Given that realignments are always after rather than before the economic fact, there no doubt are hidden economic costs, such as forgone trade or trade negotiated at higher than necessary prices, associated with the necessity of discrete and large adjustments. These costs fail to show up in any single statistic and are generally ignored in discussions of the EMS. As we will note in a moment, the Community points to the fact that the EMS has not been realigned in more than two years as an indication of its success. The issue the Community so carefully sidesteps is the opportunity cost that was being borne over this period by Germans because of the cheap mark and by Italians and French because of the expensive franc and lira.

Second, there is no indication that the existence of the EMS has disciplined the monetary and fiscal policies of governments of the member states of the Community. The strong currency countries have remained strong and the weak currency countries have remained weak, which is reflected in the revaluations shown in table 5–2 and in the inflation and budgetary statistics of these countries. It is also sometimes argued that the EMS has been a success because inflation rates have declined throughout the Community over the post-1979 period. But inflation rates have dropped worldwide during this period, thus the decline in the Community simply reflects the general change in world inflation levels (see figure 5–1). In fact, examining the differential between industrial country inflation rates and the EC average, the Community is, if anything, in a worse position relative to the remainder of the industrial world than it was in the 1970s. During the snake period from 1975 to 1978, EC inflation was 1 percent higher than the remaining industrial nations. In the early EMS period from 1979 to 1982, this differential rose

TABLE 5-2

Eleven Realignments in the European Monetary System, 1979–87

Percentage Change in Bilateral Rates

DATE	Belgian/ Luxembourg franc	Danish kroner	Deutsche mark	French franc	Italian lira	Irish pound	Dutch guilder	Greek drachma
9/24/79	—	−2.90	+2.00	—	—	—	—	—
11/30/79	—	−4.80	—	—	—	—	—	—
3/23/81	—	—	—	—	−6.00	—	—	—
10/5/81	—	—	+5.50	−3.00	−3.00	—	+5.50	—
2/22/82	−8.50	−3.00	—	—	—	—	—	—
6/14/82	—	—	+4.25	−5.75	−2.75	−3.50	+3.50	—
3/21/83	+1.50	+2.50	+5.50	−2.50	−2.50	−3.50	+3.50	—
7/22/85	+2.00	+2.00	+2.00	+2.00	−6.00	+2.00	+2.00	−13.10
4/7/86	+1.00	+1.00	+3.00	−3.00	—	—	+3.00	−25.80
8/4/86	—	—	—	—	—	−8.00	—	−1.01
1/12/87	+2.00	—	+3.00	—	—	—	+3.00	−9.11
Total since 3/13/79	−7.07	−9.76	+21.96	−16.02	−22.61	−13.77	+17.30	−59.56

Source: International Monetary Fund.

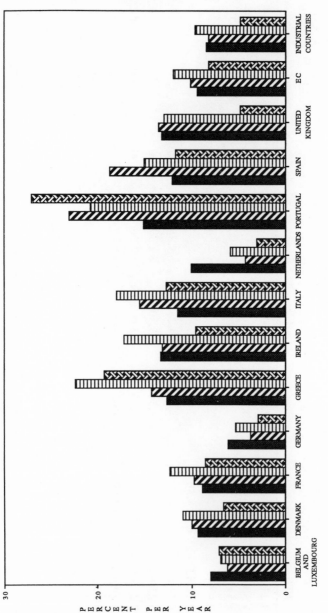

FIGURE 5–1

*Average Annual Inflation Rates in European
Community Countries*

Source: International Monetary Fund.

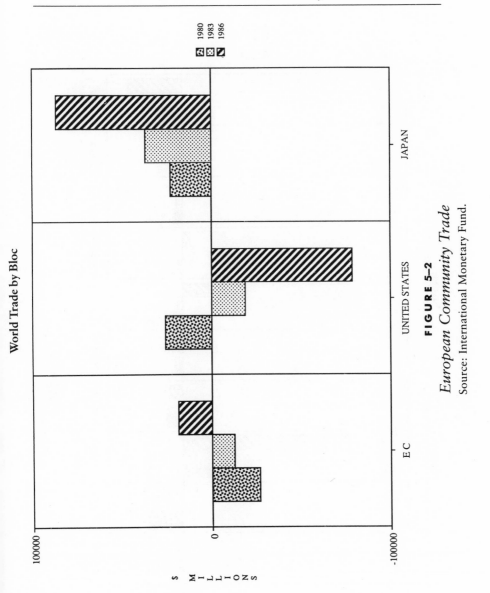

FIGURE 5–2
European Community Trade
Source: International Monetary Fund.

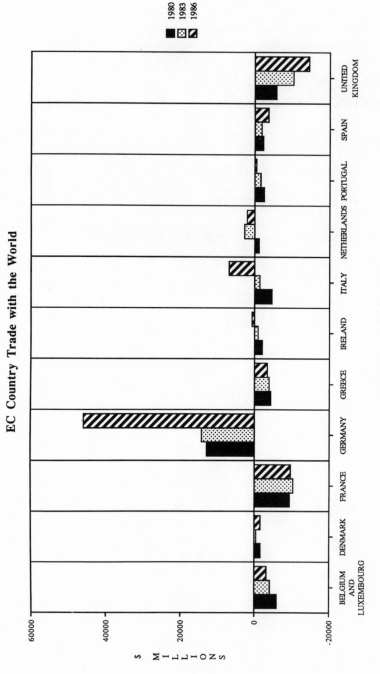

FIGURE 5–2 (continued).

to 2 percent. During the late EMS period from 1983 to 1986 it rose to 2.29 percent, and in 1987–1988 was approximately 3.35 percent. In addition, during the EMS period the relation between money supply growth and inflation has been more erratic than it was during the snake period and more erratic than that of non-EMS currencies. Although exchange-rate volatility has clearly decreased, the predictability of monetary inflation has decreased.

Third, the inability of exchange rates to adjust fully leads to trade distortions within the Community. This is seen very clearly in figure 5–2. Germany appears as a trade locomotive dragging the remainder of the EC behind. It alone is responsible for the few EC trade surpluses that have existed since the institution of the EMS. In addition, Germany's intra-Community trade surplus has risen from approximately $7.4 billion in 1983 to $10.8 billion in 1985 to the outstanding level of almost $30 billion in 1988. Either further realignments are necessary or the remainder of the Community member states must be willing to accept the position of beggar to their German neighbor.

The Delors Committee and the Single Monetary Dimension

Although the Single European Act does not specifically call for the formation of a single European monetary union, the vague language of article 201 of the Treaty of Rome leaves the door open for such integration.

> In order to ensure that the convergence of economic and monetary policies which is necessary for the further development of the Community, Member States shall cooperate in accordance with the objectives of Article 104[18] [which states:]

> Each Member State shall pursue the economic policy needed to ensure the equilibrium of its overall balance of payments and to maintain confidence in its currency, while taking care to ensure a high level of employment and a stable level of prices.[19]

At the Hanover summit of June 1988, the Council affirmed the belief that "in adopting the Single [European] Act, the Member States of the Community confirmed the objective of the progressive realization of economic and monetary union"[20] by forming a committee under the leadership of M. Jacques Delors to develop a program for establishing a European monetary union in conjunction with the single European market.

On April 17, 1988, the Delors Committee released its plan for establishing a complete European monetary union, which was effectively accepted by all members of the committee, including Bank of England governor Mr. Robin Leigh-Pemberton, in spite of the immediate reaction from Nigel Lawson (former British chancellor of the exchequer) who claimed that the committee's report endorsed "a concept of the European Community that we do not share." As Mr. Leigh-Pemberton noted, "no one should be deluded into believing that an early political gesture is a shortcut to avoiding the difficult and long drawn-out task of working towards convergent economic performance."[21]

The Delors plan contains three major stages. Stage one would entail the inclusion of the nonparticipating member states (at that time meaning only Britain) in the exchange-rate mechanism of the EMS and an expansion of the role of the Committee of Central Bank Governors in coordinating policy. Stage one was to commence on July 1, 1990. Although this deadline was not formally met, the leaders of the EC states agreed in Dublin in June 1990 to open the Intergovernmental Conference on Economic and Monetary Union, a major stepping-stone to the development of the Euro-Fed system envisioned in the Delors Report. This agreement was met by a softening of the British stance against entering into the exchange-rate mechanism.

Stage two would create a European System of Central Banks (ESCB), the so-called Euro-Fed, which would require amending the Treaty of Rome. At this stage, the Community would see a gradual transfer of power away from the individual member states and to the new Community institution. The ESCB's responsibilities would include

1. the establishment of price stability,
2. the "support of general economic policy set at the Community level,"
3. the formulation and implementation of "monetary policy,

exchange rate and reserve management, and the maintenance of a properly functioning payment system," and
4. the coordination of "banking supervision policies of the supervisory authorities."[22]

The ultimate goal of the ESCB is to narrow the existing exchange-rate bands until all twelve currencies have converged to one effective European currency.

The third stage of the Delors plan would implement the complete transference of monetary authority to the Community. The rules and procedures that the EC establishes in budgetary and macroeconomic arenas would be binding on the member governments. The Council of Ministers would be empowered to

> impose constraints on national budgets to the extent to which . . . it is necessary to prevent imbalances, make discretionary changes in Community resources to supplement structural transfers to Member States or to influence the overall policy stance in the Community, [and] to apply . . . terms and conditions that would prompt Member countries to intensify their adjustment efforts.[23]

The Delors plan is the Werner plan taken one step further. Like the earlier report, it envisions a world with completely fixed exchange rates evolving over a series of stages with individual government sovereignty being reduced as the adjustment period ends. Although the later plan is more explicit on the detail of a European central banking system, both plans recognize the impact that monetary union has on the independence of fiscal and monetary policy within the Community countries. At the Madrid summit in July of 1989, the leaders of the EC member states gave approval to the substance of the Delors Report. The blueprint set out by M. Pierre Werner in 1970 appeared to find new life after M. Delors resuscitated it in 1989. In December 1989, at the Strasbourg summit, the Community decided to hold an intergovernmental conference by the end of 1990 with the expressed purpose of proposing alterations to the Treaty of Rome that would create the legal basis for transferring monetary sovereignty to a European central bank. This decision was reaffirmed in Dublin in June 1990, and the Intergovernmental Conference was set for December 13, 1990.

What Does a Single Monetary Europe Buy?

Why does the EC need a central bank or a single currency? Taking the issue further, why should countries such as the United States and Canada not join their economies further by doing away with one or the other dollar? Could not Sweden and Norway, perhaps along with Finland, create a Nordic currency and increase the efficiency of their economies? What are the possibilities for the yen, the Korean won, or the Taiwan dollar? After all, the income and structural differences between the above countries are no greater than those between the member states of the European Community. Yet none of these countries would argue for creating a monetary union. So why is a monetary union so critical to the perceived success of the European economies? Before addressing this question directly, let us look at the specifics of the arguments put forth in support of monetary union, arguments it should be noted, that do not differ at all from those voiced by Mr. Roy Jenkins in his call for monetary union in October 1977.

One of the first and simplest arguments for a single currency centers on the inconvenience of dealing in twelve separate currencies. From a consumer standpoint one has no doubt heard stories of how the continual changing of currency on a trip from Copenhagen to Lisbon could cost the traveler as much as one-half the value of the currency in conversion fees. From the business standpoint, multinational companies suffer from the inability to form coherent financial statements for businesses being conducted in different countries and for selling products and purchasing resources in a host of different currencies. How, by committing to a regime of fixed exchange-rates, would one solve the above problems? After all, a single currency is nothing more than a fixed exchange-rate system. A single currency would mean that the businessman need not worry that exchange rates between countries have fluctuated because they could not, and the traveler would no longer have to pay a conversion fee in her trip to Lisbon. Are they better off? On the surface, the answer appears to be yes. Pan-European marketing managers would no longer need to feel that they need to be currency speculators and could focus on selling products. The Euro-accountant would no longer need any rules for which exchange rate to use in forming the balance sheet of a multinational company. Investors could more clearly measure managerial performance because financial statements would be consistent across countries. The first stop for the German tourist in Greece would be the beach and not the currency exchange. Although the rhetoric surrounding this discussion would lead us to believe that both businesses and consumers would be nothing but better off, the reality is, however, less clear.

A variant of the convenience argument is the currency risk argument. A German businessman decides to build a plant in Italy and the plant takes two years to build. By the time the plant is completed, the lira has risen against the mark and the plant is no longer profitable. Bemoans the businessman, "How am I to make a sensible business decision with those damn exchange rates fluctuating around?" The logical foundation of this point is that exchange rates randomly vary like a gas in a box, rather than being driven by underlying economic fundamentals. Let us alter the story to prove the point. Suppose our businessman is now in the single-currency Europe. After having built the plant, the manager finds that the costs of land and labor have risen, so the previously profitable investment is no longer beneficial. What should the businessman blame now? The two stories are not different. In the latter story, because the currency price is fixed—remember, no exchange rates—the increase in the demand for Italian things has forced up the price of Italian land and labor. In the former story, an increase in the demand for Italian things has forced up the value of Italian land and labor because of an increase in the value of the currency.

There is a subtle but important difference between these two stories. Suppose that there is a demand for some but not all Italian things. In a multicurrency system the lira becomes more expensive so all Italian things rise in price to foreigners. Under the single-currency system, the increase in the demand for those specific Italian articles increases the real price of those articles to everyone, foreigner and Italian alike. We now see one of the important distinctions between the single-currency Europe and a multicurrency Europe, and this concern is aptly reflected in the comments of the newer members of the EC. Should Europe move to a single currency tomorrow, the ability of low-income countries to keep their real prices from rising relative to their wealthier neighbors would prove to be impossible, and thus most poor countries would be faced with the prospect of a drastic decline in the purchasing power of their own citizenry within their country. Few of these countries want to be faced with this prospect, hence they have an obvious concern about their ability to quickly integrate their economies into the European first tier. This is not an issue of simply one more exchange rate adjustment within the EMS as *The Economist* claims.[24] The fact of the matter is countries with fundamentally different economies will not necessarily be better off operating under the same currency regime.

A further perspective on currency risk is based on the ability to hedge future fluctuations in exchange rates. Some would argue that should a business person desire to insulate himself from currency risk, futures markets exist to provide exactly the kind of currency stability that a single currency would provide, albeit at a directly observable price. This argument has been criticized because long-term futures markets do not exist to allow people to hedge anything other than short- or medium-term currency fluctuations, and a sufficient diversity of hedging instruments do not exist to hedge the currency risk completely. This latter point is clearly supported by a survey conducted by Arthur Andersen & Co. that found that innovation in and expansion of derivative security markets in Europe is high on the wish list of corporate executives.[25] Yet it is unclear how a single currency resolves the difficulty of adding derivative security markets in countries where either no such markets exist or those that exist are highly underdeveloped. As for criticism of the lack of long-term futures markets there is no doubt that it is well-founded, but it begs two fundamental questions.

First, there appears to be no strong demand for a long-term market of the kind that proponents of a single currency say cannot exist. There is no technical reason why ten-year deutsche mark futures could not exist, at some price, should there be a demand for a financial instrument of that type. But either the demand is simply not there, or the cost of handling transactions of this type, given the demand, is just too high. If this is true, why should the government bother forcing all individuals to hold a single currency only to benefit those who want to hedge long-term currency fluctuations, considering that if they alone had to pay for the hedging of their own long-term currency risk, they would admit that the transaction is either too risky or too expensive?

Second, suppose that the demand for long-term currency risk hedging existed. Is this demand by itself sufficient for arguing that permanently fixed exchange rates are the solution to the problem? Of course it is not. To argue that a single currency is the best way to satisfy the demand for long-term currency risk hedging, it is necessary to prove that an EC committee or group of central bankers would somehow be more omnipotent than an organized market when it comes to determining exactly how such exchange rate insurance could be put together.

Should Europe Have a Single Currency?

Because we understand, from a purely economic perspective, what a European central bank and single currency would buy, the question is, should Europe have a single currency? The answer, we think, is a clear no. Yet, this judgment implies neither that the EC should have twelve separate currencies nor that it should not experiment with a parallel European currency. Indeed, as one Bank of England official recently pointed out, Europe does not have twelve currencies given the dominance of the deutsche mark over its neighboring currencies. In this respect, the drive toward EMU is a reflection of the need to do away with superfluous currencies.

Money serves two primary purposes in an economy: it provides a store of value, and it facilitates transactions. In essence, a national currency represents a store of value of the wealth of the country. As a currency is inflated each unit "holds" less of the nation's wealth. When currencies are traded, one country trades its wealth for another's, although we normally think of this in terms of trading goods and services. A single currency, therefore, increases in value when the wealth levels of the individual members of a community are more equal and the desire for trade between community members is greater. A pure Friedmanite monetarist would argue that the level of money in the society should be sufficient to maintain the nominal price level, that is, there should be no reduction in the value of the money as the economy grows. That nominal price level would be determined initially by setting the supply of money at a level sufficient to permit trading as cheaply as possible.

Translating this concept to Europe, five features of European markets are important in understanding the costs and benefits of a single European currency. First, the wealth levels across the Community are extremely disparate. Sections of Greece, Portugal, Spain, and Ireland have income levels less than one-half those of countries such as Germany and the Netherlands. Second, the economic fundamentals for creating economic wealth in these countries vary significantly. For example, the United Kingdom is a curious mixture of petroleum and services economy, Germany is an industrial juggernaut, Portugal and Greece are primarily agrarian, and Luxembourg is a tax haven. Third, the level of intra-Community trade is quite high. In 1986, 23 percent of world trade and 42 percent of industrial country trade was intra-Community, with 59 percent of all EC trade being conducted with other Community countries.[26] Community members depend heavily on one another for goods and services. Fourth, government policies vis-à-vis the maintenance of price levels and budgetary finance are quite variable. Although governments have shown amazing discipline in bucking the tendency to finance their deficits monetarily, there is no indication that deficit pressures in high deficit countries have eased. Fifth, the level of trade between sections of the Community and the extra-Community world is quite disparate. As we have noted several times, only Germany has been able to maintain a positive trade balance with non-Community partners, and its balance of payments surplus appears unlikely to slow without some type of currency adjustment.

These circumstances create obvious conflicts. The existence of high trade levels within the EC leads to the obvious desire to facilitate trade by reducing difficulties with currency conversion and risk. This explains very concisely the strong pro–single-currency lobbying by European business. Notes Gino Scotti of Fiat SpA, "We have costs in one set of currencies and revenues in another. It's very complicated to manage all of this."[27] A single currency means that the problem of currency risk, as created by erratic government policy, is also resolved because now only one government—the EC—can be erratic. Many businessmen, particularly in more economically volatile countries, believe that the discipline of the Bundesbank will be imposed on their country, and their government's powers in monetary policy matters will be neutralized.

But the question of the independence of a European central bank has not been resolved, and that eleven of the twelve central banks are fairly tightly controlled by their governments is not necessarily a good sign for those hoping for an independent European monetary authority. Indeed, many European central bankers view the independence of the German central bank as an antiquated anachronism. Yet, since a majority of EC economies do not possess the monetary stability of the *mitteleuropäish* (middle European) deutsche mark zone, many EC businesses strongly believe that expanding that zone would be of benefit to them. It is equally clear that should the deutsche mark zone be expanded, those already in that zone may have to accept a level of instability that they have recently become unaccustomed to dealing with, hence the German central bank is naturally reluctant to assume the role of Europe's bank.

A single currency is also not without some direct costs. The existence of such widely disparate wealth levels and unbalanced trade within the Community means that the cost of a single currency and the consequent equalization of price levels across Europe will be borne by a group that is completely different from the group receiving the gains. Hence the less developed sections of the Community have demanded structural funds as part of the quid pro quo for accepting the notion of EMU.[28] Since they will be facing a direct reduction in wealth because of monetary union, the wealthier sections of the Community need to provide an influx of wealth to compensate for the decline. But unless the structural differences that are responsible for the initial wealth differentials are resolved, the problem will persist. We see this scenario very clearly in the United States. The poor sections of America—places like Mississippi, Arkansas, West Virginia, and so on—have remained consistently poor for as long as statistics have been gathered. This condition has persisted in spite of the influx of "structural funds" because the fundamental reason for the poverty in these areas—low education, poor land usage, racial tensions, and so on—has remained unresolved. It is equally unclear whether Europe has a plan for resolving the structural problems of its poorer areas and whether northern Europe will be willing to support continually its poorer southern neighbors. As one German official pointed out to us in private conversation, "corporate Germany has recognized its responsibility for supporting social Germany. I'm not convinced that it will be equally enamored with supporting social Europe." Now that West Germans must concern themselves with the welfare of their East German comrades, they certainly must be less willing to sacrifice themselves for European causes.

The Political Pressures for EMU

Since the economic fundamentals do not provide substantive proof that the European economy would run more efficiently with a single currency, where is the pressure coming from for such a radical change? It is in answering this question that we will see the political nature of the decision to embrace EMU.

We have briefly discussed the role that business has played in creating pressure for EMU. Business perceives three benefits from a single European monetary authority. First, a single monetary authority would impose German-like discipline. Second, business can operate more efficiently without the needless currency conversion tax. Third, financial information would be more consistent across countries thereby improving the efficiency of the marketplace.

The belief that a correctly formed central bank would severely limit the ability of individual countries to monetize their debt is based on the argument that the threat of individual governments being forced into public debt markets where they would be at the mercy of market interest rates would impose discipline. The end result of this new reality would be lower central government debt levels. Business would gain because this new monetary discipline would provide a more stable European price level, albeit perhaps at higher than current German or Dutch levels.

The other two arguments are fairly clear and have been discussed earlier. Businessmen argue that they could lower prices to consumers if they did not have to deal in so many currencies, because individual currencies are just one more regulatory hassle to harmonize. From an investor's standpoint, financial statements would make more sense since fewer accounting games would be available for massaging corporate earnings. Internal planning would be easier since currency fluctuations would no longer be such a dominant aspect of European business life.

The political pressure from business is clearly real and dominant in the thinking of European leaders. But politicians, too, have strong motives for desiring a harmonized monetary Europe, and this is where 1992 and EMU become inextricably linked. Given the Community's commitment to the 1992 program with its free movement of capital and pan-European banking and investment system, the individual member states are faced with a rather daunting prospect—the complete elimination of home country monetary control. To see the problem a European government faces, imagine a government that finds itself with an unstable currency because of inconsistent monetary and fiscal policy. In the pre-1992 days, the business sector within that country had little prospect of dealing effectively with the unstable monetary situation. Perhaps, a futures contract could provide some insurance, but currency flight was against the law and the penalties were stiff. In the all-new 1992 world, all capital flows are cheap and business has a very simple alternative for stabilizing funds: it can remove its transaction operations from the unstable country and conduct all business in a more stable currency, transacting in the unstable currency only as needed, for example, to pay workers, buy materials, and so on. Should the government take actions that make its currency even more unstable, currency flight would become even more exacerbated. Workers would begin holding accounts in other currencies and converting funds into their own country's currency as needed. The existence of a more stable currency, therefore, is an automatic hedge against fluctuations in value of less stable currencies.

The alternative to going back to the days of currency controls, clearly a step away from the impetus for more open European markets, is to attempt to harmonize the monetary systems of the EC countries so that individuals and businesses do not have the incentive to escape from what might otherwise be an unstable currency. In other words, EMU is something of a currency cartel allowing weaker currency countries to maintain some of their weakness against the dominance of stronger currency economies. The only other real option is to allow currency competition, which, given the current state of the EC economies, would imply very heavy pressure for the revaluation of the EMS currencies and ensure the dominance of the deutsche mark over the other Community economies. Through the formation of an EMU, individual member states maintain more control over their individual economies than would otherwise be possible under the single market initiative.

The Monetary Alternatives for Europe

If the EC is not ready for a single currency, what, then, is the solution? One obvious option is to leave things as they are; but most EC observers believe the sovereignty of national currencies is slowly coming to an end. Indeed, if our arguments are valid, the natural pressures of currency competition will see to it that national currencies become effectively superfluous.

A second solution would be establishing a parallel European currency alongside the individual national currencies. Whichever currency best suits the users would be their decision. This is similar to the hard-ECU proposed by John Major, the British prime minister. The parallel currency idea has several advantages. First, it permits European businesses concerned with currency risk to have an alternative hedging instrument should they desire one. Second, it assures that needless pressure is not put on the real prices of resources in less developed EC countries, thereby alleviating the pressure for massive structural fund aid. Third, it provides a testing ground for EMU without committing the Community to a course that may prove politically irreversible. Should the pan-European currency prove dominant, its dominance would be tested by its survivability and not by the fact that it would be the only legally mandated currency.

The major problem with developing a parallel currency has little to do with its theoretical properties but involves the practical factor of its use. We noted earlier that the ECU has failed as a pure monetary alternative to existing currencies. It is mainly valued by those interested in its natural hedging characteristics. A recent survey by the Association for the Monetary Union of Europe reported that while a majority of businesses desired monetary union, few would be willing to bear the additional cost of using a currency that was not already actively in use.[29] Therefore, a parallel currency, although theoretically appealing, may be practically ineffective. This is reflected in the cool reception given to the hard-ECU proposal by the British.

A third solution, and one that has received no discussion at all, would be to rearrange the currency structure of Europe to more accurately reflect the trade and wealth zones. Such a solution might lead to one zone including Portugal, Spain, southern Italy, Greece, and Ireland; a second zone that would include France and northern Italy; a third zone that would include Benelux, Denmark, and Germany; and the United Kingdom would, as ever, remain a zone in and of itself and perhaps would be slowly integrated with France and northern Italy. These new currency zones would then be permitted to float against each other. Such a system would reflect the realities associated with the wealth and trade differentials within the Community and would preclude the need for making the large structural transfers involved in imposing a single currency.

Conclusion

The concept of a European monetary union and European central bank is one of the major wild cards in the 1992 program. The political pressure for a monetary union is quite strong, but many observers are correct in being wary that, once such a union is set in stone, it will mark the death knell for independent economic action by member state governments. In other words, once a European monetary union is established, the federalization of Europe will be effectively complete, whether the fact is recognized at the time or not. The governments and political organizations of the member states will be drawn ever closer, while the hallway back to independent political action will be closed to them.

Whether the Community goes full speed ahead on monetary union will critically depend on the monetary integration of the two Germanies. If the monetary conversion of the deutsche mark and the ostmark goes well, there is little doubt that the Community politicos will herald it as evidence for the value of greater West European monetary integration. If it goes badly, and by badly we mean that the conversion causes inflation in West Germany and severe unemployment and inflation in East Germany, EC member states will definitely give monetary union another look, for three reasons. First, the West German electorate will look at their experience and ask themselves if they want to try the same thing again; only this time the conversion would be for the benefit of not fellow Germans but their European brothers and sisters. The answer will be no, of course, and West German politicians will quickly lose their enthusiasm for the Delors plan. Second, the monetary merger of East and West Germany represents approximately the same kind of monetary merger as between southern and northern Europe: the similarity being in terms of wealth, the difference in terms of economic and monetary stability. The poorer sections of Europe will look at the economic agony of East Germany and wonder whether the same thing will happen to them. They, too, will lose their interest in a monetary union. Third, troubles with the German monetary union will provide concrete evidence to back up the arguments of anti-unionists like Margaret Thatcher, who may even·come to be recognized as a "good European."

Yet German monetary union is at one and the same time easier and more difficult than European monetary union. It is more difficult because the bankruptcy of the East German economy is a daunting sum and the task of rebuilding the country is of Herculean proportions. But there the hard part ends. With German monetary union, there is little doubt that the demise of the ostmark is simply a stage in the demise of the East German state. Whether monetary union came before or after political union was simply a matter of necessity, but there was no higher law indicating that it had to be so. Such cannot be said of the EMU and the individual countries of the Community. Germany is essentially replacing the old East German government bureaucracy with a West German model that itself was built on the prewar model. Germany used to be one nation, the Community never was. It is one thing for the Bundesbank to extend its monetary arm over the six *Länder* to the east, but it is entirely another matter for the EC to build a Euro-Fed system more or less from the ground up. Finally, West Germany has made what amounts to an irrevocable agreement to stand behind its monetary unification with East Germany and appears willing to pay the bills no matter how much they amount to. Can the same be said of the EC if EMU goes wrong?

Prospects and Strategies

If our opponent is to do our will, we must put him in a position more disadvantageous to him than the sacrifice would be that we demand. The disadvantages of his position should naturally, however, not be transitory, or, at least, should not appear to be so, . . . or our opponent will refuse to yield.

—*Karl von Clausewitz,* On War

Although it is relatively simple to look back in history to see the antecedents of the current European movement toward further economic integration, speculating on the future is an entirely different matter. But speculate we must. For business in both Asia, America, and the non-Community Europe, 1992 raises some rather obvious strategic questions for which educated answers are required:

- What will the markets of Europe look like after 1992?
- What are the potential "trouble spots" in the single market program?
- What will the post-1992 corporation look like?
- What should a company do to prepare for European market changes?
- Where are the opportunities in the "new" Europe?
- Who will be the winners and losers in the restructuring of European industry?

In answering these questions we are obviously forecasting highly uncertain events. Even in late 1990, it is unclear how far the Community will ultimately move in achieving economic integration. The rapidly changing events in Eastern Europe throw another wrench into the system. The unification of Germany, a total surprise to virtually everyone, including those of us who were in East Germany shortly before the fall of Erich Honecker, has obviously distracted the German government from its support of the 1992 initiative. The events in Eastern Europe also bring to the fore Margaret Thatcher's statement that "we must not forget that East of the Iron Curtain [are] peoples who once enjoyed a full share of European culture, freedom, and identity."[1] These volatile and exciting events have yet unforeseen implications for European economic integration.

Our primary thesis in this book has been that 1992 is a European reaction to two primary threats: the external threat of the rising power of the Pacific rim countries mixed with the relative economic decline of the United States, and the threat of technological obsolescence vis-à-vis Europe's Asian and American rivals. The economic changes of the last two decades have caused a fundamental change in the technology of business and a reorientation of world economic power. The single market program slowly grew because of pressure from key European industries attempting to adapt to this change, much in the same manner as the demand for regulatory change in the United States arose from similar pressures in the 1970s. It is this thesis that will serve as the basis of our speculation about the future of the European economy.

Post–1992 European Markets

What will the European market of the late twentieth century look like? After reading Paolo Cecchini's *1992: The European Challenge,* one might be quick to assume that Europe will be populated by pan-European commercial behemoths, funded by Euro-banks and ECU-denominated equity issues, spewing forth generic Euro-services and products for the new European man, woman, and child. This is certainly a gross oversimplification that does justice to neither the Cecchini report nor the specific implications it puts forth for different industries and markets. Nevertheless, much of the EC discussion of 1992 puts heavy, almost religious, emphasis on the power of economies of scale and the role of size in international competition. This emphasis does not, however, reflect the realities of late twentieth-century production or the opportunities that information technology opens for consumer demand and its ultimate satisfaction by innovative entrepreneurs. Further, an overwhelming belief in size equals efficiency is antithetical to the growth of the service economy so necessary for Europe's future.

What a specific industry's structure will look like in the next decade is obviously a complex combination of how the new EC regulatory structure affects the industry's production technology, how its customer demand evolves, and the unforeseen political and world economic changes and innovations that occur in the interim. Assuming that the single market program proceeds as planned, post-1992 EC markets will, in general, be more heavily concentrated and more regionally focused as compared with their historic fixation on national markets. Greater emphasis will be placed on the role of integrating information technology into the production process, and the most heavily affected markets will be those most sensitive to this change, that is, financial services, telecommunications, and technologically sensitive manufacturing. In addition, the role of services employment will rise with the integration of information technology. An unforeseen consequence of these changes will not be the development of a plethora of Euro-products (although more will certainly be developed), but the more efficient satisfaction of customer variety.

The Implications for Industrial Concentration

Because 1992 is driven by commercial pressures, it must reflect the desire of specific commercial enterprises to expand beyond the reach of their former regulatory domains. In addition, that the member states of the Community, and the Commission itself, very obviously believe that a major problem with EC industry has been the fragmentation resulting from national regulatory restrictions and nontariff barriers implies that a blurred, if not blind, eye will be turned toward concentration-inducing mergers and alliances in the near future. Consequently, *there is little doubt that for many key industries the level of industrial concentration will increase.* This concentration will no doubt occur in such key areas as airlines, banking, communications equipment and technology, computers and information technology, mass retailing, and, possibly, automobile production.

Whether the increase in European industrial concentration leads to an increase or a decrease in the level of prices and profits is solely a function of the specifics of the individual markets and EC regulations. In computers, for example, the product offerings and potential competition are most likely sufficient to ensure that concentration increases will reflect efficiency gains and not attempts at monopolization. The same may be true of the increases in concentration that may be evident in automobile production. In the latter case, decreased concentration may be evident if the Community permits more liberal importation of foreign automobiles, a rather unlikely event. This would naturally lead to reduced automobile prices and more competitive satisfaction of customer demands.

Unlike the automobile and computer businesses, consolidation in the airline industry, where a tacit cartel has existed for several decades, will probably strengthen the industry's coordinated control over prices. Recent moves by Air France to lock up the prime routes within France, and the absence of intracountry airlines possessing the regional characteristics that a rival national airline might want to purchase, bodes ill for the future of true competition in the intra-Community airline market. The sole route to gaining access to intracountry routes, when they even exist, appears to be direct alliances or possible mergers between national carriers. Although the European Court has recently taken a dim view of the cartel-like tendencies of the EC carriers, the Commission itself appears to be quietly willing to permit the regionalization of the European airline market.[2]

The Regionalization of European Markets

The trend away from national markets and toward concentrated regional markets should also be evident in industries with production processes that require a trading off of scale economies in one dimension with scale diseconomies in another. *The move toward regional operations is most likely in industries where production and distribution techniques reward scale, but the retail operations and/or the demand for variety by customers, perhaps because of cultural differences, lead to more focused marketing and/or service.* Examples would include, but would not be limited to, industries such as banking and financial services, mass retailing, and durable goods production and marketing.

In banking and financial services, particularly in its retail dimension, there are several pieces of evidence pointing to the value of a movement toward satisfying regional diversity while taking advantage of production synergies. First, the United States experience has shown that retail megabanks are not necessarily the most profitable ventures. The superregional phenomenon, partially driven by regulatory factors, has provided strong evidence that retail banking does have size limitations. Even in the culturally homogeneous United States, bankers have found that Texas banks are different from Ohio banks, and New York banks are different from North Carolina banks. The inability of the Japanese and British to be successful in the American retail banking market, and the Americans in the European market, is further evidence of the cultural dependence of retail operations.[3] Second, economies of scale exist in many of the aspects of bank and financial services production, for example, clearing operations, data processing, cash management, and portfolio transactions, but not in other areas, for example deposit creation, consumer lending, private banking, and account management. This leads banks and financial services to attempt to gain production efficiency where possible, while avoiding the diseconomies of scale associated with many of the labor-intensive retail operations. Regional growth is most likely under these circumstances since the institutions can achieve scale while still promoting the retail character of the other operations of the institution.

The Amro Bank-Generale Bank agreement is an excellent example of how to take advantage of this production synergy while recognizing the strength of the merger partners in their home market retail operations. The agreements signed by the two banks permitted the Belgian Generale Bank to take over many of Amro's Belgian operations and gave Amro authority over activities in Holland that were previously handled by Generale Bank. Both banks also now operate joint payment systems, have established a series of "Eurodesks" to handle European operations, and have developed joint lending procedures.[4] The ability to develop a truly European retail bank is fanciful; it will simply never occur in the manner that many people think. One may perhaps see European bank holding companies made of decentralized regional banks, but a generic retail Euro-bank is unlikely.

Mass retailing and consumer durables marketing is another area where regional concentration may prove the norm. Mass retailing cannot be solely culturally independent. Some products are culturally neutral, but others are not, and sales techniques are rarely culturally independent. Witness the inability of mass retailers to move beyond national boundaries, both between European countries, America and Canada, and Asian countries, let alone across oceans. The woes of Printemps, a French department store, in the United States are indicative of the inability to transfer retail services expertise.[5] Yet distribution and inventory management techniques should be culturally independent. Given a set of business conditions, good distribution systems are good distribution systems, and having a warehousing and distribution network that requires a company to treat countries like markets is not necessarily efficient. Although northern Germans may differ in certain aspects of product demand from Danes or Dutch, production and transportation costs should allow them all to be serviced by a warehouse and distribution system based in Hamburg, should that prove to be most profitable. The retail operations may be uniquely "Dutch," or "Danish," or "German" and thus may require decentralized decision making at this level.

Information Technology Is the Key

The economic boom of the 1980s was driven by a combination of oil price reductions and the practical development of information technology. The revolution in corporate finance, epitomized by program trading, securitization, and the rise of derivative markets, is, pure and simple, a result of the application of computer technology. The globalization of markets, seen in the move toward twenty-four–hour stock trading, the rise of multinational companies (MNC), and production processes that require coordination across oceans, is clearly the outcome of the ability to communicate rapidly and accurately over long distances. Europe's historic regulatory and corporate structure served to protect it from this new competition for a period of time, but as the importance of technology rose, the position of the European companies fell relative to their rivals, and many commercial opportunities were forgone because of a lack of regulatory or organizational flexibility.

The importance of information technology in future European industry structure can be seen in five specific dimensions: financing, production, distribution, organizational structure and decision making, and marketing.

MODERN FINANCIAL TECHNIQUES WILL INCREASE CAPITAL ACCESS. Modern financial techniques have led to a plethora of mechanisms for corporate financing, opening up to smaller and medium-sized companies financial markets that were previously the bastion of the larger firms. As we noted earlier, the level of market capitalization in the Community and the average capitalization per firm on an exchange clearly indicates that many EC companies were either unwilling or, more likely, found it unprofitable to use financial market financing. World market pressures will force the European markets to conform. This has led to speculation of where the financial capital of Europe will reside—London, Paris, or Frankfurt? If the Community is successful in structuring a more efficient financial market, which country will not matter very much. Local markets will serve local needs with most trading and contracting occurring through an open network. The only thing that is certain is that to remain competitive in the world market post-1992 EC markets must, by necessity, increase smaller and middle market firms' access to market capital.

PRODUCTION AND DISTRIBUTION TECHNOLOGY WILL STRESS THE ABILITY TO MEET CUSTOMER VARIETY. Production techniques have radically changed the nature of modern manufacturing. Moves toward flexible manufacturing systems, more focused factories, and just-in-time (JIT) inventory techniques are the hallmark of the factory of the future. Focused factories, maintaining no inventory and tight order relations with suppliers, cannot be operated without state-of-the-art information technology. Again, the advent of information technology and its impact on production is the key.

Also, the factory of the future is more than simply intelligent robots replacing human workers. The application of modern information processing techniques has allowed the Japanese to compete based on not only quality, but variety and time as well. The ability to rapidly change product designs to meet customer needs, and to get technological and product advances to market, represents one of the focal points of competition in the future. The implication is that economies of scale are really not as important as the ability to quickly meet changing consumer needs over time. This new time-based competition, with its emphasis on meeting consumer variety with higher quality and varied products, appears tailor-made for Europe, with its culturally similar yet radically diverse customer markets.

THE MOVE TOWARD DECENTRALIZED MANAGEMENT. The last ten years have seen an upheaval in the nature of business organization that includes an increasing trend away from rigid, top-heavy managerial hierarchies and a swing toward more flexible and independent divisional operations within the firm. This trend has been part and parcel with the movement away from traditional manufacturing techniques and the integration of advanced information technology in the white-collar sector of the corporate workplace.

The traditional centralized management structure is based on the belief that goals are formulated from above as are the mechanisms for achieving those goals. Information flowed, mostly in the form of paper or direct contact, through organized channels from top to bottom or bottom to top. Performance needed to be closely monitored by supervisors. It is easy to see why such a system was necessary before the full-scale integration of information technology in the marketplace. Anything other than a rigid managerial structure would have been akin to chaos in a large organization.

The move toward decentralized operations is the logical organizational response to the effect of modern technology on the interaction between individuals within a company and between divisions of that corporation. Managerial coordination, monitoring work performance, and having access to information from any level of the company simply require less formal channels because the value of the channels in preventing organizational chaos has been superseded by technology's ability to manage information flows. Fewer managers are necessary to monitor the performance of the complex components of the operations of a company because information flows no longer need to be forced through rigid channels. Information can move not only throughout the organization but also between the organization and suppliers, further relieving the company of the necessity of being vertically integrated for quality assurance or production coordination. With a decentralized management structure, the firm begins to look less like a firm and more like a number of interrelated companies pursuing a common goal while making independent decisions. The ability to monitor becomes less important than the ability to structure incentives that assure that independent action by the divisions is in the best interests of all the divisions together.

How do decentralized operations relate to 1992? Many European companies are attempting to alter their organizational structure to meet these changes and streamline their operations to take advantage of the organizational revolution seen elsewhere, but they have suffered from several disadvantages. First, computer systems have cost more in Europe, so many firms have fallen behind in their attempts to achieve the level of office automation that is available in Japan and the United States. The deficiency was further exacerbated by the weak European position in the office automation market (see figure 4–11). Second, the percentage of managers who fall into the class of computer literate is considerably lower in Europe than in either the United States or Japan. Although one may quibble about the value of an MBA degree, few entering or apprentice managers in European companies receive the kind of "managerially oriented" computer training that is available to the average MBA student in the United States. Third, organizational restructuring is difficult and slower in countries with more stringent severance arrangements and more long-term commitments to workers. Decentralization generally implies a reduction of the managerial work force, something many European firms find politically difficult to accomplish.

The move toward decentralized operations in Europe is a given simply because European operations have the most to gain from such an organizational structure. A series of independent decision-making bodies sharing information and production when necessary, but not burdening one another when interference is unwarranted, is ideal for the culturally diverse European market. The link between our earlier statement about the conflict between the desire for scale efficiencies and the demand for variety should be clear. A flexible, decentralized organization, provided the organizational incentives are correctly structured, is the ideal post-1992 European company.

An excellent example of the move toward a more flexible European company is Allen Bradley. Before its 1992 reorganization it was a top-down company organized by operations and country. Its reorganization reduced the number of layers in management severalfold and organized operations and sales by country with pan-European oversight.[6] Allen Bradley's restructuring is perhaps a classic example of taking advantage of production economies while allowing for independence at the level of sales within a country, that is, respecting the cultural differences of the customers. And the Allen Bradley reorganization is not unique. Colgate-Palmolive, Philips, Sara Lee, and others have followed similar organizational paths.[7]

MORE FOCUSED MARKETING. The role of marketing in the post-1992 Europe has probably been the focus of more discussion than any other area. Much of this discussion has, however, been incorrectly focused on the importance of standardizing advertising, prices, and distribution. John Quelch and Robert Buzzell note in a 1989 article that the "new emphasis is on the search for similarities rather than differences across national boundaries."[8] Although they are certainly correct to the extent that firms are attempting to take advantage of the existing products and marketing by seeing where they can be easily applied or adapted, the gains from such a strategy will be short-lived. In the long term, 1992 potentially provides firms with the opportunity to search for the combinations of similarities and differences within a larger market that will allow them to better exploit their product line's strength.

In marketing, 1992 has three potential outcomes. First, there is the Euro-marketed Euro-product, which has either few attributes or product characteristics to which European consumers react similarly. The Euro-product is not only generic in content, but it is also generic in image, so differentiation through advertising or service is impossible. Second, at the other extreme, is the "focused" product, which is built to individual specifications with customers varying considerably depending on their valuation of its possible differences. The product may vary because of regional or cultural differences, but ultimately it must be marketed to individual groups independently. Third, there is the quasi Euro-product, a mixture of the focused product and the Euro-product. This product may have some similarities across regions, but it will vary slightly. Such a product may gain from general corporate image advertising or the advertising of other Euro-products or focused products in the product line.

The marketing implications of 1992 depend critically on the characteristics of the customers a company is serving. Pan-European marketing that attempts to force standardization on consumers will fail if the product demand is intrinsically diverse. Eric Friberg notes that Benetton sells sweaters of the same colors all over Europe, while Nestlé markets more than a dozen different varieties of one brand, Nescafé coffee, in deference to strong local tastes.[9] Post-1992 Euro-marketing must be more customer sensitive. For those firms marketing Euro-products, either real or potential, 1992 offers the opportunity to take advantage of the gains to scale in both production and marketing. For companies marketing focused products, little should change unless the products cater to the demands of customers of similar demand but of different nationalities. The greatest gains will accrue to those marketing quasi Euro-products, which provide the opportunity to produce with scale, both in production and marketing, while they also possess the market size limitations that provide for protection from entrants.

The Rise of Services and the Opportunities for Small Firms

The 1990s appear to be the decade when the services market comes into its own. The rise of the services industry is the outgrowth of a complex set of circumstances that are rooted in the same technological changes that have revolutionized the industrial sector. With the exception of the United Kingdom, and to a minor degree Germany, the EC has shown itself deficient in keeping up with progress in the services industry. This is mostly a function of the slow speed with which the Community has moved from an industrial society to an information society and the Community's lack of progress in developing twenty-first–century factory technology.

As the Community moves further into the information technology revolution, its shortfall in the services sector should be made up with an increasing level of direct consumer services and, more importantly, production-based services to businesses. The implications for smaller innovative ventures are significant. Since consumer services are more labor intensive, less amenable to large-scale operations, and heavily culturally sensitive in the retail dimension but relatively standardized in production, they represent tailor-made opportunities for pan-European franchising.

Production-based services represent a second area of opportunity for smaller scale operations. As firms become more decentralized and move to more advanced manufacturing systems, the opportunities for small specialized suppliers will increase. For example, a small U.S. trucking and warehouse services company specializes in JIT inventory management. It provides inventory services and quick delivery to firms that need specialized supplies but whose suppliers have yet to fully integrate these new techniques into their production process. The services company serves as the temporary intermediary between the specialized supplier and the specialized demander, providing inventory services, quality control, and JIT delivery. The firm is currently planning to move into the United Kingdom to begin offering its services through U.K. trucking and warehousing companies.

Perhaps the classic business service company is Federal Express. Heavily limited in its ability to provide services in Europe at the level of quality it provides in the United States, Federal Express focused on moving into each European country through the purchase of existing licensed trucking companies. Although Federal Express vice president David B. Schoenfeld admits that the system could be operated with fewer divisions than it is currently forced to use, he sees some advantages. The company is learning to service European markets of all sizes and is perfectly poised to take advantage of the inevitable consolidation when the transport regulatory structure is harmonized.[10]

Concerns about the Post-1992 Europe

Our earlier discussion was based on the assumption that the European single market would reflect a more laissez-faire attitude and be representative of a complete open market. But, as the previous chapters have shown, it is naive to expect this utopian outcome. Nineteen ninety-two is a politically motivated process with economic consequences, and many of the potential consequences are troubling, particularly, though not exclusively, for foreign firms. In addition, the radical changes in Eastern Europe have many concerned about the viability of the single market initiative.

Local Content and Rules of Origin

Perhaps the largest concerns of foreign companies center on the requirements pertaining to local content and rules of origin. Rules of origin determine the country of origin of a product. Local content rules specify what percentage of the value of a product must be added, either through production, materials, or marketing, in the country promulgating the rules. The Community in general has been persistent in applying rather stringent rules of origin and local content, mostly in dealings with imports from Asia and the greenfield plants (wholly owned foreign-production facilities) of Japanese manufacturers.

The political nature of these restrictions is clear. The European broadcasting lobby was successful in convincing the Commission to institute a 50 percent European content requirement on European television broadcasting, much to the chagrin of the American television and movie industry. At the other end of the spectrum, the Commission scrapped the reciprocity requirement in the Second Bank Directive for the more flexible national treatment approach. The reciprocity clause had raised cries of foul from American, Asian, and EFTA banks but was scrapped primarily at the insistence of the British and German banks. Its removal was more a reflection of the concerns of the British and German banks about foreign retribution and the weak competition that foreign banks pose for EC banks within the EC than it was a signal that the Community was easing its stance on foreign corporations.

The local content battle is also fought out between EC countries, as the Nissan Bluebird case shows. The Nissan Bluebird is constructed from both British- and Japanese-produced components and is assembled in a plant in Sunderland, England. Approximately 60 percent of the Bluebird's content is of British origin. According to the French and Italians, this percentage content is insufficient to have the car defined as "European," and they have declared the car subject to their "informal" quota for Japanese automobiles. After much public wrangling, the French and Italians eased their stance, mainly because the British committed to increasing the U.K. content of the Bluebird to 80 percent by the end of 1990.

The Social Dimension

Few studies of the management implications of the single market give more than a sentence or two to the social dimension of 1992, but the implications for corporate behavior are large. In considering the key limitations to European world competitiveness, Wisse Dekker of N.V. Philips sees the social costs of being a European company as second only to the inability to achieve scale economies and to relieve market fragmentation in limiting European world competitiveness. He estimates that Philips's social charges, "as a percentage of wages and salary are . . . about two times those of our [sic] competitors."[11]

The social dimension of 1992 includes not only basic European rights but issues such as job security, workplace control, the environment, the commitment to less developed regions of the EC, and the commitment of the commercial sector to the social integrity of the Community. The major problem with the social dimension is not that such goals are inappropriate or unwarranted but that the pressure within the Community has generally led the EC to tailor its social policy commitments to the highest common denominator. Jacques Delors has frequently expressed his contempt for "savage capitalism," and it is clear that the Community has no desire to ˉllow for competition between countries when determining workplace rules, safety, and environmental rules, and so on. The social pressure on the EC has focused and will continue to focus on improving the restrictions in countries with lower standards rather than attempting to find what might be a more "efficient" balance between the social costs and benefits.

The Lack of Accountability of Regulators

It is typical in the United States to believe that regulatory agencies are accountable to no one. Yet American government officials are accountable indirectly to elected senators and congressmen through oversight and budget committees, and directly to the president and members of the cabinet. More or less the same is true of EC countries, but the same system of checks and balances is not available within the EC bureaucracy. The Parliament is mostly ineffectual and the Commission is an unelected quasi-autonomous body with a not inconsiderable amount of independent decision-making authority. The EC regulatory process is also one that puts heavy weight on the lobbying ability of the EC parties affected by the regulations. Although this might appear to be a balanced democratic process, it serves to prevent the kind of radical change that might prove necessary for the fundamental operations of a truly open market and fosters commercial collusion that is contrary to the best interests of the consumer. Adam Smith said it best when he noted that "people of the same trade seldom meet together, even for merriment and diversion, but the conversation ends in a conspiracy against the public, or in some contrivance to raise prices. . . . [T]hough the law can not hinder people of the same trade from sometimes assembling together, it ought to do nothing to facilitate such assemblies; *much less to render them necessary*"[12] [italics added]. The Community, by rendering such meetings necessary, has assured industry groups the ability to restrict trade to their benefit or, at a minimum, to reduce the harm caused by any liberalization that might occur.

The EC lobbying rules have been a point of contention with the United States since only EC nationals are permitted to sit on working committees, whereas non-Community representatives are not even permitted to observe the deliberations. Although lobbying the European Parliament and even EC bureaucrats is considered relatively easy and cheap by United States standards, and certainly more effective than attempts to lobby Japan's rather inconsequential Diet or powerful ministries,[13] the fact of the matter remains that without direct representation within the committees commenting on the exact provisions of directives and regulations, the power of foreign firms to have their voices heard is limited. The ineffectiveness of foreign lobbyists was exemplified most markedly when Secretary of Commerce Robert Mosbacher's demands for a voice in the discussions over the Second Banking Directive were rebuffed.[14] Secretary Mosbacher recognized that EC lawmaking is almost exclusively behind a set of closed doors marked "interested Europeans only." When a piece of "legislation" comes out into the light for the world to see, there is generally little flexibility toward changing its substance or form.

The Implications of Changes in Eastern Europe

When the single market program was being developed by Lord Cockfield and his colleagues, the opening of Eastern Europe to democratic reforms was a twenty-first–century dream. Today, the dream is a 1990 reality, and the swiftness of events east of the Elbe have astonished the world. The unpredictability of these changes must have implications for the Community's integration, but probably less than we first imagined. The liberalization of Eastern Europe will most directly affect the 1992 initiative through Germany, but it will also have indirect effects because of foreign investment and the Community's need to develop a policy on trade and political interaction with these fledgling democracies.

The unification of Germany represents a major problem for the 1992 program for three reasons. First, controlling the flow of East Germans into the EC is a problem. The Schengen Agreement, an accord to open up the borders of Germany, France, and the Benelux countries, collapsed in late 1989 because the West Germans were unwilling to control the movement of East Germans into the Community. The agreement was subsequently approved in the summer of 1990 once the EC recognized the degree of West German commitment to reunification. The subsequent reunification of Germany presented the rest of the Community with an effective fait accompli.

With the West Germans preoccupied with the rebuilding, reeducation, and integration of their Eastern cousins, who is going to pay for the restructuring of the poorer sections of the Community? West Germany is the locomotive of the EC and was clearly expected to bankroll a major share of the "new" Europe. The second problem the Community faces because of a unified Germany is that not only will German time be devoted to the East, but German money will be devoted there as well.

The third problem is also of a monetary nature. German support for a Community-wide monetary union must necessarily be lessened by the preoccupation with German economic and monetary union. German inflation is estimated to rise above 4 percent next year and the real rate of interest has increased since the beginning of 1990. It is unlikely that the Bundesbank and the German *finanzministerium* will be keen to have the deutsche mark supporting too many economies.

While events in Eastern Europe have distracted the Germans, there is also concern that the opportunities arising in the East will cool the desire for not only foreign investment in the Community but intra-Community investment as well. This concern is both justified and unjustified. It is justified to the extent that investment in Eastern Europe will substitute for investment in other sections of the Community, particularly Spain, Portugal, Greece, and Ireland, but other more developed sections of the EC also. Nevertheless, since 1992 makes a distinction between an EC firm and a non-EC firm, foreign firms that desire to sell products in the Community will be under heavy pressures to invest in Community countries. Investment competition is important in the export market, therefore, building a facility to export from Hungary would be a direct substitute for building a similar facility in Italy.

Yet the rebirth of the East has enormous benefits for the Community countries. The quickest route into and out of Eastern Europe is through Western Europe, and companies desiring an Eastern European presence will most certainly need a West European operation. Also, in the next ten years the East will be attempting to make up for almost fifty years of neglect and frustrated aspirations. The tools and expertise for that rebuilding will come primarily from Community countries.

The changes in Eastern Europe create an atmosphere of confusion that must be troubling to those wanting to see a rapid integration of the EC economies. But these events are not necessarily antithetical to the theoretical concept of an open Europe and may serve to further the economic liberalization of Western Europe. What is required of the Community is a broadening of its vision of Europe and perhaps a greater willingness to listen to Mrs. Thatcher's call for a true European Community encompassing the continent from Moscow to Lisbon and Spitsbergen to Malta. Some, such as David Owen, cofounder of the British Social Democratic party and member of Parliament, feel that the Community will ultimately have to bring in the major countries of Eastern Europe simply to support their economies and aid their development. Lord Cockfield is more cautious and pragmatic, believing that these countries should be integrated into something akin to EFTA before they are considered potential Community members. Jacques Delors sees a Europe of "concentric circles" with the EC in the center.[15] Whatever the out-

come, the fact of the matter remains that the political pressures behind 1992 are the same as they were before the opening of the Berlin
Wall, and because these political pressures demand the changes that
have been proposed, those changes will occur. What else will be
demanded of the Community as the events in the East unfold is
anybody's guess.

Formulating a 1992 Strategy

Strategy specialists typically discuss strategy development in the
context of three methods: the entrepreneurial mode, the adaptive
mode, and the planning mode.[16] The entrepreneurial mode is proactive, growth oriented, flexible, and most often occurs in smaller and
newer organizations. The adaptive mode is reactive, moderately
flexible, and generally lacking in vision. The planning mode is both
proactive and reactive, stressing efficiency and growth, but also remaining somewhat inflexible and predictable. The planning mode
is the traditional mode of strategy development in large centralized
organizations.

Strategy development in firms in the 1980s has begun to move
away from the pure planning mode and to add a considerable degree of the entrepreneurial mode into decision making and strategic
development processes. The move toward decentralization with in-
terdivisional incentives is nothing more than an attempt by large
firms to foster a sort of controlled entrepreneurship and to thereby
reap the benefits of an entrepreneurial firm's unstructured style
while attempting to control the chaos that sometimes ensues.[17]

Post-1992 strategic planning will reflect this new style of strategic
development, but how will firms plan for the single market changes
themselves? This requires a very delicate balance of all three modes
of strategic development. Preparing for 1992 requires controlled
planning, quick adaptation, and, when necessary, entrepreneurial
initiative. In general, developing a single market strategy should be
easy. Companies simply need to know what the regulatory changes
are, how they will affect the nature of their business, and the likelihood that such changes will be introduced. With this combination
of information they can determine the appropriate response. But
alas, reality is not so accommodating. The regulatory changes are
not a given but will be amorphously determined within the black

box that is the EC bureaucracy, and if firms cannot understand the law or its intent, understanding its outcome is even more difficult. Therefore the path to developing a concrete strategy is less certain.

It goes without saying that any strategy must be based on an understanding of one's market, company, and external environment. We will not spend time repeating the importance of these factors, but instead we will focus on factors specific to developing a 1992 strategy.[18] The keys to developing a global 1992 strategy are

- flexibility and adaptability,
- developing standardization while respecting diversity,
- a willingness to decentralize organizational control,
- a commitment to information technology, and
- building product line strength and geographic depth.

Being Flexible and Adaptive

Perhaps the most important consideration in developing a 1992 strategy, or adapting a current 1992 strategy, is *flexibility*. No one quite knows the direction that the single market program will take as regards any specific industry, and the events in Eastern Europe show how precarious world political and economic events can be. In addition, there has always been speculation that 1992 is a boom phenomenon, ready to fail once a major recession hits some of the more critical players.

The NCR strategy is an excellent example of a flexible response strategy. NCR does not have one 1992 strategy but an umbrella strategy made up of four major scenarios: 1992 works, 1992 fails, 1992 disappoints, and the United States of Europe.[19] NCR has considered the likelihood of each scenario and has formulated its most likely response to each scenario.

Next to being flexible, the strategy must be *adaptive*. Although the two concepts appear identical, there are subtle differences. Flexibility implies having alternative scenarios, adaptability means having flexible scenarios that are easily achievable. The NCR strategy is also indicative of an adaptive strategy. Its Project 1992 is broken up into a series of phases, each of which leads into the next more or less naturally as events in the Community unfold.[20]

Seeking Standardization and Rationalization but Respecting Diversity

One of the hallmarks of the 1992 program is the reduction of nontariff barriers between EC countries through the concept of mutual recognition. This potentially allows companies to rationalize production, more efficiently map out distribution networks, and seek out the similarities in markets that can be initially exploited by existing products. In the long term, the reduction of nontariff barriers presents opportunities to find the right mixture of similarities and differences between markets to take advantage of a company's comparative advantages.

The post-1992 company will need to carefully understand what it can and cannot standardize and when it is appropriate to "think European" versus thinking regionally, culturally, or nationally. The implication is that European management will need to allow subsidiaries the flexibility to remain national or cultural while not allowing them to behave parochially. 3M has attempted to create an atmosphere where country units "think European" through multinational training programs and the establishment of European management action teams (EMATs). EMATs are grouped by product, whereas the major European subsidiaries are national units. The EMATs are charged with establishing stronger links between the strategies of the company as a whole and the product groups across countries, both on a global and a European dimension.[21]

Although the concept of "thinking European" is a bit campy, there is some value to recognizing that European companies have traditionally been organized on national lines and managers have been trained to understand their national markets. Old habits are sometimes slow to change. Karen Jackson, director of Sound Thinking, speaks of one of the major challenges of 1992 being the need to "deregulate minds"[22]; nevertheless, caution must be exercised. Thinking European should imply thinking multiculturally, respecting deep-seated cultural differences, and attempting to adapt to them rather than viewing them as antiquated idiosyncrasies that need to be "harmonized."

Decentralizing

We stated earlier that the post-1992 corporation will be considerably more organizationally decentralized. Achieving decentralization is no easy task since it requires that top management take a considerable risk in delegating authority to those closer to the final market. There are three keys to achieving a smooth transition from a centralized to a decentralized corporate structure.

First, form must follow function. When there were national regulatory structures and barriers to intercountry trade, the most efficient organizational form was nationally based. As the regulatory structure evolves around a supranational authority, the regulatory structure will become less of a constraint in the day-to-day servicing of markets. Organizational form will become more sensitive to the market function of the firm and less a creature of the economic barriers between EC countries. Nixdorf is one of many companies that has recognized this change and has moved to the strategic business unit (SBU) organizational structure.[23] The SBU structure stresses product line and market characteristics in a decentralized environment that allows the company to more efficiently mold itself around the servicing of the market.

Second, incentives must be structured so that the independent divisions still recognize their links to the parent company and the other divisions. BancOne, a United States superregional bank with offices in Wisconsin, Indiana, Ohio, Michigan, and Texas, provides an excellent example of how to manage a decentralized company. BancOne has a definite corporate philosophy that pervades almost all of its operations and is instilled in its employees with the help of the BancOne College, a corporate training facility. But the key to keeping the organization humming is information. Each BancOne subsidiary receives almost continuous information on every other subsidiary in the organization and each subsidiary always knows where it stands on key operating statistics. In addition, managers at one subsidiary are "strongly" encouraged to seek out the managers in the other subsidiaries for information and tips on performance. The information flows serve, first, to provide information about the market and, second, as a reminder of the level of corporate performance expected by central management. A decentralized firm is not simply a series of independent firms under one roof, thus it is important that critical linkages be maintained. If decentralization only brings about the transference of worker loyalty from the corporation to the division or business unit, corporation parochialism could make matters worse than if the company had remained centralized.

Third, the decentralization must allow divisional managers the opportunity to take risks and experiment. The value of decentralization can be found in the flexibility that divisional managers gain when their monetary and professional rewards are linked to their performance. Companies cannot simultaneously have both the security of control from centralization and performance from flexibility because of centralization.

Knowing How to Manage Information

Almost everything that we have spoken about in this chapter has revolved around understanding and dealing with the impact of information technology on the markets and corporations of the late twentieth century. The successful firms of the 1990s will be those that manage information most efficiently, which entails creating an "information literate" work force as well as managing information at a number of levels.

First, to solve the problem of managing information within the firm, newly independent divisions need incentives to share information. Managing information with the firm requires a centralized information structure within a decentralized organizational structure. Although one section of the corporation may desire independence in making strategic product decisions, the corporation does not desire one section to protect its information from the other sections of the company.

Second, firms need to properly manage information about their competitors. As intra-Community protectionism declines, competitor-sensitive strategic responses become more valuable. Also, since a company's competitors will be marketing many of the same product lines, it becomes critical that the decentralized divisions of a company understand the need for a coordinated effort in dealing with competitive rivals.

Third, companies need to manage information about production. The move toward more technologically based manufacturing techniques requires more control over information about the production process not only within the firm but between the firm and its suppliers. The need to coordinate information technology improvements with suppliers will become increasingly important.

Increasing Product Strength and Discontinuing Weak Products

Philips is a classic example of both the old-style European company and the emerging restructured new European company. The company has been burdened over the years with product lines that have ranged from consumer electronics and computers to saxophones and domestic appliances. Production facilities were spread all over the continent. Although an excellent engineering organization, Philips continually found itself beaten to the market when it came to the full-scale commercialization and marketing of its discoveries. Today, Philips is attempting to rationalize production by closing obsolete production facilities, centralizing distribution, and concentrating on key strategic businesses. It has laid off 24,000 workers in two years and has increased its focus on the commercialization of its discoveries.[24]

The new Philips strategy emphasizes product strength and geographic reach. This concept of building product strength and slowly expanding that strength throughout the product line and across increasing geographic coverage is well developed by Robert Gogol and Jean-Claude Larreche in a recent study.[25] According to this framework, the strongest position, and the one with the greatest long-term return, is wide geographic coverage and high product strength, what Gogol and Larreche term "kings." Our previously defined Euro-products and traditional "global" products would fall into this category. The weakest position is poor geographic coverage and weak products, or "commoners," that are subject to attack once their limited geographic position is invaded by stronger products. The two wild cards in this scheme are strong products with weak geographic coverage, "barons," and weak products with wide geographic coverage, "crusaders." Barons represent opportunities for expansion because of similarities in demand across cultures (potential Euro-products) and, with modifications in product design, barons may increase their geographic coverage and become quasi Euro-products. Crusaders can only survive with rapid increases in product line strength, either in conjunction with geographic retrenchment or with the riskier strategy of attempting to protect all the territory at once.

Therefore, post-1992 companies need to know when to cut products or product lines loose. Having a pan-European presence is valuable only so long as the products behind that presence are strong enough to withstand concerted regional attacks by strong local products or continent-wide assaults by stronger Euro-products. Many other European companies operate under conditions similar to Philips's former "imperial overstretch," and there is little doubt that the financial markets take a dim view of irrational cross-subsidization of products.

The Role of Mergers and Alliances

The prospect of 1992 has created a tremendous flurry of takeover and alliance-building activity in Europe. The question that each individual company must ask is, will mergers and/or alliances be part of our single market strategy? To answer this question requires understanding what European mergers and alliances can provide that a greenfields strategy cannot.

This is not the place to discuss a complete theory of mergers and alliances, but a few general comments are necessary. Mergers have traditionally provided the acquiring company with the opportunity to rapidly move into a geographic or product market. The acquired company also receives the benefits of market expansion, although the management normally, though not always, takes a position subordinate to the management of the acquiring company. Mergers most often take place on friendly terms and arise because production demand, customer demand, or organizational synergies exist. Takeovers, on the other hand, normally arise when one company or group sees an opportunity in reorganizing and/or managing a target firm. More often takeovers are acrimonious, unwanted by the target firm, and are generally driven by the target company's inability or unwillingness to restructure the firm in a manner more profitable for the stockholders.

Alliances represent temporary organizational partnerships generally focused around a product or product line, a line of research or product development, and/or exploitation of some technology or resource. Alliances and joint ventures allow companies to gain efficiencies in scale, to acquire knowledge, and to spread risk without the necessity of a full-scale merger.[26]

The Mergers and Acquisition Strategy

Mergers and acquisitions (M&A) as part of a 1992 strategy have value when based on the criteria that we have discussed earlier, namely, building efficient scale in production, distribution, and marketing; gaining technical expertise; gaining cultural expertise; strengthening or expanding the product line; and adding geographic coverage. But mergers and acquisitions carry the additional problems of integrating the operations of the firms, removing duplicate operations, and developing a new joint organizational structure. In addition, American-style M&As and M&A strategy do not fully translate to Europe. National restrictions still make acquisitions a difficult endeavor and, unless both parties are fully satisfied, the marriage could prove difficult. In addition, the opportunities for divestiture and consolidation, so important in U.S. M&A endeavors, are significantly more limited in Europe given the explicit social guarantees required of many European companies. The implication is that 1992-driven mergers must be carefully planned and structured for the long term since flexibility after the fact is limited.[27]

In the paragraphs that follow we explore examples of 1992 M&A strategies.

Distribution. Grampian Holdings Sporting Goods Division (makers of Mitre and Patrick sporting equipment), acquired Patrick in 1987. The attraction was Patrick's distribution network in West Germany, which is being considered on the basis of its European distribution network.[28]

Guinness PLC increased its stake in Christian Dior S.A. in April 1989, thereby increasing its holding in Louis Vuitton Möet Hennessy S.A. (LVMH). Given that LVMH holds distribution rights for Guinness's premium whiskeys and gins and Guinness is responsible for much of the worldwide marketing of Moet Hennessy champagne, Guinness's increase in LVMH holding represents a strengthening of the distribution agreements between Guinness and LVMH.[29]

Geographic Coverage and Product Line Strength. Vickers is attempting to use its merger with S & W Medico Teknik, a Danish concern, to gain access to European markets for its rather formidable product line of medical products.[30] DRG PLC and Cellux S.A. have complementary product lines, which allows DRG to further fill out its product line of adhesive products. Cellux also brought to the table a substantial distribution network and technological and marketing expertise.[31]

Many consider the Carnaud S.A./Metal Box Group merger creating CMB packaging a classic example of a 1992-induced merger. The two food packaging companies have complementary production facilities and product lines. Metal Box is strong in Italy, Greece, and the United Kingdom, and Carnaud's niches are in Belgium, France, Germany, Italy, Portugal, Spain, and Turkey. The new company is the third largest packaging company in Europe and, more importantly, is strong all over the continent.[32]

The move toward greater geographic coverage can also come from outside Europe. Microamerica, a Massachusetts-based microcomputer hardware and software company, purchased a Swiss company, Euro Software Services, and began marketing its products in Germany.[33]

Bombardier Inc. of Canada purchased Short Brothers PLC of Northern Ireland for production, capacity, and product line considerations. Both companies gain greater geographic coverage for their products because Short's products obtain a new market in North America and Bombardier's products get an expanded market in Europe.[34]

Production Efficiency. Sema Metra, a French computer services company, and CAP, a similar British concern, merged to take advantage of opportunities to consolidate operations and increase scale to remain competitive in a "rapidly maturing" industry facing increased competition from both new companies and rapidly consolidating established competitors. The driving factor behind the merger was achieving scale in the training of personnel, the key ingredient in marketing computer services.[35]

Cultural Expertise. Trusthouse Forte subsidiary Gardner Merchant is the world's largest caterer with 25 independent divisions and 34,000 employees spread over 6 EC countries. Yet this British company encountered the difficulty of moving operations into another culture when, sixteen years ago, it established its first German operation in Wiesbaden and quickly ran into trouble. Notes Managing Director Garry Hawke, "[we quickly learned] that you do not set up a business in a foreign country without a clear understanding of its culture, laws, [and] ways of doing business."[36] The Gardner Merchant strategy is to purchase strategically located firms with strong staffs who then receive training in its operational practices in the United Kingdom. The technical operations are purely Gardner Merchant's, but the local tastes, customs, and operations are the purview of the independent local division.

Technical Expertise. The international merger of accounting firms is an excellent example of strong firms merging to gain technical expertise, in this case the technical expertise necessary to provide accounting services to multinational companies faced with disparate accounting standards. The merger of Peat Marwick with KMG Main Hurdman created the world's largest accounting firm, one with the capability of serving "global" clients. The year after the merger, Peat Marwick's growth shot up to 25 percent. Arthur Andersen and Arthur Young lost several major multinational clients to the new firm, KPMG Peat Marwick, which created pressure for their own ultimate merger. The advantages of these new multinational accounting firms are obvious. When Bertelsmann A.G. bought Bantam and Doubleday publishers, it hired KPMG Peat Marwick as its auditors. KPMG Peat Marwick's purchase of the German accounting firm Treuverkehr now gives it 70 percent of Bertelsmann's auditing business.[37]

The Alliance Strategy

The alliance strategy provides a company with a European presence or geographic expansion while protecting the parent company from many of the risks associated with the complete commitment of a merger or greenfields approach. In conjunction with the purchasing of minority interests in a company, the alliance can serve as a stand-alone strategy or a cautious first step that can be more fully consummated should the partners decide that further integration would be valuable. Notes Eston Gross, corporate coordinator of acquisitions and divestments for Akzo, "a joint venture with a partner with complementary experience can be an excellent way to minimize risks in entering an unfamiliar but promising market.[38] An additional benefit of the alliance approach is that it provides the non-Community partner the opportunity to use its partner as its European spokesperson with the EC bureaucracy. Within Europe, the merger strategy appears to be dominant, at least for the time being, as small companies attempt to consolidate and larger companies reorganize. Firms moving into Europe, particularly Japanese firms, but to some extent American firms, tend to be oriented toward alliances and joint ventures. This is clearly the more cautious path and, for the Japanese in particular, it reflects the kind of political expediency that is necessary in Europe.

In general, four types of nonexclusive alliance strategies fit well into a 1992 strategy: the cautious move toward merger, the marketing alliance (cross-distribution or cross-licensing agreements), the product development alliance, and joint production agreements. Although alliance strategies are, in general, efficiency based, some, such as the alliances arising in European air transport, are clearly driven by attempts to replace the old nationally sanctioned cartels with tacit alliances to protect markets.

The Cautious Move toward Merger. Examples of alliances growing into full-scale acquisitions are common. For example, Leyland merged with Daf, but before the merger Daf had a long-standing agreement to distribute Leyland trucks on the European continent.[39] Scott Paper had traditionally handled the marketing of soft paper products through joint ventures with European companies. With the accession of Philip Lippincott to the chairmanship in 1983 and the rise of the opportunities in Europe, Scott proceeded to buy out its joint venture partners and consolidate operations.[40]

Creating a Marketing Alliance. Marketing alliances represent an opportunity to market a product without necessarily producing that product in the local market or having a native distribution system. Firms can create a marketing alliance either with manufacturer branding or through distributor or retailer branding. This strategy has value primarily for European companies since foreign manufacturers must concern themselves with local content requirements.

A large component of the 1983–89 Olivetti/AT&T alliance was devoted to marketing Olivetti personal computers under the AT&T name in the United States. The alliance linked AT&T's American awareness with Olivetti's production facilities to allow AT&T to move quickly into the personal computer market.

In Europe, Fuji-Xerox arose from the initial distribution agreement between Fuji and Rank Xerox. Rank Xerox was itself a creature of a marketing agreement between Haliod (Xerox) and Rank in 1956. Xerox had neither the cash nor the organization to expand internationally but did have a strong but limited product base, and Rank provided Xerox with the European distribution it needed.[41] More recently, Megasource, a Michigan-based computer information system manufacturer, arranged a joint venture with a French marketing firm to market their computerized pharmaceutical system to French hospitals.[42]

Creating a Production Alliance. The most obvious type of alliance is a production-based alliance. The eleven-year Honda/Rover alliance is a classic western-eastern alliance. Honda gains production facilities in Europe while Rover learns Japanese production techniques.[43] Such alliances are transportable, for example, Ford and Mazda plan to take their profitable joint production alliance and transplant it to Europe. The purchase of 50 percent of Saab by General Motors helps Saab achieve more efficient scale in automobile production and marketing and gives GM the upscale European model it has been unable to produce in-house.[44] AT&T and ITAL-TEL, the Italian telecommunications company, have formed a joint venture to modernize Italy's telephone system.

R & D and Product Development Alliances. R & D and product development alliances are similar to production alliances and are very often linked with them. The boldest of the European product development programs is the alliance established in 1987 between Philips and Siemens to develop and produce four-megabit chips by the end of the year.[45] Amper, a Spanish telecommunications equipment supplier, and APT, a joint venture between AT&T and Philips, formed a Spanish venture, APT España, devoted to research and production of advanced technology communications systems. Amper has proved itself to be a busy company, having linked its operations with the likes of Northern Telecom, DEC, Prodata, Pargon, and Olivetti.[46]

Assessing 1992's Winners and Losers

Assessing the impact of any complex endeavor on a specific group is always a difficult task, particularly when the enterprise itself is still evolving. In examining the impact of 1992 on specific industries, a threefold matrix approach is an instructive tool. The primary impact of 1992 will be felt in production technology and distribution, and these are two of the anchors of the matrix. The driving force behind the impact in these areas is information technology. The third anchor is markets. Table 6–1 provides a breakdown of how the single market may affect some selected industries on these dimensions.

Production technology will most dramatically be affected by movements toward rationalized production, modern manufacturing techniques, and so on, and the most dramatic effects will be evident in industries such as telecommunications, distribution services, electronic and computer manufacturing, and automobiles.

Distribution will be affected by the removal of nuisance trade barriers and the application of modern distribution techniques based on the integration of information technology. The most affected industries will be trucking, food sales and processing, distribution services, and consumer durables. Other potentially affected industries are electronics, computers, automobiles, and pharmaceuticals.

The third dimension is customer market changes. There are two types of customer market changes: regulatory changes and 1992-induced changes. The first type of change is the removal of restrictions that have limited customer choice and also includes the easing of restrictions in the government procurement market. Markets affected by such changes include financial services, pharmaceuticals, telecommunications, trucking, and defense and government contractors. The second type of customer market effect is the increased commercial demand that occurs because of changes in the post-

TABLE 6-1

Predicted Impact of the Single Market Program
on Selected Industries by Function

	Markets	Distribution	Production Technology
Automobiles	Moderate	Moderate	Moderate/high
Business services	High	Moderate	High
Chemicals	Low	Low	Low/moderate
Computers/office automation	High	Moderate	High
Consumer durables	Low	High	Moderate
Consumer electronics	Low	Moderate	High
Defense	Moderate	Low	Low/moderate
Distribution services	High	High	High
Financial services	High	Low	Moderate/high
Food processing and marketing	Low	High	Low
Pharmaceuticals	Low	Moderate	Moderate
Telecommunications	High	Moderate	Moderate/high
Traditional manufacturing	Low	Low	Moderate
Trucking	High	High	Low

1992 market. Such changes reflect the increased business demand, which is caused by the increased consumer demand for the business's products. These include the increased demand for computer and telecommunications services, the altered demand for trucking services, and the rise of business service companies.

There are, of course, other 1992 winners and losers, including the non-Community companies faced with the prospect of an altered regulatory structure and little prospect of having their voices heard. As we have stated earlier, non-Community companies are faced with the daunting prospect of altering the nature of their operations to accommodate these regulatory changes.

For companies currently producing products in the Community, the primary issues are local content restrictions and rules of origin. To the extent that these companies are "European" by the Community's definition, the implications of 1992 are no different for these non-Community companies than for a native EC company. If the company fails to meet the new European standards, it has no other option but to alter its operations and comply.

For companies marketing products in the Community that are produced outside the Community, the prospects are less sunny. If the products are not politically sensitive, there is little likelihood that restrictive actions will interfere. Under the opposite set of circumstances these companies are faced with the serious prospect of establishing greenfield operations in the Community, merging or aligning themselves with an existing European company, or not marketing their products in the European Community. No matter what approach is used, it represents the company's second-best alternative since it is driven by political expediency rather than the pure economics of the marketplace.

Companies moving into the Community for the first time will be facing a mixed bag. To a certain extent, the new Community rules make large-scale entrances into the Community easier; thus benefiting those larger companies that are considering moving into Europe. On the other hand, smaller companies could be at a serious disadvantage should the new EC rules settle too large a tax on setting up operations. For example, suppose a small company was considering setting up a research and development facility in Luxembourg or Ireland to take advantage of tax breaks and to establish an entrée into the Community. It is possible that because of EC requirements the company would not be able to receive these tax breaks after 1992 and, further, would have to meet more stringent EC standards. As a result the company may now opt not to open the facility.

Nineteen ninety-two is billed as the building of a "Europe for Europeans," and this statement must be taken seriously. The winners are supposed to be Europeans, but that does not mean that foreign companies do not fall into that category or that some Europeans will not lose. As Wisse Dekker notes, "Opel is GM but it is considered absolutely European."[47] And 1992 is not for all Europeans. Remembering that the program is fundamentally not a consumer movement, it is realistic to expect that consumers will benefit only as a result of secondary effects. Questions about the union orientation of 1992 still remain. The European labor movement has pulled out all the stops in making sure that its voice is heard.

Overall, the winners will primarily be in the rising industries, for example, banking, insurance, computers, telecommunications, electronics, and business and consumer services. The losers will be mostly in the declining industries—for example, steel, primary manufacturing, and chemicals—and in those industries whose protection hurts the rising industries—for example, national telephone and communications monopolies, construction, trucking, and, perhaps, airlines. This does not imply that there will not be winners in the losers' category or losers in the winners' category. For example, modern telecommunications has both winners—those attempting to provide modern communications equipment to companies—and losers—those who have relied on the largess of national PTTs.

We began this chapter with five questions pertaining to predictions about the post-1992 European market, and we will end the chapter by saying that neither we nor anyone else really knows the answers to those questions, but our analysis has allowed us to speculate about some possible answers.

Nineteen ninety-two is one more step in an evolutionary process that has brought national markets closer together. As in almost all cases of economic evolution, government and social institutions sometimes move more slowly than appears rational, but they do ultimately react to the pressure for change even if they do not completely accommodate the demands for change. For those expecting, in the words of the Monty Python troupe, "something completely different," 1992 will disappoint them; for those more realistic souls expecting something "moderately" different, it will not. In planning strategy in Europe, it is safe to bet that managers will have a freer rein in operating their companies for their shareholders' benefit, provided that they satisfy the criterion of Euro-capitalism established by the Community.

7

The Limits to
European Integration

There was also little evidence to suggest that there had developed in the Communities a sufficient degree of consensus at the popular level, and a refocusing of loyalties towards the Communities' institutions, so that any claim of the latter to sovereignty could be sustained. At the end of the day, national governments remain the responsible actors, and the separate nations the main constituencies.

—*Paul Taylor,* The Limits of European Integration

In *La Grande Illusion,* Alain Minc points out that "[i]n history, as in business, living with illusions can be very dangerous."[1] Nineteen ninety-two, he argues, is an attempt by Europeans to reach out to the ideal of Europe for a miracle to solve what are essentially national problems. In its ideal form, the single market program will fail because it does not address the fundamental political questions. Rather, it is based on the false hope that economic integration will be the spark that will lead to political integration. 1992 is an *ignis fatuus,* a deceptive goal.

Minc's book is one of the few to look at the limits of the single market program in a structured and logical manner. As a Frenchman and head of Carlo DiBenedetti's French holding company, Cerus, you might expect Minc to be a bona fide 1992 enthusiast; but more to his credit, he is a realist. His book raises a basic and all too often overlooked question: Are there natural limits to European integration? The answer is yes.

From a purely neoclassical economic perspective, there are no limits to European economic integration if that integration is nothing more than the removal of trade barriers and the instituting of free trade. Those who wish to trade, trade; those who do not wish to trade, do not. But 1992 is not about free trade, but it is about Euro-harmonized managed trade. As we have emphasized earlier, the single market program is politics with an economic face and not the victory of laissez-faire capitalism over European socialism. For these reasons, European economic integration has limits.

We can use our economic theory of regulation to explain the limits of European economic integration. Two major factors will serve to limit the ability of the European Community to complete its integration and will limit the ability of the Community to effectively expand its program to a larger future Community. First, internal political pressures will restrict the Community's ability to develop effective Euro-regulations. Second, the economic integration will create a split between the political and economic spheres of human endeavor. As the EC institutions attempt to expand their powers within the Community and the Community itself grows in size, the pressures between local interests and European interests will increase. This pressure will become even more salient if the Community chooses to expand eastward, where economic and political instability and inexperience with western-style political processes will take some time to overcome.

National Politics versus Euro-Politics

When a political coalition finds itself up against a strong rival, one solution is to attempt to negotiate an agreement whereby both the coalition and its rival are satisfied with the outcome. For example, in the United States it is not uncommon to find two groups that on the surface appear completely at odds coming together to form laws that are mutually beneficial. Such was the case with the Clean Air Act, which was supported by the industrial states of the Northeast and Midwest and the environmental states of the Rocky Mountains and the Northwest. The reason was that it helped reduce air pollution by imposing a differential tax on industrial plants, thereby making it more costly to open new plants in the South. Southern states, incidentally, voted against the law.

Before the single market initiative, European unionists found themselves viewed as quaint anachronisms, but with their linkage to pan-European commercial interests, they have become part of a formidable coalition. The stakes are a European union of sorts for the unionists and a new regulatory structure for the pan-European commercial interests. But national commercial and political interests still exist and will prove a counterweight to this group. Belgium miners and steelworkers still riot in Brussels when Community-mandated closures are imposed. German unions will continue to restrict shopping hours in German stores and limit the workweek. National agricultural lobbies will remain as strong as ever and provide ever-present pressure on their national legislatures. Portuguese farmers will still go on rampages, uprooting eucalyptus trees planted under the auspices of an EC program meant to foster the Portuguese eucalyptus paper industry, because of their belief that the trees take groundwater and devastate sections of the indigenous agriculture industry.

Although Euro-statesmen have quite effectively neutralized many national political lobbies, they have done so only with the aid of commercial interests that span national borders. But political power resides in Brussels, Luxembourg, and Strasbourg only with the grace and blessing of the member state governments. *As long as political power is kept out of the hands of the European Community institutions, the pressure of local interests will continue to limit the ability of the Community to further European integration.*

Commercial Europe versus Political Europe

Nineteen ninety-two will create two classes of Europeans, commercial Europeans and national Europeans. This is because, although European commercial interests can theoretically move anywhere in the Community, Germans are still Germans politically. They must return to Germany to vote, get a divorce, or engage in any activity of an effective political nature. *Nineteen ninety-two allows Europeans to exist as Europeans only commercially and professionally, not politically.* The reason for this separation is obvious. Although the European Parliament was given moderately expanded powers by the Single European Act and is an elected assembly, it is basically still an ineffectual body about which few Europeans really care. Although it is expected that the December 1990 Intergovernmental Conference on Political Union will increase the power of the Parliament, there is little evidence that it will play anything but a role second to that of the member states' national parliaments. The Commission is unelected, although appointed by member state governments and has more of the character of the "dictatorship of the proletariat," than a European executive branch.

The Community institutions are permitted to have power only so long as they serve the consensus formed among member state governments. This is what member state governments want, and there is no indication that European voters themselves would support a pan-European political organization meant to supersede their national governments. Germans feel safer voting for members of the Bundestag, Frenchmen for deputies of La Assemblée Nationale, and Britons for Members of Parliament. "Europe for Europeans" is a quaint saying with no real meaning unless all Europeans agree. Europe is a politically diverse continent with conservative Irish Catholics to the north, conservative Spanish Catholic socialists to the west, Italian Catholic communists to the south, and Protestant Social Democratic Germans and Danes to the east. They do not, as a group, desire political and social integration because, unlike commercial integration, it is inconsistent with their remaining English, Spanish, Greek, or Dutch.

Can the Community Expand?

With the events in Eastern Europe rapidly unfolding, the natural question of the Community's ability to expand arises. Few people disagree that had the original EC-6 decided to commercially merge, there would have been little difficulty in achieving a 1992-style integration. The EC-6 are commercially similar countries with heavy trade links and well-developed political and economic systems. The addition of the United Kingdom, southern Europe, and the Iberian peninsula to the European Community, however, has created strains in the EC system. There are now radical political differences between the countries, which create very obvious philosophical differences within the EC hierarchy. Economically, the EC countries cover the spectrum from a petro-economy (United Kingdom), to an agrarian society (Portugal), to an industrializing economy (Spain), to an exporting industrial juggernaut (Germany). The wealth levels in the Community are now almost as disparate as those between North and South America. And attempts at fully integrating newer countries into the Community system have not always been easy. For example, since its entrance into the European monetary system, the Greek economy has virtually succumbed to chaos.

These differences highlight the difficulty of integrating such radically different economic systems and show the natural limitations to forcing harmonized standards and codes on naturally disparate economic and political systems. As the Community initially expands, perhaps taking in the EFTA countries first, the strains will be minor. EFTA countries are modern well-developed economies with political systems not unlike those of the existing EC countries, nonetheless, expansion into Eastern Europe and Turkey will prove difficult.

Turkey, although a semimodern industrial society, presents several problems. First, it is a poor nation with a very large population and a weak commercial infrastructure. Second, it is politically, socially, and religiously different from the remainder of the Community. Even if it was accepted as a member of the EC, it will tend, more often than not, to be odd man out. Third, it is in a virtual state of war with one of the other Community members over the question of Cyprus. It has the benefit of being a member of NATO, and this attribute undoubtedly helped the Spanish, Portuguese, and Greeks in their EC membership bids.

The newly democratic states of Eastern Europe pose another problem. They suffer from weak commercial infrastructures and the lack, as of yet, of stable political structures. It is unlikely that fifty years of communist domination has turned the populace into political conservatives, so the likelihood that they will remain politically left of center is high. These countries will put not only enormous political strains on the Community but massive economic pressures as well. The EC could be faced with the daunting prospect of a plethora of developing economies demanding structural funds from a small number of developed economies.

The pressures for the expansion of the European Community will come from the outside and will most likely be ignored until the end of the century. Today, the EC faces the real possibility of a two-tier Community, and certainly does not want to consider either expanding that second tier or, worse, adding a third tier. Should the Community expand, its character will change so radically that true integration will never come. The political, economic, and social divisions that have kept the houses of Europe apart for centuries will simply become a means of keeping divided the separate rooms of the new larger "common European" house.

A Final Comment

We began this book by asking several fundamental questions about 1992. Why is it occurring now? Why is it structured as it is? What is its probable outcome? We hope we have provided clear answers to these questions.

In a nutshell, 1992 is the outcome of a political process that is demanding change in the regulatory structure of key European commercial sectors. It is supported by a curious coalition of old-style European unionists and pan-European commercial interests. The latter see the EC as a means of releasing them from increasingly obsolete national regulatory structures. The former see 1992 as a quest for European union, something that has eluded them for decades. Nineteen ninety-two gives the commercial interests their new and improved regulatory structure, while the unionists receive a new "social" Europe to preside over from Brussels. The pan-European commercial interests would certainly do without the social dimension of 1992 if they could, but this is the quid pro quo demanded of them by the unionists.

To understand 1992, it is important to understand the nature of this coalition. The kind of consensus that is coming out of the European Council these days simply could not occur without the political persuasion of national pressure groups. The European unionists need the pan-European industrial interests, because they can create exactly the same pressure in a number of places at one time. The pan-European commercial interests also need the EC, in fact, they are lucky that it exists, otherwise an entirely new European political structure would have to be constructed. Because European Community legislation can only originate in the Commission, any regulatory change desired by the commercial interests must be channeled through the EC.

It is unlikely that the single market program will be fully implemented by 1993. It is equally unlikely that the program will fail on its major dimensions. The political pressure for 1992 is real, and it is politically effective at the national level. When Paul Taylor notes that, "there is little evidence to suggest that there has developed . . . a refocusing of loyalties towards the Communities' institutions,"[2] he is speaking of the European population. But European commercial interests have found that there are benefits to being "good Europeans." So long as those benefits exist and can be capitalized on, the pressure and impetus for European commercial integration will continue.

Appendix A:
A Statistical Look
at the European Community

This appendix contains a small compendium of statistical information on the European Community. Although the data are not all-encompassing, they present a short look at the macroeconomics of these countries over the last several years.

The following table lists the basic statistics for EC and EFTA countries, the United States, and Japan from 1970–1988.

European Community Countries

Belgium

Year	GNP (billions of francs)	Population (millions)	Consumer Prices (1985 = 100)	Exchange Rate (francs/$)	Real GNP in Constant $ (billions/1985 $)	Real GNP/Capita (thousands $)
1970	1292.00	9.66	35.0	49.675	74.3116	7.6927
1975	2326.00	9.79	52.3	39.528	112.5131	11.4927
1980	3508.00	9.85	71.2	31.523	156.2975	15.8678
1985	4797.00	9.86	100.0	50.360	95.2542	9.6607
1986	5072.00	9.91	101.3	40.410	123.9028	12.5028
1987	5293.00	9.92	102.9	33.153	155.1543	15.6405
1988	5565.00	9.92	104.1	37.345	143.1469	14.4301

Denmark

Year	GNP (billions of kroner)	Population (millions)	Consumer Prices (1985 = 100)	Exchange Rate (kroner/$)	Real GNP in Constant $ (billions/1985 $)	Real GNP/Capita (thousands $)
1970	118.41	4.93	26.7	7.4890	59.2179	12.0118
1975	214.59	5.06	41.6	6.1775	83.5033	16.5026
1980	364.50	5.12	68.3	6.0150	88.7240	17.3289
1985	593.41	5.11	100.0	8.9690	66.1623	12.9476
1986	639.78	5.12	103.7	7.3425	84.0249	16.4111
1987	665.04	5.13	107.8	6.0965	101.1925	19.7256
1988	695.40	5.13	112.7	6.8740	89.7638	17.4978

France

Year	GNP (billions of francs)	Population (millions)	Consumer Prices (1985 = 100)	Exchange Rate (francs/$)	Real GNP in Constant $ (billions/1985 $)	Real GNP/Capita (thousands $)
1970	797.8	50.77	25.3	5.5205	571.2091	11.2509
1975	1470.8	52.79	38.6	4.4855	849.4845	16.0918
1980	2826.1	53.88	63.3	4.5160	988.6211	18.3486
1985	4700.1	55.17	100.0	7.5610	621.6241	11.2674
1986	5052.5	55.39	102.5	6.4550	763.6357	13.7865
1987	5301.3	55.63	105.9	5.3400	937.4436	16.8514
1988	5658.3	55.87	108.8	6.0590	858.3336	15.3631

Germany

Year	GNP (billions of marks)	Population (millions)	Consumer Prices (1985 = 100)	Exchange Rate (marks/$)	Real GNP in Constant $ (billions/1985 $)	Real GNP/Capita (thousands $)
1970	675.7	60.71	50.4	3.6480	367.5095	6.0535
1975	1029.4	61.83	67.8	2.6223	578.9914	9.3642
1980	1485.2	61.56	82.7	1.9590	916.7375	14.8918
1985	1844.3	61.02	100.0	2.4613	749.3195	12.2799
1986	1945.2	61.05	99.8	1.9408	1004.2757	16.4501
1987	2020.2	61.17	100.1	1.5815	1276.1188	20.8618
1988	2121.4	61.20	101.2	1.7803	1177.4673	19.2397

Greece

Year	GNP (billions of drachmas)	Population (millions)	Consumer Prices (1985 = 100)	Exchange Rate (drachmas/$)	Real GNP in Constant $ (billions/1985 $)	Real GNP/Capita (thousands $)
1970	304.4	8.79	10.3	30.000	98.5113	11.2072
1975	691.4	9.05	18.4	35.650	105.4028	11.6467
1980	1767.6	9.64	39.1	46.535	97.1466	10.0774
1985	4582.6	9.93	100.0	147.760	31.0138	3.1232
1986	5475.4	9.97	123.0	138.760	32.0809	3.2177
1987	6326.2	9.99	143.2	125.925	35.0823	3.5117
1988	7389.6	10.01	162.5	148.100	30.7052	3.0675

Ireland

Year	GNP (millions of pounds)	Population (millions)	Consumer Prices (1985 = 100)	Exchange Rate ($/pound)	Real GNP in Constant $ (billions/1985 $)	Real GNP/Capita (thousands $)
1970	1648	2.95	15.6	2.3937	4.4133	1.4960
1975	3796	3.18	29.0	2.0235	6.4688	2.0342
1980	9003	3.40	56.0	1.8975	8.4726	2.4919
1985	15654	3.55	100.0	1.2435	12.5887	3.5461
1986	16586	3.54	103.8	1.3995	11.4175	3.2253
1987	17829	3.54	107.1	1.6755	9.9356	2.8067
1988	18784	3.54	109.4	1.5075	11.3897	3.2174

Italy

Year	GNP (billions of lira)	Population (millions)	Consumer Prices (1985 = 100)	Exchange Rate (lira/$)	Real GNP in Constant $ (billions/1985 $)	Real GNP/Capita (thousands $)
1970	63.13	53.66	14.0	623.0	723.8019	13.4887
1975	124.84	55.40	24.0	683.6	760.9226	13.7351
1980	389.61	56.42	51.8	930.5	808.3212	14.3269
1985	807.62	57.13	100.0	1678.5	481.1558	8.4221
1986	892.66	57.22	105.9	1358.1	620.6666	10.8470
1987	973.92	57.35	110.9	1169.0	751.2374	13.0992
1988	892.09	57.44	116.5	1305.8	586.4164	10.2092

Luxembourg

Year	GNP (billions of francs)	Population (millions)	Consumer Prices (1985 = 100)	Exchange Rate (francs/$)	Real GNP in Constant $ (billions/1985 $)	Real GNP/Capita (thousands $)
1970	56.34	0.34	37.2	49.675	3.0488	8.9672
1975	94.33	0.36	47.6	39.528	5.0135	13.9263
1980	154.70	0.36	70.8	31.523	6.9315	19.2543
1985	251.02	0.37	100.0	50.360	4.9845	13.4717
1986	260.78	0.37	100.3	40.410	6.4341	17.3893
1987	257.77	0.37	100.1	33.153	7.7674	20.9930
(est) 1988	271.17	0.37	101.7	37.345	7.1399	19.2971

Netherlands

Year	GNP (billions of guilders)	Population (millions)	Consumer Prices (1985 = 100)	Exchange Rate (guilders/$)	Real GNP in Constant $ (billions/1985 $)	Real GNP/Capita (thousands $)
1970	115.10	13.03	40.2	3.5970	79.5992	6.1089
1975	219.94	13.65	60.9	2.6885	134.3312	9.8411
1980	336.12	14.14	81.5	2.1295	193.6686	13.6965
1985	418.86	14.48	100.0	2.7720	151.1039	10.4354
1986	429.15	14.56	100.1	2.1920	195.5845	13.4330
1987	431.81	14.66	99.4	1.7775	244.3975	16.6710
1988	447.75	17.76	100.1	1.9995	223.7073	12.5961

Portugal

Year	GNP (billions of escudos)	Population (millions)	Consumer Prices (1985 = 100)	Exchange Rate (escudos/$)	Real GNP in Constant $ (billions/1985 $)	Real GNP/Capita (thousands $)
1970	181.1	9.04	6.7	28.750	94.0169	10.4001
1975	376.8	9.43	13.3	27.472	103.1262	10.9360
1980	1223.5	9.77	35.3	53.040	65.3470	6.6885
1985	3339.9	10.16	100.0	157.487	21.2075	2.0873
1986	4267.2	10.21	111.7	146.117	26.1450	2.5607
(est) 1987	4467.76	10.25	122.2	129.865	28.1531	2.7466
(est) 1988	4650.94	10.41	133.9	146.371	23.7304	2.2796

Spain

Year	GNP (billions of pesetas)	Population (millions)	Consumer Prices (1985 = 100)	Exchange Rate (pesetas/$)	Real GNP in Constant $ (billions/1985 $)	Real GNP/Capita (thousands $)
1970	2559	33.78	13.9	69.70	264.1330	7.8192
1975	6000	35.60	24.5	59.77	409.7339	11.5094
1980	15079	37.54	56.2	79.25	338.5610	9.0187
1985	27558	38.50	100.0	154.15	178.7739	4.6435
1986	31649	38.67	108.8	132.40	219.7066	5.6816
1987	35407	38.83	114.5	109.00	283.6986	7.3062
1988	39190	39.05	120.0	113.45	287.8654	7.3717

United Kingdom

Year	GNP (billions of pounds)	Population (millions)	Consumer Prices (1985 = 100)	Exchange Rate ($/pound)	Real GNP in Constant $ (billions/1985 $)	Real GNP/Capita (thousands $)
1970	52.19	55.42	19.6	2.3937	637.3837	11.5010
1975	107.24	55.90	36.1	2.0235	601.1084	10.7533
1980	231.01	55.95	70.7	2.3850	779.2912	13.9283
1985	356.76	56.62	100.0	1.4445	515.3398	9.1017
1986	383.93	56.76	103.4	1.4745	547.4901	9.6457
1987	419.57	56.93	107.8	1.8715	728.4093	12.7948
1988	459.05	57.08	113.0	1.8095	735.0894	12.8782

European Free Trade Association Countries

Austria

Year	GNP (billions of schillings)	Population (millions)	Consumer Price (1985 = 100)	Exchange Rate (schillings/$)	Real GNP in Constant $ (billions/1985 $)	Real GNP/Capita (thousands $)
1970	373.9	7.43	42.9	25.880	33.6770	4.5326
1975	652.5	7.58	60.9	18.510	57.8838	7.6364
1980	986.4	7.55	78.8	13.809	90.6493	12.0065
1985	1347.0	7.56	100.0	17.280	77.9514	10.3110
1986	1420.8	7.56	101.7	13.710	101.9001	13.4788
1987	1474.9	7.58	103.1	11.250	127.1603	16.7758
1988	1554.0	7.60	105.1	12.265	120.5538	15.8623

Iceland

Year	GNP (millions of kronur)	Population (millions)	Consumer Prices (1985 = 100)	Exchange Rate (kronur/$)	Real GNP in Constant $ (billions/1985 $)	Real GNP/Capita (thousands $)
1970	432	0.205	0.8	0.881	6.1294	29.8995
1975	1928	0.221	2.4	1.708	4.7034	21.2822
1980	15069	0.228	13.9	6.239	1.7376	7.6211
1985	113591	0.240	100.0	42.060	2.7007	11.2529
1986	151938	0.240	121.3	40.240	3.1128	12.9699
1987	201261	0.250	144.0	35.660	3.9194	15.6775
1988	245971	0.250	179.5	46.220	2.9648	11.8590

Norway

Year	GNP (billions of kroner)	Population (millions)	Consumer Prices (1985 = 100)	Exchange Rate (kroner/$)	Real GNP in Constant $ (billions/1985 $)	Real GNP/Capita (thousands $)
1970	79.26	3.88	29.0	7.1400	38.2788	9.8657
1975	146.79	4.01	43.4	5.5850	60.5597	15.1022
1980	275.53	4.09	64.9	5.1800	81.9586	20.0388
1985	490.69	4.15	100.0	7.5825	64.7135	15.5936
1986	504.63	4.17	107.2	7.4000	63.6131	15.2549
1987	553.68	4.19	116.5	6.2325	76.2554	18.1994
1988	581.14	4.20	124.3	6.5700	71.1614	16.9432

Sweden

Year	GNP (billions of kroner)	Population (millions)	Consumer Prices (1985 = 100)	Exchange Rate (kroner/$)	Real GNP in Constant $ (billions/1985 $)	Real GNP/Capita (thousands $)
1970	172.17	8.04	26.9	5.1700	123.7983	15.3978
1975	301.59	8.19	39.5	4.3855	174.1008	21.2577
1980	521.08	8.31	65.0	4.3728	183.3291	22.0613
1985	838.37	8.35	100.0	7.6155	110.0873	13.1841
1986	914.49	8.37	104.2	6.8190	128.7036	15.3768
1987	988.99	8.40	108.6	5.8480	155.7237	18.5385
1988	1077.23	8.44	114.9	6.1570	152.2717	18.0417

Switzerland

Year	GNP (billions of francs)	Population (millions)	Consumer Prices (1985 = 100)	Exchange Rate (francs/$)	Real GNP in Constant $ (billions/1985 $)	Real GNP/Capita (thousands $)
1970	93.9	6.19	49.9	4.3160	43.5997	7.0436
1975	144.6	6.41	72.3	2.6200	76.3359	11.9089
1980	177.3	6.39	81.1	1.7635	123.9688	19.4004
1985	241.4	6.47	100.0	2.0765	116.2533	17.9681
1986	254.9	6.50	100.8	1.6235	155.7604	23.9631
1987	266.3	6.54	102.2	1.2780	203.8869	31.1754
1988	279.1	6.51	104.1	1.5040	178.2630	27.3830

United States

Year	GNP (billions of $)	Population (millions)	Consumer Prices (1985 = 100)	Exchange Rate	Real GNP in Constant $ (billions/1985 $)	Real GNP/Capita (thousands $)
1970	1015.5	205.50	36.1		2813.02	13.69
1975	1598.4	215.97	50.0		3196.80	14.80
1980	2732.0	227.76	76.6		3566.58	15.66
1985	4014.9	239.28	100.0	N/A	4014.90	16.78
1986	4240.3	241.62	101.9		4161.24	17.22
1987	4526.7	243.93	105.7		4282.59	17.56
1988	4864.3	246.33	109.9		4426.11	17.97

Japan

Year	GNP (billions of yen)	Population (millions)	Consumer Prices (1985 = 100)	Exchange Rate (yen/$)	Real GNP in Constant $ (billions/1985 $)	Real GNP/Capita (thousands $)
1970	80592	104.34	36.9	357.65	610.6711	5.8527
1975	148170	111.57	63.3	305.15	767.0845	6.8754
1980	240098	116.78	87.2	203.00	1356.3633	11.6147
1985	317252	120.75	100.0	200.50	1582.3042	13.1040
1986	331254	121.49	100.6	159.10	2069.6312	17.0354
1987	345292	122.09	100.7	123.50	2776.4515	22.7410
1988	366366	122.61	101.4	125.85	2870.9392	23.4152

European Community Total

Year	Population (millions)	Real GNP in Constant $ (billions/1985 $)	Real GNP/Capita (thousands $)
1970	303.08	2977.1563	10.1802
1975	312.04	3750.5996	8.3197
1980	317.63	4448.1198	7.1408
1985	321.90	2928.5280	10.9919
1986	322.77	3635.3643	8.8786
1987	323.77	4558.5904	7.1024
1988	327.78	4174.7554	7.8515

EFTA Countries Total

Year	Population (millions)	Real GNP in Constant $ (billions/1985 $)	Real GNP/Capita (thousands $)
1970	25.75	245.4832	9.5352
1975	26.41	373.5835	14.1450
1980	26.57	481.6435	18.1287
1985	26.77	371.7062	13.8852
1986	26.84	453.0899	16.8811
1987	26.96	566.9457	21.0291
1988	27.00	525.2146	19.4524

Source: International Monetary Fund, *International Financial Statistics*, various issues.

The following table gives the relative economic statistics for EC and EFTA countries, the United States, and Japan for 1988.

Real GNP Shares

	EC & EFTA Alone	EC & EFTA Together	EC, EFTA, U.S., & Japan	Relative Real Per Capita GNP (U.S. = 100)
Belgium	3.43%	3.05%	3.05%	80.31
Denmark	2.15%	1.91%	0.75%	97.38
France	20.56%	18.26%	7.15%	85.50
Germany	28.20%	25.05%	9.81%	107.08
Greece	0.74%	0.65%	0.26%	17.07
Ireland	0.27%	0.24%	0.09%	17.91
Italy	14.05%	12.48%	4.89%	56.82
Luxembourg	0.17%	0.15%	0.06%	107.40
Netherlands	5.36%	4.76%	1.86%	70.10
Portugal	0.57%	0.50%	0.20%	12.69
Spain	6.90%	6.12%	2.40%	41.03
U.K.	17.61%	15.64%	6.13%	71.67
EC	100.00%	88.83%	36.65%	43.70
Austria	22.95%	2.56%	1.00%	88.28
Iceland	0.56%	0.06%	0.02%	66.00
Norway	13.55%	1.51%	0.59%	94.30
Sweden	28.99%	3.24%	1.27%	100.41
Switzerland	33.94%	3.79%	1.49%	152.40
EFTA	100.00%	11.17%	4.38%	108.26
U.S.			36.89%	100.00
Japan			23.93%	130.31
U.S. & Japan			60.82%	

Population Shares

	EC & EFTA Alone	EC & EFTA Together	EC, EFTA, U.S., & Japan
Belgium	3.03%	2.80%	1.37%
Denmark	1.57%	1.45%	0.71%
France	17.04%	15.75%	7.72%
Germany	18.67%	17.25%	8.46%
Greece	3.05%	2.82%	1.38%
Ireland	1.08%	1.00%	0.49%
Italy	17.52%	16.19%	7.94%
Luxembourg	0.11%	0.10%	0.05%
Netherlands	5.42%	5.01%	2.45%
Portugal	3.18%	2.93%	1.44%
Spain	11.91%	11.01%	5.40%
U.K.	17.41%	16.09%	7.89%
EC	**100.00%**	**92.39%**	**45.29%**
Austria	28.15%	2.14%	1.05%
Iceland	0.93%	0.07%	0.03%
Norway	15.56%	1.18%	0.58%
Sweden	31.26%	2.38%	1.17%
Switzerland	24.11%	1.83%	0.90%
EFTA	**100.00%**	**7.61%**	**3.73%**
U.S.			34.04%
Japan			16.94%
U.S. & Japan			**50.98%**

Source: International Monetary Fund, *International Financial Statistics,* various issues.

The table below rates exports from EC countries in millions of 1980 dollars:

Exports to	1980	1981	1982	1983	1984	1985	1986
United States	$38,421	$42,460	$42,952	$46,031	$57,668	$65,381	$73,963
Japan	$6,694	$6,609	$6,521	$6,852	$7,444	$8,048	$11,344
Belgium/Luxembourg	$46,897	$38,750	$37,737	$36,668	$36,848	$38,823	$50,505
Denmark	$9,846	$8,730	$8,473	$8,184	$8,177	$9,303	$12,234
France	$71,903	$63,624	$66,665	$63,016	$63,779	$66,630	$84,361
Germany	$87,492	$75,828	$71,414	$73,098	$72,687	$77,174	$96,456
Ireland	$8,341	$7,860	$7,119	$6,613	$6,627	$7,051	$8,146
Italy	$46,164	$38,394	$36,427	$34,600	$36,786	$39,772	$52,881
Netherlands	$47,797	$40,285	$39,333	$39,800	$39,685	$43,321	$52,261
Spain	$11,263	$10,340	$10,824	$10,563	$10,674	$12,051	$19,203
United Kingdom	$44,878	$41,174	$42,993	$44,148	$46,575	$46,698	$62,738
Greece	$5,980	$6,093	$5,950	$5,420	$5,436	$5,671	$6,880
Portugal	$4,610	$4,715	$4,416	$3,672	$3,418	$3,645	$5,663
Total EC	$385,171	$335,793	$331,351	$325,782	$330,692	$353,139	$451,328
Industrial Countries	$502,896	$447,139	$440,715	$438,724	$458,885	$496,235	$625,748
Developing Countries	$161,127	$164,893	$151,435	$136,540	$131,360	$129,924	$144,278
Asia	$20,982	$21,153	$21,602	$21,546	$22,230	$25,791	$30,897
Africa	$41,996	$40,684	$35,941	$30,100	$20,030	$28,144	$29,485
Middle East	$46,512	$54,332	$52,168	$48,863	$43,142	$37,154	$35,625
Western Hemisphere	$21,489	$21,668	$17,629	$13,881	$14,309	$13,917	$17,174

Source: International Monetary Fund, *Direction of Trade Statistics*, various issues.

The table below rates imports into EC countries in millions of 1980 dollars:

Imports from	1980	1981	1982	1983	1984	1985	1986
United States	$66,287	$60,403	$56,295	$51,581	$52,570	$52,927	$57,151
Japan	$19,680	$19,491	$19,392	$19,977	$20,960	$22,689	$33,980
Belgium/Luxembourg	$46,124	$38,185	$36,825	$36,220	$35,373	$37,569	$49,801
Denmark	$8,832	$7,745	$7,934	$7,962	$7,194	$7,806	$10,061
France	$64,014	$55,150	$53,292	$52,035	$51,679	$54,955	$71,149
Germany	$92,434	$80,673	$81,734	$79,278	$79,150	$86,042	$117,622
Ireland	$6,881	$6,037	$6,020	$6,127	$6,377	$7,013	$8,749
Italy	$41,887	$35,137	$35,419	$34,943	$34,496	$36,747	$51,361
Netherlands	$55,757	$51,509	$50,066	$49,639	$50,492	$52,775	$60,963
Spain	$11,942	$10,439	$10,847	$10,973	$12,187	$13,438	$16,991
United Kingdom	$47,256	$42,631	$40,710	$40,019	$42,256	$46,352	$49,529
Greece	$3,282	$3,026	$2,781	$2,950	$3,122	$3,160	$3,982
Portugal	$2,921	$2,499	$2,670	$2,981	$3,385	$3,797	$5,314
Total EC	$381,330	$333,031	$328,298	$323,127	$325,711	$349,654	$445,522
Industrial Countries	$541,867	$479,700	$466,564	$457,483	$463,509	$492,043	$616,958
Developing Countries	$205,726	$182,960	$163,561	$144,865	$145,342	$146,283	$138,451
Asia	$25,781	$22,368	$21,404	$20,918	$22,407	$22,556	$29,120
Africa	$41,996	$40,684	$35,941	$30,100	$29,030	$28,144	$29,485
Middle East	$90,214	$82,952	$65,903	$49,158	$43,001	$38,785	$29,102
Western Hemisphere	$26,117	$25,276	$23,941	$23,779	$24,202	$24,861	$21,715

Source: International Monetary Fund, *Direction of Trade Statistics*, Various issues.

Appendix B:
European Community Directives, Decisions, Proposals, and Regulations

Appendix B contains a detailed listing of the directives and regulations of the European Community that make up the 1992 single market program and their status as of March 28, 1990. We have arranged the directives and regulations by area, but it should be recognized that any such ordering is necessarily weak because many of the legal documents do not fit perfectly into any one category. The groupings are

- border controls,
- technical standards and regulations,
- transport,
- movement of people,
- technology,
- medicine,
- health and safety (including food),
- consumer protection,
- environment,
- public procurement,
- taxation,
- business and finance, and
- agriculture.

To find a specific regulation one should look under more than one category. For example, items pertaining to the licensing of medical professionals might be found under medicine and movement of people, whereas some health rules might be under agriculture and some under health and safety.

In addition to a description of the directive or regulation, the listing includes the Official Journal (OJ) identification number, the date of the OJ listing, the current status, and the proposed date of implementation by the member states. The OJ number column will contain either an "L" number, a "C" number, a Commission number (in the form (year)number), or no number at all. "L" documents are those rules and regulations that have been approved by the Council and are binding on the member states. "C" documents are those rules and regulations that have been proposed by the Commission but have yet to be approved by the Council. "C" documents normally have a proposed implementation date. Commission documents are Commission proposals that either do not need Council approval or have not reached the "C" document stage. The final set of documents are those containing no number at all. These are items that the Commission has committed to proposing but for which no official published version presently exists.

TABLE B-1

European Community Decisions, Directives, Proposals, and Regulations Underlying the Single Market Program

Directive	Official Journal	Date of OJ	Current Status	Date of Implementation
Border Controls				
Duty-free admission of fuel contained in the fuel tanks of commercial motor vehicles, lorries, and coaches	L 183	7/16/89	Adopted	10/1/85
Single Administrative Document (SAD)—third country aspects	L 179	7/11/85	Adopted	1/1/88
Simplification of Community transit procedure: amendment to Regulation 222/77	L 157	6/17/87	Adopted	7/1/88
Abolition of customs presentation charges	L 157	6/12/86	Adopted	1/1/88
Elimination of customs formalities in the framework of the TIR Convention and the introduction of common border posts—"banalisation"	L 341	12/4/86	Partially Adopted	7/1/87
Sixth Directive relative to exemptions in international travel: increase to 350 ECUs	L 183	6/16/85	Adopted	10/1/85
17th VAT Directive concerning the temporary importation of goods other than means of transport	L 192 L 130 C 324	7/24/85	Adopted (amendment) (amendment)	1/18/86; Germany and Greece: Derogation

TABLE B-1 (continued).

Directive	Official Journal	Date of OJ	Current Status	Date of Implementation
Introduction of common border posts ("banalisation")	L 382 C 29	12/31/88 2/4/89	Adopted Amended proposal	7/1/89
Introducing Community export and import declaration forms	L 179	7/11/85	Adopted	1/1/88
Duty-free admission of fuel contained in the fuel tanks of commercial motor vehicles lorries and coaches	(84)171 (86)383 C 183	7/22/86	Adopted	See "L183"
Introduction of common border posts ("banalisation")			Adopted	See "L 123"
Directive on the easing of controls at intra-Community borders	(84)749 (85)224 C 47	2/19/85	Proposal	TBA
Proposal for a Directive amending for the first time Directive 83/182 on temporary importation of certain means of transport (motor vehicle)	C 184 (87)14 C 40	7/14/88 2/18/87	(amendment) Proposal	TBA
Harmonization information given by customs agents on goods classification	(88)839 C 28	2/3/89	Proposal	TBA
Technical Standards and Regulations				
Simple pressure vessels	L 220 L13	8/8/87 1/1/90	Adopted (amendment)	7/1/90 7/1/92
Type approval of motor vehicles and their trailer, Directive 70/156	L 192	7/11/87	Adopted	10/1/88
Rollover protection structures	L 220	8/8/81	Adopted	6/26/89

Description		Reference	Date	Status	Deadline
(incorporating two pillars and mounted in front of the driver's seat on narrow-track wheeled agricultural and forestry tractors)	(88)640	C 324	12/17/88	(amendment)	
	(88)629	C 305	11/30/88	(amendment)	
	(89)681	L 398	12/30/89	(amendment)	1/3/91
	(88)326	C 311	12/16/89	(amendment)	
	(89)592	C 30	2/8/90	(amendment)	
Tire pressure gauge		L 152	6/6/86	Adopted	11/30/87
Amending 80/181/EEC on units of measurement: Metric vs. Imperial systems		L 357	12/7/89	Adopted	
Extension of information procedures on standards and technical rules (amendment to Directive 83/189)		L 81	3/27/92	Adopted	1/1/89
		L 100	4/26/83	Adopted	
Modification of framework (tractors)		L 126	5/20/88	Adopted	12/31/88
Amendment of Directive on making up by volume of certain prepackaged liquids		L 143	6/10/88	Adopted	6/30/88
		L 42	12/19/74	Adopted	7/1/90
		L 398	12/30/89	(amendment)	
Commission Directive on field of vision of motor vehicle drivers		L 181	7/12/88	Adopted	10/1/88
Amends 84/529 relating to standards applied to electrically operated lifts	(89)638	C 17	1/24/90	Proposal	Immediately
Commission Directive adapting to technical progress 76/758/EEC on the approximation of the laws of the member states relating to the end-outline marker lamps, front, rear, and stop lamps for motor vehicles and their trailers.		L 265	9/12/89	Adopted	

TABLE B-1 (continued).

Directive	Official Journal	Date of OJ	Current Status	Date of Implementation
Commission Directive adapting to technical progress 76/761/EEC on the approximation of the laws of the member states relating to the motor vehicle headlamps that function as main beam or dipped beam headlamps.	L 265	9/12/89	Adopted	
Commission Directive adapting to technical progress 76/538/EEC on the approximation of the laws of the member states relating to the rear fog lamps for motor vehicles and their trailers	L 265	9/12/89	Adopted	
Self-propelled industrial trucks*	L 384 C 31	12/31/87 2/9/90	Adopted (communication)	1/1/89
Adopting 71/127 on rearview mirrors of motors vehicles	L 147	6/14/88	Adopted	1/1/89
Amending 85/3 on weights dimension and characteristic of certain road vehicles	C 45 L 98 L 2	2/24/89 4/15/88 1/3/85	(amendment) Adopted Adopted	1/1/89
Adopting 71/320 on braking devices of motor vehicles and trailers	L 92	4/9/88	Adopted	10/1/88
Adopting 80/1269 on engine power of motor vehicles	L 92	4/9/88	Adopted	10/1/92

				Not Applicable
Recommendation on standardized information in existing hotels	L 384	12/31/86	Adopted	
Roadworthiness tests for motor vehicles and their trailers	L 222 C 74	8/12/88 3/22/89	Adopted Adopted (amendment)	7/28/90
Driver's seat on wheeled agricultural and forestry tractors	L 228	8/17/88	Adopted	9/30/88
Radio interferences (electromagnetic compatibility)	L 139	5/23/89	Adopted	1/1/92
Implementation of Directive 74/150 (weight and dimensions, driveshaft, engine stopping device, windscreen wipers, footrest) tractors	L 67	3/10/89	Adopted	12/31/89
Construction products	L 40	2/11/89	Adopted	6/28/90
Adapting to technical progress concerning electrical equipment for use in potentially explosive atmospheres employing certain types of protection (79/196)	L 311	11/10/88	Adopted	12/31/89
Test methods for industrial trucks	L 100	4/12/89	Adopted	1/1/89
Side guards of certain motor vehicles	L 124	5/5/89	Adopted	10/30/89
Adapting to technical progress 76/759 on directional indicator lamps of motor vehicles	L 109	4/20/89	Adopted	
Adapting to technical progress 76/756 on installation of lighting and light signaling on motor vehicles and tractors	L 109	4/20/89	Adopted	9/30/89
Low Voltage: electrical appliances: standards (73/23 EEC)	L 77	3/26/73	Adopted	8/1/75

TABLE B-1 (continued).

Directive	Official Journal		Date of OJ	Current Status	Date of Implementation
Approximation of laws in member states relating to appliances burning gaseous fuels	(88)786 (88)459	C 42 C 260	2/21/89 10/13/89	Common Position (amendment)	12/31/92 12/31/92
Directive amending 85/3/EEC on weights and dimensions of certain road vehicles	88/214/01	C 214	2/5/89	Adopted	7/1/89
Directive on safety glazing in motor vehicles	(89)653	C 95	4/12/90	Proposal	10/1/92
Directive on masses and dimensions of motor vehicles	(89)453	C 95	4/12/90	Proposal	10/1/92
Directive on pneumatic tires for motor vehicles and trailers	(89)653	C95	4/12/90	Proposal	10/1/92
Amends machinery standards Directive to include mobile machinery	(89)624	C 37	2/17/91	Proposal	1/1/92
Radio interferences (electromagnetic compatibility)				Adopted	See "L 127"
Directive on safety glass for use in motor vehicles	(72)981	C 119		Proposal Deleted by Commission	
Spray suppression devices of certain categories of motor vehicles	(89)377	C 263	10/16/89	Proposal	10/1/91
Directive on the approximation of laws relating to weights and dimensions of certain motor vehicles				Adopted	See "L 106"

	COM/OJ No.	OJ Ref	Date	Status	Implementation/Notes
Directive on the approximation of laws relating to tires of motor vehicles and their trailers	(76)712	C 37	2/14/77	Proposal	
Implementation of Directive 74/150 (weight and dimensions, driveshaft, engine stopping device, windscreen wipers, footrest) tractors					See "L 129"
Extraction solvents	(83)626 (85)79 (88)227	C 312 C 77 C 152	11/17/83 3/23/85 6/10/88	Adopted Proposal	36 mos. after notification
Obligation to indicate strength and rules on volume of containers	(82)626 (83)638	C 312	11/17/83	Partially Adopted	1/1/85
Definition of spirituous beverages and aromatized wines				Adopted	See "L 159"
Construction products				Adopted	See "L 140"
Directive amending 85/3/EEC on weights and dimensions of certain road vehicles				Adopted	See "L 174"
Proposal for Council Decision on global approach to testing and certification for industrial products	(89)209 90/C 10/01	C 267 C 310	10/19/89 12/21/89	Common Position Resolution	1/1/93
Proposal for a Directive to protect computer programs	(88)816	C 91	4/12/89 5/8/89	Proposal Proposal	
Earth-moving and mobile machines	(88)740	C 70	3/20/89 1/17/90	Proposal (amendment)	1989–1993
Harmonization of laws in member states relating to nonautomatic weighing instruments				Adopted	See "L 213"

TABLE B-1 (continued).

Directive	Official Journal	Date of OJ	Current Status	Date of Implementation
Council Directive on furniture flammability safety requirements				
Technical standards for civil aviation				
Essential requirements for safety in large pressure vessels				
Interpretation of standards for construction products: Eurocodes				
Transport				
Fares for scheduled air services	L 374	12/31/87 10/11/89	Adopted Proposal (Implement Reg.)	12/31/87
Air transport: sharing of passenger capacity	L 374	12/31/87 10/11/89	Adopted Proposal (Implement Reg.)	1/1/88
Air transport: application of Articles 85 and 86 (rules of competition)	L 374	12/31/87 10/11/89	Adopted Proposal (Implement Reg.)	1/1/88
Maritime transport: 1. freedom to provide services in the sea transport sector: (a) between member states and between member states and third countries	L 378	12/31/86	Adopted	7/1/87

			Not Adopted	
(b) within member states				
2. application of Articles 85 and 86 of Treaty of Rome to maritime transport	L 378	12/31/86	Adopted	7/1/87
3. unfair pricing practices	L 378	12/31/86	Adopted	7/1/87
4. coordinated action to safeguard free access to cargoes in oceanic trades	L 378	12/31/86	Adopted	7/1/87
Commission regulations on air transport and coordination of capacity, revenues, tariffs, and slot allocations at airports*	L239	8/30/88	Adopted	Immediately
Road transport: organization of the market (Community quota) for the carriage of goods by road between member states transitional and final stages	L 163 C 87	6/30/88 4/5/90	Adopted Proposal	7/1/88 12/31/95
Code of conduct for computerized reservation systems	L 220	7/29/89	Adopted	8/1/89 1/1/90
Road transport: organization of the market (Community quota) for the carriage of goods by road between member states—transitional and final stages			Adopted	See "L 153"
Inland waterways: goods and passengers, freedom to provide services by nonresident carriers within member states	(85)610 C 331	12/20/85	Proposal	TBA

TABLE B-1 (continued).

Directive	Official Journal	Date of OJ	Current Status	Date of Implementation
Road transport: goods, freedom to provide services by nonresident carriers within a member state	(85)611 C 349	1/1/90	Proposal	TBA
Road transportation: conditions for nonresident carriers providing services within a member state	L 390	12/30/89	Adopted	7/1/90: Applies until 12/31/92
Abolishment of transit advice notes on crossing internal frontiers	L 51	2/27/90	Adopted	7/1/90
Road transport: passengers, freedom to provide services by nonresident carriers within a member state	(87)31 C 77	3/24/87	Proposal	TBA
Maritime transport: goods and passengers, freedom to provide services in the sea transport sector within a member state by nonresident carriers	(85)90 C 212	8/23/85	Adopted	TBA
Road transport: common rules for the international carriage of passengers by road	(87)79 C 120	5/6/87	Proposal	1/1/88
Community railway policy:				
a) development of community railways	(89)564 C 34	2/14/90	Proposal	
b) obligations inherent in public service in rail transport	(89)564 C 34	2/14/90	Proposal	
c) establish a network of high-speed trains	(89)564 C 34	2/14/90	Proposal	

d) common rules for combined carriage	(89)564	C 34	2/14/90	Proposal	
Directive on the stores of ships, aircraft, and international trains	(79)794	C 31	2/8/80	Proposal	TBA
Amendment to the Proposal for Council Directives amending Council Directives 83/416/EEC concerning the authorization of scheduled interregional air services for the transport of passengers, mail, and cargo between member states	(88)126	C 78	3/25/88	Proposal	
Action program for transport infrastructure to complete an integrated transport market by 1992	(88)238 (88)340	C 170 C 270	7/5/89 10/19/88	(amendment) Proposal	
Code of conduct for computerized reservation systems (Regulation)					See "L 170"
Abolition of controls related to means of transport	(88)800			Adopted	See "L 180"
Adaptation of Community transit legislation to take account of abolition of internal frontiers (amendment to Regulation 222/77)					
Air crew qualifications					
Revision of air services (fares) Directive					
Movement of People					
Proposal amending Directive 75/318 concerning the testing of medical specialties	L 15		1/17/87	Adopted	7/1/87 Portugal: 1/1/1991

TABLE B-1 (continued).

Directive	Official Journal	Date of OJ	Current Status	Date of Implementation
Comparability of vocational training qualifications	L 199	7/31/85	Adopted	7/16/87 report due
Coordination relating to commercial agents	L 382	12/31/86	Adopted	1/1/90 U.K. and Ireland: 1/1/94; Italy: 1/1/1993
Mutual recognition of diplomas in pharmacy	L 253	9/24/85	Adopted	10/1/87; Greece: 1997
Specific training in general medical practice	L 267	9/19/86	Adopted	1/1/95
Right of establishment proposal for a Directive setting up a general system of mutual recognition of higher education diplomas	L 19	1/24/89	Adopted	1/4/91
Mutual recognition of diplomas, certificates, and qualifications of goods haulage operators and road passenger transport operators	L 212	7/22/89	Adopted	1/1/90
Council Directive on the right of residence:				
retired people	L 180	7/13/90	Adopted	
general Directive	L 180	7/13/90	Adopted	
students	L 180	7/13/90	Adopted	
Council Directive on package travel, including package holidays	L 158 (90)232 C 158	6/23/90	Adopted (reexamination)	12/31/92

Proposal for a Council Directive on mutual acceptance of personnel licenses for the exercise of functions in civil aviation	(89)472 C 10	1/16/90	Proposal	
Proposal for Council Decision proposing the adoption of a Community action program for the development of continuing vocational training	(89)567 C 12	1/18/90	Proposal	
Right of establishment proposal for a Directive setting up a general system of mutual recognition of higher education diplomas			Adopted	See "L 143"
Right of residence for nationals of member states not yet or no longer employed	(79)215 C 207 / (85)292 C 171	8/17/79 / 7/10/85	Proposal	12 mos. after notification
Community charter of fundamental social rights	(89)248	5/30/89	Preliminary Draft (communication)	
Directive on the coordination of rules concerning the right of asylum and the status of refugees	(89)568			
Proposal concerning the elimination of cumbersome administrative procedures relating to residence permits				
Proposal concerning the introduction of European vocational training card proving the qualification of its holders				

TABLE B-1 (continued).

Directive	Official Journal	Date of OJ	Current Status	Date of Implementation
Technology				
Cooperation between higher education and industry for advanced training relating to new technologies (COMET)	L 222	8/9/86	Adopted	Not Applicable
Pan-European cellular, digital, land-based mobile communications	L 196	7/17/87	Adopted	12/26/88
Legal protection of microcircuits	L 24	1/27/87	Adopted	11/7/87
Directive on the initial stage of the mutual recognition of type approval for telecommunications terminal equipment*	L 217	8/5/86	Adopted To be repealed as of 1/1/90	
Recommendation on the coordinated introduction of ISDN*	L 382	12/31/86	Adopted	TBA
Directive on standardization in the field of information technology and telecommunications*	L 36	2/7/87	Adopted	2/7/88
Directive on competition in the markets for telecommunications terminal equipment*	L 131	5/27/88	Adopted	6/30/90
Establish a plan of action for information services market*	L 288	10/21/88	Adopted	Not Applicable

Description	Number	Date	Status	
Community action in field of information technology and telecommunications in health care (AIM)*	L 314	11/22/89	Adopted	Not Applicable
Five R&D programs in technology (Particularly controlling harmful organisms)	L 355	12/17/88	Adopted	Not Applicable
Establishment at Community level of a policy and plan of priority action for the development of an information services market	(87)360 C 30	2/4/88	Proposal	TBA
Proposal Directives on the contained use of genetically modified microorganisms			Adopted	See "L 203"
Contained use of genetically modified microorganisms	L 117	5/8/90	Adopted	10/23/91
Proposal Directives that relate to environment of genetically modified organisms			Adopted	See "L 204"
Green Paper on copyright and the challenge of technology	(88)172			Not Applicable Not Applicable
Community action on information technology and telecommunications in health care	(88)588 C 299 (88)315 C 214	11/24/88 8/16/88	Proposal Proposal	7/1/88
Community resolution on the development of a common market on telecommunications services and equipment up to 1992	(88) C 257	10/4/88	Proposal	
Legal protection of biotechnology inventions	(88)496	1/13/89	Proposal	12/31/90

TABLE B-1 (continued).

Directive	Official Journal		Date of OJ	Current Status	Date of Implementation
Agreement relating to Community patents		L 401	12/30/89	Adopted	
Establishing an internal market for telecommunication services with open network provisions (ONP)				Adopted	See "L 217"
Green Paper on the development of the Common Market for telecommunications services and equipment			6/30/87	Proposal	
Coordinated introduction of pan-European land-based public radio paging in the EC	(89)166	C 193	2/23/90	Proposal	TBA
Frequency bands reserved for pan-European public radio paging	(89)166	C 193	2/23/90	Proposal	TBA
Directive on competition in the markets for telecommunications services (draft)					
Medicine					
Directive concerning the placing on the market of high-technology medicinal products including those derived from biotechnology		L 15	1/17/87	Adopted	7/1/87
Council Recommendation concerning tests relating to the placing on the market of medicinal products		L 73	3/16/87	Adopted	Nonbinding Council Recommendation

	Document	Date	Status	Implementation
Council Directive concerning the approximation of laws relating to proprietary medicinal products				See "L 139 part B"
Coordination of provisions in respect to certain activities in the field of pharmacy	L 253	9/24/85	Adopted	10/1/87
Extension of Directives to medicinal products not already included:				
a) blood products	L 181	6/28/89	Adopted	12/31/92
b) proprietary medicinal products	L 142	5/25/89	Adopted	12/31/92
c) radiopharmaceuticals	L 142	5/25/89	Adopted	12/31/92
d) serums, toxins, vaccines	L 142	5/25/89	Adopted	12/31/92
Medicinal Products				
a) wholesale distribution of medicinal products for human use	(89)607 C 58	3/8/90	Proposal	1/1/92
b) legal status for supply of medicinal products for human use	(89)607 C 58	3/8/90	Proposal	1/1/92
c) labeling of medicinal products for human use and package leaflets	(89)607 C 58	3/8/90	Proposal	1/1/92
Wider scope of 65/65/EEC and 75/319/EEC laying down additional provisions on homeopathic medicinal products	(90)72 C 108	5/1/90	Proposal	12/31/90
Wider scope of 81/851/EEC	(90)72 C 108	5/1/90	Proposal	12/31/90
Proposal for a Council Regulation concerning the creation of a supplementary protection certificate for medicinal products	(90)101	4/11/90	Proposal	
Extension of Directives to medicinal products not already included			Adopted	See "L 139"

TABLE B-1 (continued).

Directive	Official Journal	Date of OJ	Current Status	Date of Implementation
Proposal for a Council Directive on advertising of medicinal products for human use	(90)212 C 163	7/4/90	Proposal	1/1/92
Active implantable medical devices			Adopted	See "L 212"
Directive on measures for control of foot-and-mouth disease			Adopted	See "L 215"
Establishment of a system of EC-wide authorizations and administration in medicinal products:				
• to establish a European agency for the evaluation of medicinal products				
• amendment of 65/65 on medicinal products				
• amendment of 81/851 on veterinary medicinal products				
• repeal 87/22 on high-tech medicinal products				
Harmonization of conditions of distribution to patients				
Information for doctors and patients				
Active medical devices (nonimplantible)				
Nonactive medical products (sterile)				
In vitro medical diagnostic products				

Health and Safety (including food)

Medical examination of personnel	L 168 85/326 85/327	6/28/85	Adopted	1/1/86
Preservatives (modification)	(81)712 L 372	12/31/85	Partially Adopted	12/31/86
Simulants (plastic materials in contact with foodstuffs)	L 372	12/31/85	Adopted	1/1/86
Protection of hotels against fire	L 384	12/31/86	Adopted	Nonbinding Council Recommendation
Good laboratory practices in the nonclinical testing of chemicals	L 145 L 315	6/11/88 12/28/89	Adopted Adopted	1/1/89
Protection of workers by banning certain chemical agents and activities	L 179	7/9/88	Adopted	1/1/90
Amendment 76/769 on restrictions to marketing and use of certain dangerous substances: procedures for amendment	L 398	12/30/89	Adopted	
Amendment 76/769 on restrictions to marketing and use of certain dangerous substances: Benzene	L 398	12/30/89	Adopted	
Adoption to technical progress of motor vehicle standards	L 238	8/15/89	Adopted	
Directive relating to flavorings for use in foodstuffs and to sources of materials for this production	L 184	7/15/88	Adopted	7/1/90
Conditions for preparation, marketing, and use of medicated feedingstuffs	L 92	4/7/90	Adopted	10/1/91 12/31/92
Council decision to established inventory of source materials for preparation of flavorings	L 184	7/18/88	Adopted	7/1/90

TABLE B-1 (continued).

Directive	Official Journal	Date of OJ	Current Status	Date of Implementation
Machine safety	L 183	6/29/89	Adopted	12/31/92
Minimum safety and health for workplace: design of physical plant	L 393	12/30/89	Adopted	12/31/92, Greece: 12/31/94
Minimum safety and health for work equipment used by workers at the workplace	L 393	12/30/89	Adopted	12/31/92
Minimum safety and health for personal protective equipment in the workplace	L 393	12/30/89	Adopted	
Minimum safety and health on visual display units (CRT)	L 156	6/21/90	Adopted	12/31/92
Commission communication for implementing Directive on safety aspects of personal protective equipment	89/328/02 C 328	12/30/89	(communication)	
General Directive on quick frozen foods	L 40	2/11/89	Adopted	7/10/90
Food additives (modification of existing Directives)	L 40	2/11/89	Adopted	6/28/90
Materials and articles in contact with food	L 40 L 297	2/11/89 10/23/82	Adopted Adopted	(permit) 7/10/90 (prohibit) 1/10/92
Commission Directive on plastic materials and articles intended to come into contact with foodstuffs	L 297 L 75	10/23/82 3/21/90	Adopted Adopted	12/31/90

Food for particular nutritional use (amendment)	L 186	6/30/89	Adopted	(permit) 5/16/90 (prohibit) 5/16/91
Food inspection			Adopted	See "L154"
Cosmetics—4th modification to Directive 76/768	L 382	12/31/88	Adopted	12/31/89
	L 64	3/8/89	Adopted (amendment)	
	C 296	11/24/89	(reexamination)	
	L 398	12/30/89	(amendment)	
Amending Second Directive 82/434/EEC on laws relating to methods of analysis necessary to checking composition of cosmetics products:	(89)537			
Free formaldehyde	L 108	4/28/90	Adopted	12/31/90
Adaptation to technical progress	L 71	3/17/90	Adopted	12/31/90
Reference methods and list of national laboratories for detecting residues	L 351	12/2/89	Adopted	1/1/91
Council Directive on laws relating to personal protective equipment	L 399	12/30/89	Adopted	12/1/91
Encourage improvements in safety and health of workers at work	L 183	6/29/89	Adopted	12/31/92
	C 172	7/7/89	Adopted (amendment)	
Machine safety			Adopted	See "L 128"
General Directive on quick frozen foods			Adopted	See "L 130"
Flavorings			Adopted	See "L 100"
Preservatives (modification)	(81)712 C 330	12/17/81	Partially Adopted	12/31/82
Infant formulae and follow-up milk (dietetic foods)	(84)703 C 28	1/30/85	Proposal	18 mos. after notification
Food additives (modification of existing Directives)	(86)564 C 285	11/12/86	Adopted	See "L 131"

TABLE B-1 (continued).

Directive	Official Journal		Date of OJ	Current Status	Date of Implementation
Materials and articles in contact with food (amendment)				Adopted	See "L 132"
Municipal wastewater treatment	(89)518	C 300	11/29/89	Proposal	12/31/91
	(89)518	C 1	1/4/90	Proposal	
Pesticide residues in fruits and vegetables	(88)798	C 46	2/25/89	Proposal	12/31/89
Food for particular nutritional use (amendment)				Adopted	See "L 133"
Food inspection				Adopted	See "L 137"
Cosmetics—4th modification to Directive 76/768				Adopted	See "L 141"
Council Directive concerning maximum tar yield in cigarettes	(87)720	C 48	2/20/88	Proposal	18 mos. after notification of approval
Council Directive on minimum safety requirements for use by workers of personal protective equipment				Adopted	See "L 188a"
Protection of workers from risks of biological agents at work		C 150	6/8/89	Proposal	
	(89)404	C 218	8/24/89	(amendment)	
Protection of workers from risks to exposure to carcinogens at work	(87)641	C 34	2/8/88	Proposal	
	(89)405	C 229	9/6/89	(amendment)	

Council Directive concerning minimum health and safety of machine equipment and installations at the workplace	(89)85 C 106	4/26/89	Proposal	
Council Directive for measures encourage improvements in safety and health of workers at the workplace			Adopted	See "L 157"
Council Directive concerning minimum safety and health of workers at the workplace			Adopted	1/1/91
Council Directive on laws relating to personal protective equipment			Adopted	1/1/90
Proposal for a Council Directive on the minimum health and safety requirements for handling heavy loads where there is a risk of back injury for workers	(89)213 C 129 (88)78 C 117 (90)131 C 118	5/25/89 5/4/88 5/12/90	Proposal Proposal Proposal	
Minimum safety and health on visual display units (Visual display units = CRT)			Adopted	1/1/91
Harmonized rules for foods and food ingredients treated with ionizing radiation	(88)654 C 336 (89)576 C 303	12/31/88 12/2/89	Proposal (amendment)	2 yrs. after adoption to permit, banned after 3 yrs.
Regulation on health rules for production and marketing of fresh meat	(89)673 C 84	4/2/90	Proposal	1/1/93
Council Regulation on health rules for producing and marketing fresh poultry	(89)668 C 84	4/2/90	Proposal	1/1/93
Council Regulation on health rules for producing and marketing meat products	(89)669 C 84	4/2/90	Proposal	1/1/93

TABLE B-1 (continued).

Directive	Official Journal	Date of OJ	Current Status	Date of Implementation
Council Regulation on health rules for producing and marketing raw milk and milk for manufacturing of milk-based products	(89)667 C 84	4/2/90	Proposal	1/1/93
Council Regulation on health rules for producing and marketing minced meat			Adopted	See "L 126"
Council Regulation on health rules for producing and marketing heat-treated milk	(89)672 C 84	4/2/90	Proposal	1/1/93
Health rules for production and marketing of animal fat, graves, and rendering by-products for human consumption	(89)490 C 327	12/30/89	Proposal	1/1/93
Seventh Amendment 67/548/EEC on classification, packaging, and labeling of dangerous substances (related to "L 87")	(89)575 C 33	2/13/90	Proposal	1/1/92
Health rules for production and marketing products of animal origin	(89)492 C 327	12/30/89	Proposal	1/1/93
Trade in fish and fish products	(89)665 C 84	4/2/90	Proposal	1/1/93
Trade in mollusks	(89)648 C 84	4/2/90	Proposal	1/1/93
Harmonized health on milk	(89)670 C 84	4/2/90	Proposal	1/1/93
Safeguard measures in veterinary field in framework of internal market	(89)490 C 327	12/30/89	Proposal	1/1/93

Health requirements regarding trade in frozen semen of bulls	(89)490 C 327	12/30/89	Proposal	1/1/93
Game meat and rabbit meat	(89)496 C 327	12/30/89	Proposal	4/1/90
Approximation of laws concerning general product safety	(89)162 C 193	7/31/89	Proposal	1/1/91
Proposal for a Council Directive on batteries and accumulators containing dangerous substances	(88)672 C 6 (89)454 C 11	1/8/93 1/17/90	Proposal (amendment)	7/1/89
Application of health standards to national products				
Consumer Protection				
Obligation to indicate ingredients and alcoholic strength	L 144	5/29/86	Partially Adopted	5/1/88 (permit) 5/1/89
Directive on products misleadingly defined	L 192	7/11/89	Adopted	10/1/88
Safety of toys (including chemical properties and electrical toys) (References to standards)	L 187 C 155	7/16/88 6/23/89	Adopted	6/30/89
Classification, packaging, and labeling of dangerous preparations	L 187 L 64 L 19	7/16/88 3/8/89 1/24/90	Adopted Adopted (amendment)	6/30/89 6/1/91
Directive amending Directive 79/581 on consumer protection in the indication of the prices of foodstuffs	L 142	6/9/88	Adopted	6/9/90
Consumer protection in respect of the indication of prices for nonfood products	L 142	6/9/88	Adopted	6/9/90

TABLE B-1 (continued).

Directive	Official Journal	Date of OJ	Current Status	Date of Implementation
Directive on liability of defective products*	L 210	8/7/85	Adopted	7/1/88
Food labeling (amendment)	L 186	6/30/89	Adopted	(permit) 12/20/90 (prohibit) 6/20/92
Labeling of tobacco products	L 359	12/8/89	Adopted	12/31/91 with exception to cigarettes and tobacco products
Price transparency in the prices of medicines and social security refunds	L 40	2/11/89	Adopted	12/31/89
Eighth amendment to 76/769 on restrictions to marketing dangerous substances	(88)7 C 43	2/16/88	Proposal (reexamination)	
Definition, description, and presentation of spirit drinks	L 160	6/12/89	Adopted	12/15/89
Indication of marks identifying the lot to which a foodstuff belongs	L 186	6/30/89	Adopted	(authorize) 6/20/90 (prohibit) 6/20/91
Decision to create a Consumers' Consultative Council	L 38	2/10/90	Adopted	Immediately
Food labeling (amendment)			Adopted	See "L 134"
Price transparency in the prices of medicines and social security refunds			Adopted	See "L 138"

Description	COM No.	OJ Ref	Date	Status	Note
Council Directive on package travel, including package holidays				Adopted	See "L 219"
Council Directive on approximation of laws concerning labeling of tobacco products				Proposal / Proposal / Adopted	See "L 190"
Eighth amendment to 76/769 on restrictions to marketing dangerous substances	(89)606	C 41 / C 30	2/19/87 / 2/8/90	Proposal (reexamination)	See "L 156"
Dangerous Substances					
a) tenth amendment on dangerous substances	(89)548	C 8	1/13/90	Proposal	TBA
b) eleventh amendment 76/769 on dangerous substances: DDBBT Ugilec 121, Ugilec 141	(89)665	C 24	2/1/90	Proposal	TBA
Compulsory nutritional labeling of foodstuffs intended for sales to consumers	(88)489 / (89)420	C 282 / C 296	11/5/88 / 11/11/89	Proposal / Proposal (amendment)	TBA
Motor vehicle liability insurance	(88)791	C 65	3/15/89	Common Position	
Third Directive on civil liability in motor vehicles				Adopted	See "L 205"
Strict liability of services with a safety defect					TBA
Council resolution on relaunching consumer protection policy	89/294/01	C 294	9/22/89	Adopted	
Environment					
Council Directive on freedom of access to information on the environment		L 158	6/23/90	Adopted	
Gaseous emissions, passenger cars		L 36	2/9/88	Adopted	7/1/88

TABLE B-1 (continued).

Directive	Official Journal	Date of OJ	Current Status	Date of Implementation
Gaseous emissions, commercial cars	L 36	2/9/88	Adopted	7/1/88
Council Directive relating to restriction on the marketing and use of PCBs (polychlorinated biphenyls)	L 269	10/11/85	Adopted	6/30/86
Council Directive relating to "Restrictions on the marketing and use of asbestos"	L 375	12/31/85	Adopted	12/31/87
Nonionic detergents (modification of existing Directive)	L 80	3/25/86	Adopted	1/1/90
Membership of the European agreement on detergents	L 350	1/1/90	Adopted	12/31/87
Tower cranes: permissible sound levels	L 220	8/8/87	Adopted	6/26/89
Household appliances: airborne noise	L 344 90/C 28/20 C 28	12/6/86 2/7/90	Adopted (amendment)	12/4/89
Hydraulic diggers (noise)	L 384 L 253	12/31/86 8/30/89	Adopted Adopted	12/29/88
Protection of hotels against fire	L 384	12/31/86	Adopted	Nonbinding Council Recommendation
Directive modifying 84/538 on lawn mower noise	L 81 L 300	3/27/88 11/19/84	Adopted Adopted	7/1/91
Amending 84/631 on supervision and control within EC of transfrontier shipment of hazardous waste	L 181	7/4/86	Adopted	1/1/87

Directive	Reference	Date	Status	Effective
Directive amending 70/220 on air pollution by gases from car diesel engines	L 214	8/6/88	Adopted	10/1/88
Amendment of 78/1015 on permissible sound levels and exhaust systems of motorcycles	L 98	4/11/89	Adopted	10/1/89
Programs for reduction and eventual elimination of pollution caused by waste from titanium oxide industry	L 201	7/14/89	Adopted	12/31/89
Amendment to 80/779/EEC on air quality limit volumes and guide volumes for sulfur dioxide and suspended particles	L 201	7/14/89	Adopted	1/11/91
Diesel particulates—passenger cars			Adopted	See "L 111"
Directive modifying Directive 78/1015 concerning motorcycle replacement exhaust systems			Adopted	See "L 150"
Modification to Directive 70/220 revision of limit values for gaseous emissions of cars (vehicles below 1400 cc)	L 226	8/3/89	Adopted Adopted	See "L 173" 12/31/89
Amends Council Directive 75/442 on waste	(88)399 C 295 (89)560 C 326	11/19/88 12/30/89	Proposal (amendment)	1/1/90
Directive on hazardous waste	(88)391 C 295 (89)560 C 326 (89)560 C 42	11/19/88 12/30/89 2/22/90	Proposal (amendment) (amendment)	1/1/90
Civil liability for damage caused by waste	(89)518 C 251	10/4/89	Proposal	1/1/91

TABLE B-1 (continued).

Directive	Official Journal	Date of OJ	Current Status	Date of Implementation
Directive amending 76/464/EEC on pollution caused by certain dangerous substances discharged into aquatic environment	(90)9 C 55	3/7/90	Proposal	12/31/91
Approximation of laws in member states relating to appliances burning gaseous fuels			Adopted	See "L 223"
Amendment to Council Directive 70/220/EEC on measures taken against air pollution by emissions from motor vehicles	(89)662 C 81	3/30/90	Proposal	1/1/91
Proposal for a Council Directive on the freedom of access to information on the environment	(88)484 C 335 (90)91 C 102	12/30/88 4/24/90	Proposal (amendment)	12/30/90
Proposal for a Council Regulation on the establishment of the European Environment Monitoring and Information Network	(89)303 C 2117 (90)114	8/23/89 3/22/90	Proposal (amendment)	
Public Procurement				
Coordination of procedures on the award of public supply contracts (amendment of Directive 77/62) and deletion of certain provisions of Directive 80/767	L 127 L 13	5/20/88 1/15/77	Adopted Adopted	1/1/89; Greece, Portugal, and Spain: 1992

Description					
Coordination of procedures for the award of public works contracts		L 210	7/22/93	Adopted	
		L 185	8/25/71	Adopted	7/19/90; Spain, Greece, and Portugal: 3/1/92
Application of community rules on procedures for the award of public works contracts		L 395	12/30/89	Adopted	12/1/91
Coordination of procedures for the award of public works contracts				Adopted	See "L 142"
Application of Community rules on procedures for the award of public works contracts					See "L 155"
Communication on a Community regime for procurement in the excluded sectors	(88)380	C 264	10/16/89	Common Position	
Opening up of public procurement in the energy, water, and transport services	(89)380	C 264	10/16/89	Common Position	
Opening up of public procurement in the telecommunication sector	(89)380	C 264	10/16/89	Proposal	
	(89)217	C 40	2/17/89	Common Position	
Proposal for a Council Directive relating to the coordination of procedures on the award of public service contracts			4/17/90	Proposal	
Public procurement in the field of services					
Taxation					
Tax reliefs to be allowed on the importation of goods in small consignments of a noncommercial character		L 372	12/31/85	Adopted	
		L 183	7/11/85	Adopted	10/1/85

TABLE B-1 (continued).

Directive	Official Journal		Date of OJ	Current Status	Date of Implementation
Thirteenth VAT Directive concerning tax refunds to persons not established in the Community		L 326	11/21/86	Adopted	1/1/88
Small consignments: exemption from value-added tax on the final importation of certain goods	(86)383 (87)272	C 183 C 183	7/22/86 7/11/87	Proposal (amendment)	TBA
Modification of Directive 83/183 on tax exemptions applicable to permanent imports from a member state of the personal property of individuals (removals)	(86)584	C 5	1/9/87	Proposal	TBA
Harmonization of income taxation provisions with respect to freedom of movement of workers within the Community	(79)737	C 21	1/26/80	Proposal	January 1st of third year after adoption
Arbitration procedure concerning the elimination of double taxation	(76)611	C 301	12/21/76	Proposal	January 1st on the second year after adoption
Common system of taxation applicable to parent companies and their subsidiaries	(69)6	C 39	3/23/69	Proposal	TBA
Common system of taxation of mergers, divisions, and contribution of assets	(69)5	C 39	3/22/69	Proposal	TBA

	Document No.	Official Journal	Date	Status	January 1st on the second year after adoption
Harmonization of taxes on transaction in securities	(76)124 (87)139	C 133 C 115	6/14/76 4/30/87	Proposal Proposal	
Harmonization of member state laws relating to tax arrangements for carryover of losses of undertakings	(84)404 (85)319	C 253 C 170	9/20/84 7/9/85	Proposal Proposal	TBA
Proposal for Council Directive instituting a process of convergence of rates of VAT and excise duties (This proposal replaces the standstill proposal on both VAT and excise duties withdrawn by the Commission)	(87)324	C 250	9/18/87	Proposal	12/31/92
Proposal on special schemes for small business (includes flat rate farmers' proposal now no longer necessary)	(86)444 (87)501	C 272 C 310	10/28/86 11/20/86	Proposal Proposal	TBA 11/1/87
Twelfth VAT Directive concerning expenditure on which tax is not deductible	(82)870 (84)84	C 37 C 56	2/10/83 2/29/84	Proposal Proposal	TBA
Eighteenth VAT Directive concerning the abolition of certain derogations (Article twenty-eight(3) of Directive 77/388/EEC)	(86)383 (87)272 (84)649	C 183 C 183 C 347	7/22/86 7/11/87	Proposal Proposal Proposal	TBA
Nineteenth VAT Directive miscellaneous supplementary and amending provisions of Directive 77/388/EEC	(84)648 (87)315	C 347	12/29/84	Proposal	TBA
Approximation of VAT rates	(87)321	C 250	9/18/87	Proposal	TBA
Harmonization of the structure of excise duties on alcoholic drinks	(72)225/2	C 43 L 106	4/29/72 4/27/88	Proposal Adopted	See "C 104"
Harmonization of the structure of excise duties on alcoholic drinks	(85)150	C 114	5/8/85	Proposal	TBA

TABLE B-1 (continued).

Directive	Official Journal	Date of OJ	Current Status	Date of Implementation
Harmonization of the structure of excise duties on alcoholic drinks (fortified wine and similar products)	(85)151　C 114	5/8/85	Proposal	TBA
Excise duty on wine	(72)225/3　C 43	4/29/72	Proposal	TBA
Introduction of a third stage concerning the harmonization of the structure of cigarette duty	(80)69　C 264	10/11/80	Proposal	TBA
Harmonization of the structure of excises on mineral oils	(73)1234　C 92	10/31/73	Proposal	TBA
Consumption taxes on manufactured tobacco other than cigarettes	(87)326　C 251 (89)525　C 12 (89)551	9/19/87 1/18/90	Proposal (amendment) (communication)	12/31/92
Consumption taxes on cigarettes	(87)325　C 251 (89)525　C 12 (89)551	9/19/87 1/18/90	Proposal (amendment) (communication)	12/31/92
Common rate bands for all harmonized duties on alcoholic beverages	(87)328　C 250 (89)527　C 12 (89)551	9/18/87 1/18/90	Proposal (amendment) (communication)	12/31/92
Common rates bands for all harmonized excise duties on mineral oils	(87)327　C 262 (89)526 (89)551	10/1/87	Proposal (communication) (communication)	12/31/92
Completion of internal market and approximation of indirect taxes	(89)260	6/14/89	Proposal	Not Applicable

Common system for withholding tax on interest income	(89)60 C 141	6/7/89	Proposal	7/1/90
Mutual assistance in the field of direct taxation and value-added tax	(89)61 C 97	4/18/89	Proposal	7/1/90
Business and Finance				
Decision on attainment of progressive convergence of economic policies during stage one of economic and monetary union	L 78 90/C 100/04	3/24/90 4/20/90	Adopted Recommendation	
Decision on cooperation of central banks of member states	L 78 90/C 100/03 C 100	3/24/90 4/20/90	Adopted Recommendation	
Account of banks: 1. first banking Directive	L 372 L 322 L 183	12/31/86 12/7/77 7/16/85	Adopted Adopted Adopted	12/31/90 1/1/93 1/1/93
2. recommendation on the setting up of a guarantee system of deposit within the community	L 33	2/4/87	Adopted	Nonbinding Council Recommendation
3. recommendation on control of large exposures	L 33	2/4/87	Adopted	Nonbinding Council Recommendation
Commission Recommendation on transparency of banking conditions relating to cross-border financial transactions	L 67	3/15/90	Adopted	9/1/90
Coordination of laws relating to legal expenses insurance	L 185	7/4/87	Adopted	1/1/90; applied: 7/1/90
Credit Insurance	L 185	7/4/87	Adopted	1/1/90; applied: 7/1/90
Council Directive amending 87/102 concerning consumer credit	L 61	3/10/90	Adopted	12/31/92

TABLE B-1 (continued).

Directive	Official Journal	Date of OJ	Current Status	Date of Implementation
Collective investment undertakings for transferable securities	L 375	12/31/85	Adopted	10/1/89 or 10/1/90; Greece and Portugal: 4/1/92
Coordinating regulations on insider dealing	L 334	11/18/89	Adopted	6/1/92
Recommendation on a European code of conduct relating to electronic payment (relations between financial institutions traders and service establishments and consumers)	L 365	12/24/87	Adopted	Nonbinding Council Recommendation
Liberalization of units in collective investment undertakings for transferable securities	L 372	12/31/85	Adopted	10/1/89; Portugal: 12/3/90
Liberalization of operations such as transactions in securities not dealt in on a stock exchange, admission of securities on the capital market and long-term commercial credits	L 332	11/26/86	Adopted	2/28/87; Portugal: 1990; Spain: 1992
UCITS Directive: Special measure concerning certain investments like mutual bonds	L 100	4/19/88	Adopted	10/1/89
Council Directive on Article 67 of the EC Treaty regarding freedom of capital flows	L 178	7/8/88	Adopted	7/1/90

Description	Number	Date	Status	Date of effect
Facilitation of freedom to provide services in insurance other than life insurance	L 172	7/4/88	Adopted	1/1/90 applied: 7/90
Recommendation concerning payment systems particularly relating cardholders to card issues	L 317	11/24/88	Adopted	11/18/89
Harmonization of the concept of own funds	L 124 C 131 (89)208	5/5/89 5/27/89	Adopted Adopted (amendment)	1/1/93
Information to be published when major holdings in the capital of a listed company are acquired or disposed of	L 348	12/17/88	Adopted	1/1/91
Regulation No. 4064/89 on control of concentrations between undertakings (mergers and acquisitions)	L 395	12/30/89	Adopted	9/21/90
First Directive to approximate the laws of member states relating to trademarks	L 40	2/11/89	Adopted	12/28/91
Insurance for civil liability in motor vehicles	L 129	5/19/90	Adopted	12/31/90 Greece, Spain: 1995 Ireland: 1998
Coordination of the requirements for the drawing up, scrutiny, and distribution of the prospectus to be published when securities are offered for subscription or sale to the public	L 124	5/5/89	Adopted	4/17/89
Amendment to 80/390/EEC	L 112	5/3/90	Adopted	
Laws relating to the exploitation and marketing of natural mineral waters	L 224	8/30/80	Adopted	11/30/80

TABLE B-1 (continued).

Directive	Official Journal	Date of OJ	Current Status	Date of Implementation
Amended Council Directive on the obligation of branches established in a member state by credit institutions and financial institutions having their head offices outside that member state regarding the publications of annual accounting documents	L 44	2/16/89	Adopted	1/1/91
Second banking Directive	Common Position (L 386)	12/30/89	Adopted	1/1/90
Directive of a solvency ratio for credit institutions	Common Position (L 386)	12/30/89	Adopted	1/1/91
Freedom of establishment and freedom to supply services in the field of mortgage credit	(84)730 C 42 (87)255 C 161	2/14/85 6/19/87	Proposal Proposal	TBA 2 yrs. after adoption
Reorganization and winding up of credit institutions	(85)788 C 356 (88)4 C 36	12/31/85 2/8/88	Proposal Proposal	TBA
Proposal on the obligations of branches established in a member state by credit institutions and financial institutions with their head offices outside that member state regarding the publication of annual accounting documents	(88)118 C 143 (86)396 C 203 (86)397 C 230	6/1/88 8/12/86 9/11/86	Proposal Proposal Proposal	12/31/90 1/1/90 1/1/90
Harmonization of the concept of own funds			Adopted	See "L 144"

Second Directive on coordination of credit institutions			Adopted	See "L 160"
Directive on prevention of use of financial system for money laundering	(90)106	4/28/90	Proposal	1/1/92
Insurance contracts	(79)355 C 190	7/28/79	Proposal	18 mos. from notification
	(80)854 C 335	12/31/80	Proposal	
Annual accounts—Insurance undertakings	(86)764 C 131	5/18/87	Proposal	1/1/89
Winding up of insurance undertakings	(86)768 C 71	3/19/87	Proposal	TBA
	(89)394 C 253	10/6/89	Proposal (amendment)	
Information to be published when major holdings in the capital of a listed company are acquired or disposed of			Adopted	See "L 145"
Directive on insider trading			Adopted	See "L 178"
Fifth company law Directive (structure of public limited companies)	(83)185 C 240	9/9/83	Proposal	TBA
Tenth Directive concerning cross-border mergers	(84)727 C 23	1/25/85	Proposed	1/1/88
Statute for a European company	(89)268 C 263	12/16/89	Proposal	TBA
Proposal for eleventh company law: Directive to dispense branches of certain types of companies from publishing separate accounts	(86)397 C 203	8/12/86	Adopted	TBA
	88/105/08 C 105	4/21/88		TBA
				See "C 81"

TABLE B-1 (continued).

Directive	Official Journal	Date of OJ	Current Status	Date of Implementation
Proposal for Council Directive amending Directive 78/660/EEC on annual accounts and Directive 83/349/EEC on consolidated accounts as regards the scope of those Directives (fourth and seventh company law Directives)	(86)238 C 144	6/11/86	Common Position	TBA
Regulation on Community trademarks	(80)635 C 351 (84)470 C 230	12/31/80 8/31/84	Proposal	TBA
First Directive to approximate the laws of member states relating to trademarks			Adopted	See "l 146"
Regulation on the rules needed for implementing the Community trademark regulation	(85)844			
Regulation on rules of procedures for the Boards of Appeal of the Community's trademark office	(86)731			
Community trademark office regulation on fees	(86)742 C 67	3/14/87	Proposal	3/14/88
Abolition of fiscal frontiers	(87)322 C 252	9/22/87	Proposal	TBA
Council Regulation on control of concentrations between industries (mergers and acquisitions)			Adopted	See "L 196"

Description	Document	Date	Status	Implementation
Council Regulation on operation of air cargo services	(90)63 C 88	4/6/90	Proposal	1/1/90
Proposal Directive on published accounts of branches of banks and other financial institutions	(88)602			
Proposal Twelfth Council Directive on company law concerning single members' private limited companies	(89)193 C 173 (89)591 C 30	5/24/89 2/8/90	Proposal Proposal	
Amended proposal for a Council Directive on the obligation of branches established in a member state by credit institutions and financial institutions having their head offices outside that member state regarding the publications of annual accounting documents				See "L 149"
Solvency ratios for credit institutions				See "L 167"
Framework for investment services with the securities field	(88)778 C 43 (89)629 C42	2/22/89 2/22/90	Proposal (amendment)	1/1/93
Thirteenth Council Directive law concerning takeover and other general bids	(88)823 C 64	3/14/89	Proposal	TBA
Second Directive on direct life insurance	(88)729 C 38 (90)46 C 72	2/15/89 3/22/90	Proposal Common Position	TBA
Guarantees issued by credit institutions or insurance undertakings	(88)805 C 51	2/28/89	Proposal	TBA
Directive on solvency ratios				See "L 167"
Amends Directive 87/102/EEC on approximation of laws concerning consumer credit	(89)271 C 155 (88)201 C 155 (89)592 C 30	5/23/89 6/14/88 2/8/90	Proposal Proposal Proposal	12/31/92

TABLE B-1 (continued).

Directive	Official Journal	Date of OJ	Current Status	Date of Implementation
Council Regulation on statistical classification of economic activities in EC (NACE)	(90)241 C 58	3/8/90	Proposal	1/93
Commission Communication relating to an action program to promote the development of the European audiovisual industry	(90)132	5/4/90	Proposal	
Amendment to Council Directive 79/695/EEC on the harmonization of procedures for the release of goods for free circulation	(89)385 C 235	9/13/89	Proposal	1/1/93
Liquidation of companies				
A framework directive for insurance sector including a single insurance license				
Harmonization of EC member state laws covering company credit organizations and consumer credit organizations				
Pension fund Directive covering harmonization of rules and laws on pensions				
Preliminary draft on the third Directive on non-life insurance				

Proposal for a Directive on the relationship of undertakings in a group

Agriculture

Production and trade in milk	L 226	8/24/85	Adopted	1/1/89
Live animals of the bovine species: amended eradication Directives to provide for final eradication of brucellosis tuberculosis and leukosis in all member states including Spain and Portugal	L 24	1/27/87	Adopted	Binding Council Decision, Eradication Plans Prepared
Live animals of the porcupine species: eradication of African swine fever in Portugal	L 382	12/31/86	Adopted	3/16/87
Live animals of the porcupine species: eradication of African swine fever in Spain	L 382	12/31/86	Adopted	3/16/87
Eradication of classical swine fever in the Community as a whole	L 99	4/11/87	Adopted	1/1/87
	L 280	3/10/87	Adopted	12/31/87
Hormone growth promoters	L 191	7/23/85	Adopted	12/31/85
Microbiological controls (meats, poultry, red meat)	L 168	6/28/85	Adopted	1/1/86
Antibiotic residues	L 275	9/26/86	Adopted	Art. 3 and 4, 4/1/87 other 12/31/87
Control of residues	L 275	9/26/86	Adopted	12/31/87 4/1/87 (permit) 12/31/88 (permit)
Swine fever	L 168	6/28/85	Adopted	1/1/86
Control of foot-and-mouth disease	L 315	11/26/85	Adopted	1/1/87

TABLE B-1 (continued).

Directive	Official Journal	Date of OJ	Current Status	Date of Implementation
Amendment to Directive 77/93 (plant health)	L 26 L 65	1/31/77 3/6/85	Adopted Adopted	1/1/85
Maximum levels for pesticide residues in cereals and foodstuffs of animal origin	L 221	8/7/86	Adopted	6/30/88
Amendment of Directive 79/117/EEC on the prohibition of certain plant protection products (ethylene oxide)	L 212 L 159	8/2/88 6/10/89	Adopted (amendment)	7/1/87
Directive on the fixing of guidelines for the evaluation of additives used in animal foodstuffs	L 64	3/7/87	Adopted	12/31/87
Modification of Directive 72/461 on health problems affecting intra-Community trade in fresh meat and Directive 72/462 on health and veterinary inspection problems upon importation of bovine animals and swine and fresh meat from third countries	L 87 (rules) L 93 (amend) L 34	3/31/89 6/1/89 5/1/87	Adopted Adopted Adopted	6/30/90 1/1/88
Acceptance for breeding purposes of purebred breeding animals of the bovine species	L 167	6/26/87	Adopted	1/1/89
Amendment to Directive 80/215 on animal health problems affecting intra-Community trade in meat products	L 279	10/2/87	Adopted	1/1/88

Description	Reference	Date	Status	Effective
Amendment to Directive 74/63 on undesirable substances and products in animal nutrition (maximum pesticide residues in animal feedingstuffs)	L 304	10/27/87	Adopted	12/31/90
Emulsifiers (modification)	L 88	4/3/86	Adopted (amendment)	1/1/85
	L 186	6/30/89		
Coffee extracts, chicory extracts	L 372	12/31/85	Adopted (modification)	1/1/87 (permit) 7/1/88
Directive amending 81/852 concerning veterinary medicinal products	L 15	1/17/87	Adopted	7/1/87
Liquid fertilizers	L 83	3/29/88	Partially Adopted	3/1/89
Commission Directive adapting to technical progress 76/538/EEC on the approximation of the laws of the member states relating to the methods of sampling and analysis for fertilizers	L 265	9/12/89	Adopted	
Directive on eradication of brucellosis in sheep and goats	90/242		Adopted	
Amendment to Directive 64/433 on health problems affecting intra-Community trade in fresh meat	L 124	5/18/88	Adopted (amendment)	1/1/89
	L 49	2/12/89		
Amendment to Directive 72/462 on health and veterinary inspection problems upon importation of bovine animals and swine and fresh meat from third countries	L 124	5/18/88	Adopted (amendment)	1/1/89
	L 49	2/12/89		
Directive on animal health requirements applicable to intra-Community trade in deep-frozen semen of bovine species	L 194	7/22/88	Adopted (amendment)	1/1/90
	L 71	3/17/90		

TABLE B-1 (continued).

Directive	Official Journal	Date of OJ	Current Status	Date of Implementation
Commission decision on equivalence of field inspection carried out in third countries on seed producing crops	L 147	6/14/88	Adopted	Not Applicable
Additives to animal feedingstuffs	L 237	8/27/88	Adopted	6/30/89
	L 343	12/13/88	(amendment)	
Amending Directive 77/93/EEC on protective measures against introduction into EC of harmful organisms to plants or plant products*	L313	11/19/88	Adopted	1/1/89
Zootechnical standards applicable to breeding animals of the porcupine species	L 382	12/31/88	Adopted	1/1/91
	L 71	3/17/90	(extension)	1/1/91
	L 71	3/17/90	(extension)	1/1/91
Modification of Directive 77/99/EEC on meat products	L 382	12/31/88	Adopted	7/1/90
				1/1/92
				12/31/92
Directive on health problems relating to minced meat and similar products: import from third countries	(89)667 L 382	12/31/88	Adopted	1/1/91
	C 84	4/2/90	Proposal	1/1/93
Jams	L 318	11/25/88	Adopted	12/31/89
Fruit juices	L 186	6/30/89	Adopted	(permit) 5/16/90
				(prohibit) 5/16/91
Approximation of laws on the official control of foodstuffs	L 186	1/30/89	Adopted	6/20/91

Directive	Number	Date	Status	Deadline
Supplements and amends Directive 76/116: calcium magnesium, sodium, and sulfur content of fertilizer	L 111	4/22/89	Adopted	4/17/90
Directive on hygiene and health of producing and marketing egg products	L 212	7/22/89	Adopted	12/31/91
Imports of meat products from third countries (animal and public health)	L 93	4/6/89	Adopted	
Secondary fertilizers	L 111	4/22/89	Adopted	4/16/90
Trade in embryos of domestic animals of bovine species	L 302	10/19/89	Adopted	1/1/91
Veterinary checks in intra-Community trade	L 395	12/30/90	Adopted	12/31/90
Veterinary rules on disposal of animal waste and prevention of pathogens in feedingstuffs	(89)509 C 327	12/30/89	Proposal	
Production and trade in medicated feeding stuffs			Adopted	See "L 201"
Boar meat	(83)655	9/7/83	Proposal	
Personnel responsible for inspection	(81)504 C 262	10/14/81	Proposal	TBA
Zootechnical standards applicable to breeding animals of the porcupine species			Adopted	See "L 124"
Imports of meat products from third countries (animal and public health)			Adopted	See "L 171"
Aujesky disease and swine vesicular disease	(82)529 C 249	9/23/82	Proposal	TBA
Semen of animals			Adopted	See "L 102" and "L 124"

TABLE B-1 (continued).

Directive	Official Journal	Date of OJ	Current Status	Date of Implementation
Modification of Directive 77/99/EEC on meat products			Adopted	See "L 125"
Proposal to amend Directive 77/93 (plant health)	(84)288 C 134	5/22/84	Proposal	1/1/89
Proposal to amend annex of Directive 76/895/EEC concerning residues of pesticides in and on fruits and vegetables (ethoxyquin and diphenylamine)	(88)798 C 46	2/25/89	Proposal	12/31/89
Proposal for the placing of plant protection products on the market	(76)427 C 212	9/9/76	Proposal	18 mos. after notification
Products of animal origin not covered by other directives	(89)658 C 84	4/2/90	Proposal	1/1/93
Proposal for the improvement of Community systems of certification of seeds	(85)782 C 356	12/31/85	Proposal	TBA
Proposal health conditions for production and trade in food products of animal origin not covered by existing legislation: eggs			Adopted	See "L 168"
Proposal for Directive on health problems relating to minced meat and similar products: imports from third countries			Adopted	See "L 126"

Description	Document	Reference	Date	Status	Implementation
Harmonized health and hygiene conditions: fish and fish products—health guarantees	(88)47 (89)428 (89)645	C 66 C 282 C 84	3/11/88 9/8/89 4/2/90	Proposal (amendment) Proposal Proposal	TBA TBA 1/1/93
Regulation on trade in fresh poultry meat and fresh meat of reared game birds	(89)503	C 327	12/30/89	Proposal Withdrawn by Commission	
Modified starches					
Jams				Adopted	See "L 135"
Fruit juices				Adopted	See "L 136"
Secondary fertilizers Directive					See "L 172"
Council Directive amending 77/93/EEC on protective measures against harmful organisms to plants and plant products				Adopted	See "L 166"
Proposal for a Council Regulation amending Regulation EEC No. 1468/81 on mutual assistance between the administrative authorities of the member states and cooperation between the latter and the Commission to ensure the correct application of the law on custom or agricultural matters	(85)467	C 267	10/18/85	Proposal	
Veterinary checks in intra-Community trade				Adopted	See "L 184"
Intensifying controls on the application of veterinary rules	(88)383	C 225	8/3/188	Proposal	4/1/89
Mutual assistance over agriculture matters	(88)383	C 225	8/31/88	Proposal	4/1/89

TABLE B-1 (continued).

Directive	Official Journal		Date of OJ	Current Status	Date of Implementation
Further modifications to emulsifiers, stabilizers, thickeners for food				Adopted	See "L 35"
Oligo-elements fertilizers	(88)562	C 304	11/29/88	Proposal	1/1/91
Zootechnical and pedigree requirements for marketing purebred animals	(88)598	C 304	11/29/88	Proposal	30 days after publication
Formulation of Directives health problems concerning animals relating to trade in dogs and cats (measures against rabies)	(88)836	C 85	4/6/89	Proposal	
Animal health in bovine and caprine species	(88)742	C 48	2/27/88	Proposal	8/1/89
Veterinary medicine	(88)779	C 61	3/10/89	Common Position	1/1/92
Veterinary Medicine	(88)779	C 61	3/10/89	Common Position	1/1/92
a) procedure to establish tolerance for residues of veterinary medicine products				Adopted	See "L 216"
b) amendment to 81/851/EEC on veterinary products					
c) extends scope of 81/8511/EEC to include immunological veterinary medicine products					
Animal embryos				Adopted	See "L 175"

			Date	Status	Target
Concerning veterinary checks in intra-Community trade and controls on the application of veterinary rules	87(591)	C 348	12/23/87	Adopted	See "L 184"
Purebred breeding sheeps and goats				Proposal	1/1/90
Animal health governing trade in poultry and hatching eggs	(89)9	C 89	4/10/89	Proposal	9/1/89
Conditions for marketing plant protection products	(89)34	C 89	4/10/89	Proposal	TBA
Protective measures against the introduction of organisms harmful to plants or plant products (proposed amendment to affect intra-EC trade)		L 212	7/22/89	Adopted	1/1/90
	90/22/03	C 22	1/30/90	(amendment)	1/1/91
	90/29/09	C 29	2/8/90	(amendment)	1/1/91
		L 92	4/7/90	(amendment)	1/1/91
Improvement of conditions under which fishery and aquaculture products are processed and marketed	(89)605	C 4	1/9/90	Proposal	
Equidae Products a) regulation intra-Community trade and imports of equidae				Adopted	See "L 214"
b) regulation on zootechnical and genealogical conditions for intra-Community trade in equidae				Adopted	See "L 214"
c) regulation on intra-Community trade in equidae intended for participation in competitions				Adopted / Adopted	See "L 214"
Veterinary Medicine a) procedure to establish tolerance for residues of veterinary medicine products				Adopted	
b) amendment to 81/851/EEC on veterinary products				Adopted	

TABLE B-1 (continued).

Directive	Official Journal	Date of OJ	Current Status	Date of Implementation
c) extends scope of 81/851/EEC to include immunological veterinary medicine products				
Decision on eradication of brucellosis in sheep and goats			Adopted	See "L 211"
Formulation of Directives on animal health problems relating to trade in fish and fish products				
Brucellosis in small ruminants				
Echinococcosis				
Directive on veterinary inspection problems not already covered by existing Directives				
Harmonized health and hygiene conditions for production and trade in shellfish and crustacea and preparation				
Harmonized health and hygiene conditions for production and trade in fish and fish products (one proposal already made on this subject)				
Pathogens in feedingstuffs				
Suppression of veterinary certificates for animal products and simplification of certificates for live animals				

Proposal for a system of certification of reproductive materials in fruit plants

Establishment of certain rules on liability in respect of plant health

Simplification of annexes in Directive 77/93/EEC (plant health)

Alignment of national standards and intra-Community standards in plant health

Reduction of role of phytosanitary certificate in intra-Community trade

Proposal for a system of certification in reproduction materials for decorative plants

Reinforcement of controls of harmful organisms especially in seed potatoes and in fruit plant reproductive material

Extension of application Directives 66/401/EEC and 70/458/EEC to seedlings

Proposal for creation of a European law on plant breeders

Suppression of plant health certificates

Directive on organic production of foodstuffs and marketing of organically produced foodstuffs

Amendment to Directive on veterinary medicines

TABLE B-1 (continued).

Directive	Official Journal	Date of OJ	Current Status	Date of Implementation
Miscellaneous				
General Directive on sampling and methods of analysis	L 372	12/31/85	Adopted	12/23/87
Proposals for regulation for a European economic interest grouping	L 199	7/31/85	Adopted	Conformance by 7/1/89
Action program for improving efficiency of electricity use	L 157	6/9/89	Adopted	Not Applicable
Directive on the control of the acquisition and possession of arms	(87)383 C 235 (89)446 C 299	9/1/87 11/28/89	Proposal (amendment)	6/30/90
Establishing an internal market for telecommunications services with Open Network Provisions (ONP)			Adopted	
Proposal for approximation of laws of member states on telecommunications terminal equipment including mutual recognition of conformity	(89)289 C 211	8/17/89	Proposal	1/1/90
Commission Directive on competition in the markets for telecommunications services	90/703		Adopted	
Broadcasting activities			Adopted	See "L 179"
Coordination concerning pursuit of television broadcast activities	L 298	10/17/89	Adopted	10/3/91

Measure	Document	Date	Status	Deadline
Alternative system on trade statistics after the abolition of all remaining internal frontiers	(88)810 C 84	4/5/89	Proposal	12/31/92
Transit of electricity through transmission grids	(89)336 C 8	1/13/90	Proposal	7/1/90
	(90)207	5/21/90	Proposal	
Harmonization of regulatory meaning of the "EC Mark" of conformity with EC essential requirements				
Green Paper on the future of EC standards policy				
Patent term Directive				
Harmonization of laws in member states relating to nonautomatic weighing instruments			Adopted	

*These measures are not a formal part of the 1992 Single Market Initiative.
Source: European Commission, U.S. Department of Commerce.

Appendix C:
A Checklist of Strategic Questions

Appendix C contains a short checklist of strategic questions of value in developing a single market strategy. The questions are broken down into four areas: country considerations, operational considerations, industry considerations, and marketing considerations.

Country Considerations

What are the host country's historical and present attitudes toward foreign business? Toward small/large business?

Does the country have a special U.S. trade relationship?

Does the country have a history of trade disputes, for example, dumping actions?

Operational Considerations

Is the local labor supply sufficient?

What will be the source of the inputs to production if you produce in the EC?

Why are you interested in the EC home-market stagnation? growth opportunities? future security? and so on.

What taxes or duties will affect you and your customers?

Is there an advantage to entering into an EC country that is lagging in EC directive implementation?

What type of alliance, if any, will be best for your purposes?

How will the local laws, such as local content, personnel, financing, unions, and so on (EC directed or not) affect your operation now or in the future?

Is your host country strategically located for future growth?

Is there patent/intellectual property protection available?

Who are your suppliers and where are they located?

Are there incentives, for example, contract length, margin, services, and so on, that are appropriate for your EC distributors?

Is there a less expensive alternative to locating in the EC?

How will the business of your product be different in the EC?

Are your expectations of the country work ethic accurate?

Industry Considerations

Are your competitors moving to the EC?

Is there EC assistance for your type of operation?

Will your EC competition be local, regional, or national?

Will EC and local interest groups influence your business favorably/ unfavorably?

How much will the government be involved in your industry?

Where do you go for information regarding your industry?

Should operations be controlled at a global, regional, or local headquarters?

Do different substitute products exist in the EC for your product?

Will customer service and warranty expectations in the community be higher/lower with your product?

Is the information you are receiving regarding EC markets accurate?

What nontariff barriers will you confront in both the immediate and the long term?

Marketing Considerations

Does your product carry any national qualities?

Will national qualities interfere with your marketing effort?

Will you market your product as an American or a European product?

Is your product marketable to Eastern Europe?

Must your marketing strategy be oriented nationally, regionally, or Europe-wide?

Is your pricing strategy determined? Is price segmentation possible?

Are your traditional buyer incentives appropriate?

What advertising media can you use?

How will different advertising media affect the image of the product?

Does the fact that your product is coming from the United States make it more desirable?

Can your product be easily adapted to new markets? How?

Does your product rely on another product's use, and is that product readily available?

What standardization should your product carry to take advantage of commonalities among markets?

Will your product complement or interfere with regional traditions or habits?

Notes

Chapter 1

1. Commission of the European Communities, *Completing The Internal Market: White Paper from the Commission to The European Council*, Luxembourg, 1985.
2. John F. McGee, "1992: Moves Americans Must Make," *Harvard Business Review* (May–June, 1989): 78.
3. From a speech delivered to the College of Europe, Bruges, Belgium, September 20, 1988.
4. As quoted in Dominic Lawson, "Saying the Unsayable about the Germans," *The Spectator*, 14 July 1990, 8.
5. Indeed, some, most notably the Bruges group, argue that the EC Commission is providing exactly this remedy, that is, governmental action, through its almost three hundred directives. See Kenneth Minogue, "Europe's Historical Passion for Cooperation," *Wall Street Journal*, 8 May 1989, A15.
6. See "EC Citizens Elect New European Parliament," *Europe* (July–August 1989): 24.
7. We have defined the Asian NICs to include Hong Kong, Malaysia, Singapore, South Korea, Taiwan, and Thailand.
8. The percentages in figure 1–1 were constructed using a smoothed exchange rate (an average over several years) so as not to confuse the change in GDP with exchange-rate changes. If the figures were constructed using current exchange rates (1975 and 1987 rates only) the United States percentage would decline considerably and the Japanese percentage would rise. The EC figures would remain approximately the same.
9. As quoted in Phillip Revzin, "Welcome to Their Party," *Wall Street Journal*, 30 December 1988, A6.
10. Paolo Cecchini, *1992: The European Challenge* (Hants, England: Wildwood House, 1988), 103.
11. Ibid., 13. The exchange rate used was $1 = 1.1 ECU.
12. Paul Kennedy, *The Rise and Fall of the Great Powers* (New York: Random House, 1987), 533.

Chapter 2

1. Mancur Olson, *The Rise and Decline of Nations: Economic Growth, Stagflation, and Social Rigidities* (New Haven, Conn.: Yale University Press, 1982), 129.
2. Sidney Pollard, *European Economic Integration 1815–1970* (London: Thames and Hudson Ltd., 1974), 35.
3. Ibid., 15–16.
4. Ibid., 19.
5. Ibid., 23.
6. Ibid., 29–30.
7. Dennis Swann, *The Economics of the Common Market,* 5th ed. (Harmondsworth, England: Pelican Books, 1984), 12.
8. James Robert Rhodes, ed., *Winston S. Churchill: His Complete Speeches 1897–1963,* vol. 7 1943–1949 (London: Chelsea House Publishers, 1974), 7323.
9. The ECE was established by the United Nations in 1947 and was located in Geneva. Its primary purpose was to enhance the cooperation between the war-ravaged European states, both east and west, as well as to aid in the economic reconstruction of Europe. See United Nations, *ECE in Action* (New York: United Nations, 1949).
10. See President's Committee on Foreign Aid, *European Recovery and American Aid* (Washington, D.C.: U.S. Government Printing Office, 1947). The OEEC subsequently became the Organization for Economic Cooperation and Development (OECD).
11. See *Steps to European Unity; Community Progress to Date: A Chronology,* 6th ed. (Luxembourg: Office of Official Publications of the European Communities, 1987), 12–14 (hereinafter cited as *Steps to European Unity*); and Dennis Swann, *Economics of the Common Market,* 5th ed. (Harmondsworth, England: Pelican Books, 1984), 18–19.
12. Anthony J.C. Kerr, *The Common Market and How it Works,* 2nd ed. (Oxford: Pergamon Press, 1980), 5–7.
13. *Treaty Establishing the European Economic Community* (Rome: March 25, 1957).
14. *Steps to European Unity,* 23–24.
15. The ESC is composed of twenty-four members from each of the largest countries—France, Germany, Italy, and the United Kingdom; twenty-one members from Spain; twelve members from each of the intermediate countries—Belgium, Greece, the Netherlands, and Portugal; nine members from Denmark and Ireland; and six members from Luxembourg.
16. See *Treaty Establishing the European Economic Community,* section 3, article 155, 25 March 1957.
17. Michael Calingaert, *The 1992 Challenge from Europe: Development of the European Community's Internal Market* (Washington, DC: National Planning Association, 1988), 14.

18. Emile Noel, *Working Together: The Institutions of the European Community* (Luxembourg: Office for Official Publications of the European Communities, 1988), 13.
19. Ibid., 14.
20. *The Court of Justice of the European Community*, 4th ed. (Luxembourg: Official Publication of the European Communities, 1986), 14.

Chapter 3

1. See Pierre Gebert, "In Search of Political Union: The Fouchet Negotiations (1960–62)," in *The Dynamics of European Union*, ed. Roy Pryce (New York: Croom Helm, 1987).
2. See Jacques Vandamme, "The Tindeman's Report (1975–76)," in *The Dynamics of European Union*, ed. Roy Pryce (New York: Croom Helm, 1987).
3. For more on the European Union Treaty, see Francesco Capotorti et al., *The European Union Treaty* (Oxford: Clarendon Press, 1986).
4. Frances Nicholson and Roger East, *From the Six to the Twelve: The Enlargement of the European Communities* (Harlow, England: Longman), 255.
5. *Single European Act* (Luxembourg: Office for Official Publications of the European Communities, 1986), section 2, subsection 1, article 8A.
6. D. Lasok and J. W. Bridge, *Law & Institutions of the European Communities*, 4th ed. (London: Butterworths, 1987), 26.
7. Denmark, Greece, Ireland, and Italy initially refused to sign the act. Although this provision was itself not directly responsible for the referenda in Denmark, nor the other countries' reservations, it was indirectly responsible. In Ireland, the pervasiveness of the act was thought to possibly violate Irish constitutional neutrality. In Denmark, the opposition was concerned about the country's ability to maintain its environmental and welfare policies and special relations with its nordic neighbors. Italian concerns were mostly minor and reflected a desire for further institutional and procedural reforms. Greece was apparently acting out of solidarity with Denmark.
8. See *Single European Act*, Hans-Joachim Glaesner, "The Single European Act: Attempt at an Appraisal" *Fordham International Law Journal* (Spring 1987): 446–502.
9. *Completing the Internal Market: White Paper from the Commission to the European Council* (Luxembourg: Commission of the European Communities, June, 1985), part 1, paragraph 27.
10. Ibid., Introduction, paragraph 12.
11. Ibid., part 1, paragraph 36.
12. *Research on the "Costs of Non-Europe": Basic Findings*, Vol. 1, "*Basic Studies: Executive Summaries*" (Luxembourg: Commission of the European Communities, 1988), 15. See also Paolo Cecchini, *1992: The European Challenge*, (Hants, England: Wildwood, 1988), 9.
13. Judgment of the European Court of Justice in case 178/84, *Commission of the European Communities v. Federal Republic of Germany*.

14. Preliminary ruling of the European Court of Justice in case 407/85, *Drei Glocken GmbH and Gertrude Kritzinger* v. *U.S.L Centro-Sud and Provincia Autonoma di Bolzano.*
15. As reported in David Buchanon, "The Quest for Tax Harmony," *Financial Times,* 22 August 1988.
16. Paolo Cecchini, *1992: The European Challenge,* 5.
17. See Group MAC, *The "Cost of Non-Europe" in the Foodstuffs Industry* (Luxembourg: Office of Official Publications of the European Communities, 1988).
18. J. Pelkmans and A. Winters, "Europe's Domestic Market," Chatham House, Paper no. 43, the Royal Institute of International Affairs (London: Routledge, 1988).
19. Ernst & Whinney, *"The Cost of Non Europe": Border-Related Controls and Administrative Barriers* (Luxembourg: Office of Official Publications of the European Communities, 1988), 120.
20. Ibid., 56. Differences in agent's cost are a good measure of excessive procedures and paperwork since there is no reason to believe that the basic cost of handling a consignment should differ across countries for any other reason.
21. Ibid., annex 12.
22. "Ploughing a Furrow to 1992," *Financial Times,* 6 June 1988.
23. As quoted in "Ploughing a Furrow to 1992," *Financial Times,* 6 June 1988.
24. Jürgen Müller, *The Benefits of Completing the Internal Market for Telecommunications Equipment/Service in the Community* (Luxembourg: Office of Official Publications of the European Communities, 1988), 14.
25. *The Commission of the European Communities, Telecommunications: Green Paper on the Development of the Common Market for Telecommunications Services and Equipment* (Brussels: Directorate-General, Information Industries and Innovation, 1989).
26. All the examples in this section are taken from Group MAC, *The "Cost of Non-Europe" in the Foodstuffs Industry.*
27. The Lee, Pearson, and Smith results are reported in John Kay, "Europe without Fiscal Frontiers: An Assessment," *European Managment Journal* (Winter 1988): 338–44.
28. See "The Smug Debtor," *The Economist,* 3 September 1988.
29. See Krish Bhaskar, *Car Pricing in Europe* (England: Motor Industry Research Institute, University of East Anglia, 1984).
30. Paolo Cecchini, *1992: The European Challenge,* 73.
31. Ibid., 98–102.
32. See F. Brown and J. Whalley, "General Equilibrium Evaluations of Tariff-Cutting Proposals in the Tokyo Round and Comparisons to More Extensive Liberalization of World Trade," *Economic Journal* (December 1980) 838–865; Alan Deardorff and Robert Stern, "An Economic Analysis of the Effects of the Tokyo Round of MLN on the U.S. and Other Industrialized Countries," United States Senate, 1979.
33. Stephan Magee, "The Welfare Effects of Restrictions on U.S. Trade," *Brookings Papers on Economic Activity,* no. 3 (1972).

34. Noel Malcolm, "Europe's Unholy Godfathers," *The Spectator,* 23 September 1989.

Chapter 4

1. Noel Malcolm, "Mr. Kinnock Takes a Walk on the Supply Side," *The Spectator,* 7 October 1989, 6.
2. The major initial works in this field include: James Buchanan and Gordon Tullock, *The Calculus of Consent* (Ann Arbor: University of Michigan Press, 1962); Mancur Olson, *The Logic of Collective Action* (Cambridge, Mass.: Harvard University Press, 1971); Sam Peltzman, "Toward a More General Theory of Regulation," *Journal of Law and Economics* (Spring 1976); Richard Posner, "Taxation by Regulation," *Bell Journal of Economics* (Spring 1971); and Stigler, G., "The Theory of Economic Regulation," *Bell Journal of Economics* (Spring 1971).
3. The inputs being money and votes.
4. The free rider problem occurs because the benefit received by a group cannot normally be restricted to members of the group who do not pay for achieving the benefit. As the group gets larger, policing the organization to make sure everyone pays his or her way becomes increasingly difficult.
5. Ambrose Bierce, *The Devil's Dictionary* (New York: Sagamore Press, 1957), 143.
6. It is possible, of course, to consider the supply of regulation as having some upper limit, beyond which more regulation is simply impossible. We will ignore this possibility.
7. These figures exclude communist parties unless they represent a significant popular party, that is, more than 10 percent of the vote. The voting percentages are, therefore, underestimates of the popularity of left-leaning political parties.
8. Commission of the European Communities, *Eurobarometer,* no. 30 (Brussels: Directorate-General Information, Communication, Culture, Surveys, Research, Analyses, December 1988), B48.
9. As quoted in OECD, *STI Review* (April) (Washington: OECD, 1989), 26.
10. Robert Lawrence and Charles Schultze, *Barriers to European Growth: A Transatlantic View* (Washington: Brooking Institution, 1987), 6.
11. We are defining the electronics industry to include consumer electronics, electronic parts, data processing, software, and automation equipment, and so on.
12. These statistics, unless otherwise stated, are for all of Western Europe and not just the EC.
13. See, for example, Electronic Industries Association, *1989 Electronic Market Data Book* (Washington: Electronics Industries Association, 1989); and Computer and Business Equipment Manufacturers Association, *The Information Technology Industry Data Book, 1960–1998* (Washington: Computer and Business Equipment Manufacturers Association, 1989).

14. See Electronics International Corporation, *Electronics in the World* (New York: EIC, 1988).

15. See Rob Van Tulder and Gerd Junne, *European Multinationals in Core Technologies* (New York: John Wiley & Sons, 1988), 134.

16. Ibid., 190.

17. See also Economic Commission for Europe, *The Telecommunications Industry: Growth and Structural Change* (New York: United Nations, 1987).

18. BRITE (Basic Research in Industrial Technologies for Europe) is a general information technology organization and the twelve major telecommunications companies represent about 22 percent of the participants. ESPRIT (European Strategic Program for R & D in Information Technology) and RACE (R & D in Advanced Communications Technologies for Europe) are more oriented toward telecommunications and between 65 and 75 percent of the participating companies are the major telecommunications companies. See Rob Van Tulder and Gerd Junne, *European Multinationals in Core Technologies* (New York: John Wiley & Sons, 1988), 226.

19. Also, the United States figures are biased downward by the exclusion from our sample of many of the regional exchanges, which are larger than the national regional exchanges in Europe.

20. Gabriel Hawawani, *European Equity Markets: Price Behavior and Efficiency* (New York: Salomon Brothers Center for the Study of Financial Institutions, 1984), 23.

21. Arthur Andersen & Company, *European Capital Markets: A Strategic Forecast* (London: The Economist Publications, 1989).

22. *Europe 1992: Less Change than Anticipated* (Greenwich, Conn.: Greenwich Associates, 1988).

23. "Factory of the Future," *The Economist,* 30 May 1987, 15.

24. James Abegglen and George Stalk, *Kaisha: The Japanese Corporation* (New York: Basic Books, 1985), 131.

25. William Pfaff, "Trade Bouts: Japan vs. Europe is the Main Event," *International Herald Tribune,* date unknown.

26. Michael Heseltine, *The Challenge of Europe: Can Britain Win?* (London: Weidenfeld & Nicholson, 1989), 104.

27. Paul Kennedy, *The Rise and Fall of the Great Powers* (New York: Vintage Books, 1989).

28. United Nations, *Statistical Yearbook, 1985/86* (New York: United Nations, 1988), 89; T. Kang, *Is Korea the Next Japan?* (New York: Free Press, 1989).

29. Paul Kennedy, *The Rise and Fall of the Great Powers,* 514–535.

30. Karel van Wolferen, *The Enigma of Japanese Power* (London: Macmillan, 1989), 5–6.

31. *Single European Act,* section 2, subsection 3, articles 118A and 188B; subsection 4, article 130A, subsection 6, article 130R.

32. Editorial, "The Social Dimension," *Financial Times,* 1 June 1989.

33. See Joel Kotkin and Sara Baer-Sinnott, "Hotspots," *Inc.,* March, 1989, 90–92; and Kenneth Labich, "The Best Cities for Business," *Fortune,* 23 October 1989, 56–93.

34. See Wolfgang Glage, "The High Cost of Dismissals and Layoffs in Europe," *The Journal of European Business* (September/October 1989): 31–33.

35. Catherine Morrison, *1992: The Leading Issues for European Companies* (Washington: The Conference Board, 1989).

36. Richard Hudson, "Europeans Are Learning that Pollution Must Be Attacked in a Coordinated Way," *Wall Street Journal*, 1 November 1988, A24.

37. See Commission of the European Communities, *General Report of the Activities of the European Communities* (Luxembourg: Office of Official Publications of the European Communities, various years).

38. Commission of the European Communities, *Report by the Commission to the Council and Parliament on the Financing of the Community Budget*, COM(87) 101 Final (Brussels: Commission of the European Communities, 1987), 23.

39. "EEC Regional Aid: The Budget-buster of the 1990s?" *The Economist*, 15 July 1989, 42.

40. Alan Philip, "Management and 1992—Illusions and Reality," *European Management Journal* (Winter 1988): 345.

Chapter 5

1. Committee for the Study of Economic and Monetary Union, *Report on Economic and Monetary Union in the European Community* (Brussels/Luxembourg, 1989).

2. During the meeting of EC leaders in Dublin in June 1990, it was agreed that two intergovernmental conferences would be held in December. These conferences are necessary for considering changes in the Treaty of Rome. Set for 13 December is the Conference on European Monetary Union, to be followed the next day by the Conference on Political Union. The importance of the back-to-back timing of these events cannot be underestimated.

3. *The Guardian*, 20 October 1977.

4. As quoted in Mark Nelson, "EC Members Agree to Work Toward a Common Goal of Monetary Union," *Wall Street Journal*, 18 April 1989, A21.

5. Karl Otto Pöhl, "A Vision of a European Central Bank," *Wall Street Journal*, 15 July 1988, A14.

6. Karl Otto Pöhl, "Herr Pöhl Reviews Current Progress Towards European Monetary Union," *BIS Review*, 8 January 1990, 1.

7. "No Sign of Softening on Delors Stance," *The London Times*, 24 November 1989, 5.

8. As quoted in Mark Nelson, "EC to Proceed with Work on Plan for Monetary Union," *Wall Street Journal*, 18 April 1989, A21.

9. Jacques van Ypersele, *The European Monetary System* (Brussels: Commission of the European Communities, 1984).

10. Ranier Masera and Robert Triffin, *Europe's Money: Problems of European Monetary Coordination and Integration* (New York: Oxford University Press, 1984), 273.

11. European Commission, *Commission Memorandum to the Council on the Co-ordination of Economic Policies and Monetary Cooperation within the Community*, Brussels, 12 February 1969, 5.

12. Ibid., 8.

13. European Commission, *Commission Memorandum to the Council on the Co-ordination of Economic Policies and Monetary Cooperation within the Community*, Brussels, 12 February 1969, 10.

14. Stephen George, *Politics and Policy in the European Community* (New York: Oxford University Press, 1985), 133–34.

15. Loukas Tsoukalis, *The Politics and Economics of European Monetary Integration* (London: Allen and Unwin, 1977), 130.

16. Peter Ludlow, *The Making of the European Monetary System* (London: Butterworths, 1982).

17. Directorate-General Economic and Financial Affairs, *The EMS: Ten Years of Progress in European Monetary Co-operation*, Brussels, 3.

18. *Single European Act*, section 2, subsection 2, article 102A, paragraph 1.

19. *Treaty of Rome*, title 2, chapter 2, article 104.

20. Committee for the Study of Economic and Monetary Union, *Report on Economic and Monetary Union in the European Community*, Brussels, 3.

21. Both Mr. Lawson and Mr. Leigh-Pemberton are quoted in "Britain Rejects EC Plan for Economic Union," *International Herald Tribune*, 18 April 1988.

22. Committee for the Study of Economic and Monetary Union, *Report on Economic and Monetary Union in the European Community*, Brussels.

23. Ibid., p. 36.

24. See *The Economist*, "Straighten Europe's Snake," 3 June 1989, 17–18.

25. See Arthur Andersen & Co., *European Capital Markets: A Strategic Forecast* (London: The Economist Publications, 1989).

26. Bank of Japan, *Comparative International Statistics* (Tokyo: Bank of Japan, 1988).

27. As quoted in Tim Carrington and Mark Nelson, "For Monetary Union in Europe, Question Is When, Not Whether," *Wall Street Journal*, Date unknown.

28. In 1978, the French and Germans were able to generate a consensus for the EMS through the use of structural grants as bribes. These grants clearly did not increase the economic parity of the economies of the Community then and there is no reason to believe that they will now. The magnitude of the wealth transfer between West and East Germany associated with German monetary union, estimated at DM 50 billion in direct government aid and as much as DM 600 billion in total investment, exhibits that monetary union cannot be accomplished without a transfer of both sovereignty and wealth.

29. See "Plotting Monetary Union," *The Economist*, 19 May 1990, 87–88.

Chapter 6

1. Quoted from a speech delivered at the College of Europe, Bruges, Belgium, 20 September 1988.

2. See "Will the EC Let Air France Spread its Wings?" *Business Week,* 29 January 1990.

3. See, for example, Peter Bellows, "1992—An American Banker's View," in IFR, *1992—The Single European Market* (London: IFR Books, 1988), 165–72.

4. See "The Alliance with Amro Bank," *Generale Bank Annual Report* (Brussels, 1988).

5. Mark Ivey, "Printemps Finds Tough Climbing in the Rockies," *Business Week,* 28 November 1988, 101–2.

6. See Business International Corporation, *Gaining a Competitive Edge in the New Europe: Strategic Responses of Non-European Companies to 1992* (New York: Business International Corporation, 1989), 41–46.

7. See, for example, Helmut Maucher, "Global Strategies at Nestlé," *European Management Journal* (Spring 1989): 92–96.

8. John Quelch and Robert Buzzell, "Marketing Moves through the EC Crossroads," *Sloan Management Review* (Fall 1989): 71.

9. See Eric Friberg, "1992: Moves Europeans Are Making," *Harvard Business Review* (May-June 1989): 88–89.

10. Larry White, "Federal Express: Managing Ahead for 1992 is Risky," *Business Month* (August 1989): 32–34.

11. Nan Stone, "The Globalization of Europe: An Interview with Wisse Dekker," *Harvard Business Review* (May-June 1989): 92.

12. Adam Smith, *An Inquiry into the Nature and Causes of the Wealth of Nations* (Chicago: University of Chicago Press, 1976) book 1, chapter 10, part 2, 144.

13. See Michael Bartholomew, "Lobbying Brussels in Anticipation of 1992," *Wall Street Journal,* 6 March 1989, A12.

14. See Philip Rezvin, "European Bureaucrats Are Writing the Rules Americans Will Live By," *Wall Street Journal,* 17 May 1989, 1.

15. See Philip Rezvin, "Fast Changing House of Europe Defies Single Blueprint," *Wall Street Journal,* 22 February 1990, A10.

16. See Henry Mintzberg, "Strategy Making in Three Modes," *California Management Review* (Winter 1973): 44–53.

17. See Gray Hamel and C. K. Prahalad, "Strategic Intent," *Harvard Business Review* (May-June 1989): 63–76, for a good discussion of strategy formulation in the modern corporation.

18. A nice summary of basic strategic considerations as they relate to 1992 can be found in James Dudley, *1992: Strategies for the Single Market* (London: Kogan Page, 1989).

19. See Business International Corporation, *Gaining a Competitive Edge in the New Europe,* 68.

20. Ibid., 64–66.

21. "How 3M Has Responded to 1992," *Management Europe,* 31 July 1989, 10–13.

22. Karen Jackson, "Deregulating Minds—A Response to the Challenge of 1992," *European Management Journal* (Spring 1989): 113–19.

23. See Richard Kirkland, Jr., "Europe's New Managers," *Fortune,* 29 September 1986, 58.

24. See "Look Out, World, Philips is on a War Footing," *Business Week,* 15 Jan-

uary 1990, 44–45; and Gerrit Jeelof, "Global Strategies of Philips," *European Management Journal* (Spring 1989): 84–91.

25. Robert Gogol and Jean-Claude Larreche, "The Battlefield for 1992: Product Strength and Geographic Coverage," *European Management Journal* (Summer 1989): 132–40.

26. For a discussion of alliances, see Business International Corporation, *Competitive Alliances* (New York: Business International Corporation, 1987).

27. See Tim Line, "The Acquisition Route to a European Presence," *European Management Journal* (Winter 1988): 359–66.

28. Hill Samuel Bank, Ltd., *Mergers, Acquisitions and Alternative Corporate Strategies* (London: W. H. Allen & Co., 1989), 137–39.

29. Barbara Toman, "Guinness Plans to Buy Stake on 16.8 Percent in Dior," *Wall Street Journal*, 7 April 1989, A6.

30. Hill Samuel Bank, Ltd., *Mergers, Acquisitions and Alternative Corporate Strategies*, 77–79.

31. "DRGs Double-Barreled Move into Europe," *M&A Europe* (March-April 1989): 76–77.

32. "Carnaud Wins Metal Box as Greenmail Arrives in London," *M&A Europe* (March-April 1989): 77–78.

33. See Stephen Quickel, "Target: Europe," *Business Month* (August 1989): 27.

34. Alan Freeman and G. Pierre Goad, "Bombardier to Buy Short Brothers PLC from British Government for $50 Million," *Wall Street Journal*, 8 June 1989, A16.

35. Hill Samuel Bank, Ltd., *Mergers, Acquisitions and Alternative Corporate Strategies*, 80–83.

36. As quoted in "Business in Europe Awards 1989," *Management Today* (May 1989): 79.

37. Lee Berton, "Peat Experience Shows Why Accountants Are Rushing to Merge," *Wall Street Journal*, 17 July 1989, A1.

38. "Akzo's Acquisition Policy," *Management Europe*, 8 May 1989, 7.

39. See Hill Samuel Banks, Ltd., "Routes for Expansion," *Mergers, Acquisitions and Alternative Corporate Strategies*, 67.

40. Hope Lampert, "Scott Paper: Managing to Local Tastes," *Business Month* (August 1989): 37–41.

41. See Business International Corporation, *Competitive Alliances* (New York: Business International Corporation, 1987), 61; and Business International Corporation, *Gaining a Competitive Edge in the New Europe*, 87–92.

42. Deborah Dine, "Global Markets Await," *Modern Healthcare*, 9 June 1989, 24.

43. "Honda/Rover-Strains in the System," *Management Europe*, 1 December 1989, 8–10.

44. Bradley Stertz and Stephen Moore, "GM to Purchase 50 Percent Saab Stake for $500 Million," *Wall Street Journal*, 18 December 1989, A3.

45. Richard Evans, "The Illusion of Recovery," *International Management* (May 1989): 29.

46. "Amper: How the Prospect of 1992 Provoked Global Reach," *Management Europe*, 8 May 1989, 2–3.

47. Nan Stone, "The Globalization of Europe: An Interview with Wisse Dekker," *Harvard Business Review* (May-June 1989): 94.

Chapter 7

1. Alain Minc, *La Grande Illusion* (Paris: Grasset, 1989).
2. Paul Taylor, *The Limits of European Integration* (New York: Columbia University Press, 1983), 300.

Bibliography

Abbati, C. 1986. *Transport and European Integration*. Luxembourg: Office of Official Publications of the European Communities.

Abegglen, J., and G. Stalk. 1985. *Kaisha: The Japanese Corporation*. New York: Basic Books.

Ackermann, C., and J. Harrop. 1985. "The Management of Technological Innovation in the Machine Tool Industry: A Cross-National Regional Survey of Britain and Switzerland." *R & D Management* 15, no. 3 (July).

Advokaterne Bredgade 3, et al. 1988. *Merger Control in the EEC*. Deventer, The Netherlands: Kluwer Law and Taxation Publishers.

Agnelli, G. 1989. "The Europe of 1992." *Foreign Affairs* 68, no. 4 (Fall).

Albert, M., and R. Ball. 1983. *Towards European Economic Recovery in the 1980s*. Report for the European Parliament. Brussels.

Aldcroft, D. 1978. *The European Economy 1914–1970*. London: Croom Helm.

Allen, H. 1979. *Norway and Europe in the 1970s*. London: Global Book Resources Ltd.

Arbuthnott, H., and G. Edwards. 1979. *A Common Man's Guide to the Common Market*. London: Macmillan.

Ardagh, J. 1982. *France in the 1980s*. Harmondsworth, England: Penguin.

Armstrong, H., and J. Taylor. 1986. "An Evaluation of Current Regional Policy." *Economic Review* 4, no. 2 (November).

Arthur Andersen & Co. 1989. *European Capital Markets: A Strategic Forecast*. London: The Economist Publications.

Balassa, F. 1967. "Trade Creation and Trade Diversion in the European Common Market." *Economic Journal* 77 (March).

———. 1975. *European Economic Integration*. Amsterdam: North-Holland.

Baldwin, R. 1989. "On the Growth Effect of 1992." Working paper no. 3119. Cambridge, Mass.: National Bureau of Economic Research.

Baldwin, R., C. Hamilton, and A. Sapir, eds. 1988. *Issues in US–EC Trade Relations*. Chicago: University of Chicago Press.

Bank of Japan. 1988. *Comparative International Statistics*. Tokyo: Bank of Japan.

Barber, J., and B. Reed, eds. 1973. *European Community: Vision and Reality*. London: Croom Helm.

Barclays Bank. 1985. "Comecon." *Barclays Bank Review* (August).

Bartholomew, M. 1989. "Lobbying Brussels in Anticipation of 1992." *Wall Street Journal*, 6 March.

Bayliss, B. 1985. "Competition and Industrial Policy." In *The Economics of the European Community,* edited by A. El-Agraa. Oxford: Philip Allan.

Bellows, P. 1988. "1992—An American Banker's View." In IFR, *1992—The Single European Market,* London: IFR Books.

Berton, L. 1989. "Peat Experience Shows Why Accountants Are Rushing to Merge." *Wall Street Journal,* 17 July.

Berwin, S.J. 1989. *Company Law and Competition.* London: Mercury Books.

Berwin, C., and R. MacAllister. 1986. "Annual Review of the Activities of the European Communities in 1986." *Journal of Common Market Studies* 25, no. 4 (June).

Bierce, Ambrose. 1957. *The Devil's Dictionary.* New York: Sagamore Press.

Blackwell, M. 1985. "Lomé III: The Search for Greater Effectiveness." *Finance and Development* 22, no. 3 (September).

Booz Allen and Hamilton Inc. 1986. "Europe's Fragmented Markets—A Survey of European Chief Executives." *The European Wall Street Journal.*

Bourguignon-Wittke, R., E. Grabitz, O. Schmuck, S. Steppat, and W. Wessels. 1985. "Five Years of the Directly Elected European Parliament: Performance and Prospects." *Journal of Common Market Studies,* 24, no. 1 (September).

Bracewell-Milnes, B. 1976. *Economic Integration in East and West.* London: Croom-Helm.

Bhaskir, K. 1984. *Car Pricing in Europe.* Norwich, England: Motor Industry Research Institute, University of East Anglia.

BIPE avec ses partenaires d'Euroconstruct. 1988. *Le «Cout de la Non-Europe» des produits de construction.* Luxembourg: Office of Official Publications of the European Communities.

Brown, A. 1985. "The General Budget." In *The Economics of the European Community,* edited by A. El-Agraa. Oxford: Philip Allan.

Brown, F., and J. Whalley. 1980. "General Equilibrium Evaluations of Tariff-Cutting Proposals in the Tokyo Round and Comparisons to More Extensive Liberalization of World Trade." *Economic Journal* 90, no. 360 (December).

Buchanan, J., and G. Tullock. 1962. *The Calculus of Consent.* Ann Arbor: University of Michigan Press.

Buchanon, D. 1988. "The Quest for Tax Harmony," *Financial Times,* 22 August.

Buckwell, A., D. Harvey, K. Thomson, and K. Parton. 1982. *The Costs of the Common Agricultural Policy.* London: Croom Helm.

Budd, S. 1987. *The EEC: A Guide to the Maze.* London: Kogan Page.

Business Week. 1990a. "Look Out, World, Philips is on a War Footing." 15 January.

———. 1990b. "Will the EC Let Air France Spread Its Wings?" 29 January.

Butler, M. 1986. *Europe: More than a Continent.* London: Heinemann.

Butt Phillip, A. 1983. "Industrial and Competition Policies: A New Look." In *Britain within the European Community: The Way Forward,* edited by A. El-Agraa. London: Macmillan.

Cairncross, A., et al., eds. 1974. *Economic Policy for the European Community: The Way Forward.* London: Macmillan.

Calingaert, M. 1988. *The 1992 Challenge from Europe: Development of the European Community's Internal Market.* Washington: National Planning Association.

Capotorti, F., H. Meinhard, F. Jacobs, and J-P Jacques. 1986. *The European Union Treaty.* Oxford: Clarendon Press.

Capstick, M. 1970. *The Economics of Agriculture.* London: Allen and Unwin.

Carrington, T., and M. Nelson. 1989. "For Monetary Union in Europe, Question Is When, Not Whether." *Wall Street Journal,* date unknown.

Castles, S., and G. Kosack. 1973. *Immigrant Workers and Class Structure in Western Europe.* London: Oxford University Press.

Cecchini, P. 1988. *1992: The European Challenge.* Brookfield, Vt.: Wildwood House, Gower.

Cecco, M. de, ed. 1983. *International Economic Adjustment: Small Countries and the European Monetary System.* New York: St. Martin's Press.

Cecco, M. de, and A. Giovannini, eds. 1989. *A European Central Bank? Perspectives on Monetary Unification After Ten Years of the EMS.* Cambridge: Cambridge University Press.

Central Intelligence Agency. 1988. *Handbook of Economic Statistics.* Washington, D.C.; see also other issues.

Chalkley, M. 1986. "Selling Mountains and Lakes." *The Economic Review* 4, no. 2 (November).

Coffey, P. 1975. "The Lomé Agreement and the EEC: Implications and Problems." *The Three Banks Review,* no. 108 (December).

———. 1976. *The External Relations of the EEC.* London: Macmillan.

———. 1977. *Europe and Money.* London: Macmillan.

———. 1979. *Economic Policies of the Common Market.* London: Macmillan.

Coffey, P., ed. 1983. *Main Economic Policy Areas of the EEC.* The Hague: Martinus Nijhoff.

Coffey, P., and J. Presley. 1971. *European Monetary Integration.* London: Macmillan.

Cohen, C., ed. 1983. *The Common Market—Ten Years After.* Oxford: Philip Allan.

Collins, C. 1985. "Social Policy." In *The Economics of the European Community,* edited by A. El-Agraa. Oxford: Philip Allan.

Commission of the European Communities. 1969. *Commission Memorandum to the Council on the Coordination of Economic Policies and Monetary Cooperation within the Community.* Brussels, 12 February.

———. 1984. *Working for Europe.* Luxembourg.

———. 1985. *Completing the Internal Market: White Paper from the Commission to the European Council.* Luxembourg.

———. 1986. *The Agricultural Situation in the Community.* Brussels.

———. 1987a. *Bulletin,* nos. 1, 2, and 3, Vol. 20, Brussels.

———. 1987b. *Report by the Commission to the Council and Parliament on the Financing of the Budget.* COM(87) 101 Final 1/2, Brussels.

———. 1987c. *Commission Communication on Budgetary Discipline.* COM(87) 430 Final, Brussels.

———. 1987d. *Reform of the Structural Funds.* COM(87) 376 Final, Brussels.

———. 1987e. *Making a Success of the Single Act.* February. Brussels.

———. 1987f. *A New Frontier for Europe.* COM(87) 100 Final, Brussels.

———. 1987g. *Own Resources Decision.* COM(87) 420 Final, Brussels.

———. 1987h. *Review of Action Taken to Control the Agricultural Markets and Outlook for the Agricultural Policy.* COM(87) 410 Final, Brussels.

———. 1987i. *Research and Technological Development in the Less Favoured Regions of the Community.* Final Report. Brussels.

———. 1988a. *Basic Studies: Executive Summaries.* Brussels/Luxembourg.

———. 1988b. *Eurobarometer: Public Opinion in the European Community,* no. 30 (December), Brussels: Directorate-General Information, Communication, Culture, Surveys, Research, Analyses; see also other issues.

———. 1988c. *Social Dimension of the Internal Market.* SEC (88) 1148 Final, Brussels.

———. 1988d. *Studies on the Economics of Integration.* Brussels/Luxembourg.

———. 1988e. *Twenty-Second General Report on the Activities of the European Communities (1988).* Brussels/Luxembourg; also earlier reports.

———. 1989a. *European Economy.* Brussels: Directorate-General for Economic and Financial Affairs; see also other issues.

———. 1989c. *Green Paper on the Development of the Common Market for Telecommunication Services and Equipment.* Brussels: Directorate-General Telecommunications, Information Industries and Innovation.

———. 1989d. *Takeovers and Other General Bids: Proposals for a Thirteenth Company Law Directive.* Bulletin of the European Communities, supplement 3/89. Luxembourg: Office for Official Publications of the European Communities.

———. 1990. *Fifth Progress Report of the Commission to the Council and the European Parliament Concerning the Implementation of the Commission's White Paper on the Completion of the Internal Market.* Brussels/Luxembourg.

Computer and Business Equipment Manufacturers Association. 1989. *The Information Technology Industry Data Book, 1960–1998.* Washington, D.C.: Computer and Business Equipment Manufacturers Association.

Cook, C., and J. Paxton. 1986. *European Political Facts, 1918–84.* New York: Facts on File Publications.

Coombes, D. 1970. *Politics and Bureaucracy in the European Community.* London: Allen and Unwin.

Cooper, C., and B. Massel. 1965. "A New Look at Customs Union Theory." *Economic Journal* 75.

Cosgrave, C. 1969. "The EEC and Developing Countries." In *Economic Integration in Europe,* edited by G. Denton. London: Weidenfeld and Nicholson.

Cosgrave-Twitchett, C. 1981. *A Framework for Development?: The EEC and the ACP.* London: Allen and Unwin.

Daltrop, A. 1982. *Politics and the European Community.* London: Longman.

Darden, S. 1986. "EEC Membership and the United Kingdom's Trade in Manufactured Goods." *National Westminster Bank Quarterly Review* (February).

Deardorff, A., and R. Stern. 1979. "An Economic Analysis of the Effects of the Tokyo Round of MLN on the U.S. and Other Industrialized Countries." United States Senate.

De Jong, H., ed. 1981. *The Structure of European Industry*. The Hague: Martinus Nijhoff.

Deloitte, Haskins & Sells. 1989. *Deloitte's 1992 Guide*. London: Butterworths.

Delors, J. 1988. "1992: The Social Dimension." Speech to the Trades Union Congress, 8 September.

Dennis, G. 1985. "The European Monetary System." In *The Economics of the European Community*, edited by A. El-Agraa. Oxford: Philip Allan.

Denton, G., M. Forsyth, and M. Maclennan. 1968. *Economic Planning and Policies in Britain, France and Germany*. London: Allen and Unwin.

Denton, G., ed. 1969. *Economic Integration in Europe*. London: Weidenfeld and Nicholson.

———. 1974. *Economic and Monetary Union in Europe*. London: Croom Helm.

———. 1984. "Restructuring the European Community Budget." *Journal of Common Market Studies* 23, no. 2 (December).

Derthick, M., and P. Quirk. 1985. *The Politics of Deregulation*. Washington: Brookings Institution.

Dine, D. 1989. "Global Markets Await." *Modern Healthcare*, 9 June.

Dinkelspiel, U. 1987. "Eureka: Co-operation in High Technology." *EFTA Bulletin* 27, no. 1 (January-March).

Directorate-General Economic and Financial Affairs. *The EMS: Ten Years of Progress in European Monetary Co-operation*. Brussels.

Dosser, D., D. Gowland, and K. Hartley, eds. 1982. *The Collaboration of Nations*. Oxford: Martin Robertson.

Drenowski, J., ed. 1982. *Crisis in the Eastern European Economy*. London: Croom Helm.

Duchêne, F., E. Szczepanik, and W. Legg. 1985. *New Limits on Agriculture*. London: Croom Helm.

Dudley, J. 1989. *1992: Strategies for the Single Market*. London: Kogan Page.

Economic Commission for Europe. 1987. *The Telecommunications Industry: Growth and Structural Change*. New York: United Nations.

The Economist. 1987. "Factory of the Future." 30 May.

———. 1988. "The Smug Debtor." 3 September.

———. 1989. "Straighten Europe's Snake." 3 June.

———. 1990. "Plotting Monetary Union." 19 May.

Economists Advisory Group, Ltd. 1988. *The "Cost of Non-Europe" in the Pharmaceutical Industry*. Luxembourg: Office of Official Publications of the European Communities.

Electronics Industries Association. 1989. *Electronic Market Data Book*. Washington: Electronics Industries Association.

Einzig, P. 1971. *The Case Against Joining the Common Market*. London: Macmillan.

Electronics International Corporation. 1988. *Electronics in the World*. New York.

El-Agraa, A., ed. 1983. *Britain within the European Community: The Way Forward*, London: Macmillan.

———. 1985. *The Economics of the European Community*, 2nd ed. Oxford: Philip Allan.

Ernst & Whinney. 1988. *The "Cost of Non-Europe": Border Related Controls and Administrative Formalities/An Illustration in the Road Haulage Sector.* Luxembourg: Office of Official Publications of the European Communities.

Euromoney. 1988. *1992: Towards a Single Market,* Euromoney and Corporate Finance (Suppl.), September.

European Community. 1986. *The Court of Justice of the European Community,* 4th ed. Luxembourg: Office of Official Publications of the European Communities.

———. 1987. *Steps to European Unity,* 6th ed. Luxembourg: Office of Official Publications of the European Communities.

European Council. 1986. *Single European Act.* Luxembourg: Office of Official Publications of the European Communities.

European Investment Bank. 1986. *Annual Report.* Luxembourg.

European Parliament. 1978. *Powers of the European Parliament.* London.

European Research Associates & Prognos. 1988. *The "Cost of Non-Europe": Obstacles to Transborder Activity.* Luxembourg: Office of Official Publications of the European Communities.

Eurostat. 1988. *Basic Statistics of the Community.* Brussels: Commission of the European Communities; see also other issues.

Evans, D., ed. 1973. *Britain in the EC.* London: Gollancz.

Evans, R. 1989. "The Illusion of Recovery." *International Management* (May).

Fennell, R. 1985. "A Re-consideration of the Objectives of the Common Agricultural Policy." *Journal of Common Market Studies* 23, no. 3 (March).

———. 1979 and 1988. *The Common Agricultural Policy of the Community.* London: Granada.

Financial Times. 1988. "Ploughing a Furrow to 1992." 6 June.

———. 1989. "The Social Dimension." 1 June.

Freeman, A., and G. Pierre Goad. 1989. "Bombardier to Buy Short Brothers PLC from British Government for $50 Million." *Wall Street Journal,* 8 June.

Friberg, E. 1989. "1992: Moves Europeans are Making." *Harvard Business Review* (May-June).

Gebert, P. 1987. "In Search of Political Union: The Fouchet Negotiations (1960–62)." In *The Dynamics of European Union,* edited by R. Pryce, New York: Croom Helm.

Generale Bank. *Annual Report.* Brussels.

George, K., and C. Joll. 1975. *Competition in the United Kingdom and the European Economic Community.* Cambridge: Cambridge University Press.

George, K., and T. Ward. 1975. "The Structure of Industry in the EEC." Occasional paper, Cambridge University: Cambridge, England.

George, K., and C. Joll. 1978. "EEC Competition Policy." *The Three Banks Review* (March).

George, S. 1985. *Politics and Policy in the European Community.* Oxford: Clarendon.

———. 1987. *The British Government and the European Community Since 1984.* University Association for Contemporary European Studies No. 4.

Glaesner, Hans-Joachim. 1987. "The Single European Act: Attempt at an Appraisal." *Fordham International Law Journal* (Spring).

Glage, W. 1989. "The High Cost of Dismissals and Layoffs in Europe." *The Journal of European Business* (September/October).

Gogol, R., and J. Larreche. 1989. "The Battlefield for 1992: Product Strength and Geographic Coverage." *European Management Journal* 7 (Summer).

Greenway, D. 1987. "Intra-industry Trade, Intra-firm Trade and European Integration." *Journal of Common Market Studies* 26, no. 2 (December).

Greenwich Associates. 1988. *Europe 1992: Less Change Than Anticipated.* Greenwich, Conn.

Groeben, H. von der. 1985. *The European Community: The Formative Years.* European Commission, Brussels/Luxembourg.

Group MAC. 1988. *The "Cost of Non-Europe" in the Foodstuffs Industry,* 2 vols. Luxembourg: Office of Official Publications of the European Communities.

The Guardian. 1977. October 20.

Hamel, G., and C.K. Prahalad. 1989. "Strategic Intent." *Harvard Business Review* (May-June).

Han, S., and H. Liesner. 1970. "Britain and the Common Market." Cambridge occasional paper no. 27.

Harrison, G. 1988. "The European Communities 1992 Plan: An Overview of the Proposed 'Single Market.'" Congressional Research Service, Washington.

Harrop, J. 1973. "The Rise and Fall of EFTA." *The Bankers' Magazine* (March).

———. 1978a. "The European Investment Bank." *National Westminster Bank Quarterly Review* (May).

———. 1978b. "An Evaluation of the European Investment Bank." *23A Société Universitaire Européene de Recherches Financières.* Tilburg, Netherlands.

———. 1978c. "Convergence in Europe." In *Workbook on Testing Ten Economies,* edited by R. Wilson. Sutton, England: Economics Association.

———. 1985. "Crisis in the Machine Tool Industry: A Policy Dilemma for the European Community." *Journal of Common Market Studies* 24, no. 1 (September).

———. 1989. *The Political Economy of Integration in the European Community.* Brookfield, England: Gower.

Hartley, K. 1982. "Defence and Advanced Technology." In *The Collaboration of Nations,* edited by D. Dosser, D. Gowland and K. Hartley. Oxford: Martin Robertson.

Hawawani, G. 1984. *European Equity Markets: Price Behavior and Efficiency.* New York, NY: Salomon Brothers Center for the Study of Financial Institutions.

Healey, N. 1988. "The Case for Britain Joining the EMS," *Economic Affairs* (February/March).

Heertje, A., ed. 1983. *Investing in Europe's Future.* Oxford: Blackwell.

Heller, R., and N. Willat. 1975. *The European Revenge: How the American Challenge was Rebuffed.* London: Barrie and Jenkins.

Hellman, R. 1979. *Gold, the Dollar, and the European Currency Systems: The Seven Year Monetary War,* translated by M. Freidberg. New York: Praeger.

Henderson, D. 1989. "1992: The External Dimension." Occasional papers, no. 25. London: Group of Thirty.

Henderson, P. 1977. "Two British Errors: Their Probable Size and Some Possible Lessons." *Oxford Economic Papers,* no. 2 (July).

Henig, S. 1980. *Power and Decision in Europe.* London: Europotentials Press.

Heseltine, M. 1989. *The Challenge of Europe: Can Britain Win?* London: Weidenfeld & Nicholson.

Hewitt, A. 1984. "The Lomé Conventions: Entering a Second Decade." *Journal of Common Market Studies* 23, no. 2 (December).

Hewstone, M. 1986. *Understanding Attitudes to the European Community.* Cambridge: Cambridge University Press.

Hill, B. 1984. *The Common Agricultural Policy: Past, Present and Future.* London: Methuen.

Hill Samuel Bank, Ltd. 1989. *Mergers, Acquisitions and Alternative Corporate Strategies.* London: Mercury Books.

Hindley, B. 1989. *Europe: Fortress or Freedom?,* Occasional paper, no. 2. The Bruges Group, London.

Hine, R. C. 1985. *The Political Economy of European Trade.* Brighton, England: Wheatsheaf.

Her Majesty's Stationery Office. 1971. White Paper, *The United Kingdom and the European Communities,* Cmnd 4715, London.

———. 1978. Green Paper, *The European Monetary System,* Cmnd 7405, November, London.

———. 1987. Central Statistical Office, Pink Book, *United Kingdom Balance of Payments,* London.

Hodges, M., ed. 1972. *European Integration.* Harmondsworth, England: Penguin.

Hoffman, G., ed. 1983. *A Geography of Europe,* 5th ed. New York: John Wiley.

Hoffman, S. 1989. "The European Community and 1992." *Foreign Affairs* 68, no. 4 (Fall).

Holland, S., ed. 1972. *The State as Entrepreneur.* London: Weidenfeld and Nicholson.

Holland, S. 1976a. *Capital Versus the Regions.* London: Macmillan.

———. 1976b. *The Regional Problem.* London: Macmillan.

———. 1980. *Uncommon Market: Capital, Class and Power in the European Community.* London: Macmillan.

Holmes, P. 1983. "The EEC and British Trade." In *The Common Market: Ten Years After,* edited by C. Cohen. Oxford: Philip Allan.

Holmes, M. 1989. *Britain and the EMS?* Occasional paper, no. 3. The Bruges Group, London.

Holt, S. 1967. *The Common Market.* London: Hamish Hamilton.

Honore, T., and J. Raz. 1988. *The Foundations of European Community Law,* 2d ed. Oxford: Clarendon Press.

House of Lords. 1983. Select Committee on the European Communities. *European Monetary System,* fifth report.

Hu, Yao-Su. 1981. *Europe Under Stress.* London: Butterworths.

Hudson, R. 1988. "Europeans Are Learning that Pollution Must Be Attacked in a Coordinated Way." *Wall Street Journal,* 1 November.

Hutchinson, P. 1929. *The United States of Europe.* Chicago: Willett, Clark & Colby.

Ilgen, T. 1985. *Autonomy and Interdependence: U.S.–Western European Monetary and Trade Relations, 1958–1984.* Totowa, N.J.: Rowman & Allenheld.

Institut für Wirtschaftsforschung—Prometeia Calcolo SRL 1988. *The "Cost of Non-Europe" in the Textile-Clothing Industry.* Luxembourg: Office of Official Publications of the European Communities.

IFR. 1988. *1992—The Single European Market.* London: IFR Publishing.

International Herald Tribune. 1988. "Britain Rejects EC Plan for Economic Union," 18 April.

International Monetary Fund. 1983. *The European Monetary System: The Experience, 1979–82.* Occasional paper, no. 19. International Monetary Fund, Washington.

———. 1988a. *International Financial Statistics Yearbook.* Washington: International Monetary Fund; see also other issues.

———. 1988b. *Policy Coordination in the European Monetary System.* Occasional paper, no. 61. International Monetary Fund, Washington.

Ionescu, G., ed. 1979. *The European Alternatives.* Alphen aan den Rijn, The Netherlands: Sijthoff and Noordhoff.

Ivey, M. 1988. "Printemps Finds Tough Climbing in the Rockies." *Business Week,* 28 November.

Jackson, K. 1989. "Deregulating Minds—A Response to the Challenge of 1992." *European Management Journal* (Spring).

Jacquemin, A. 1974. "Size, Structure and Performance of the Largest European Firms." *The Three Banks Review* (June).

Jacquemin, A., and H. De Jong. 1977. *European Industrial Organization.* London: Macmillan.

Jay, D. 1968. *After the Common Market.* Harmondsworth, England: Penguin.

Jeelof, G. 1989. "Global Strategies of Philips." *European Management Journal* 7 (Spring).

Jenkins, R. 1978. "European Monetary Union." *Lloyds Bank Economic Bulletin,* no. 41 (May).

Jenkins, R., ed. 1983. *Britain and the EEC.* London: Macmillan.

Johnson, C. 1982. "The Fall in Farm Prices." *Lloyds Bank Economic Bulletin,* no. 41 (May).

———. 1987. "How Well Are We Doing?" *Lloyds Bank Economic Bulletin,* no. 100 (April).

Johnson, H. 1973. "An Economic Theory of Protectionism, Tariff Bargaining and the Formation of Customs Unions." In *The Economics of Integration,* edited by M. Krauss. London: Allen and Unwin.

Jones, A. 1979. "The Theory of Economic Integration." In *Inflation, Development and Integration: Essays in Honour of A. J. Brown,* edited by J. Bowers. Leeds: Leeds University Press.

―――. 1985. "The Theory of Economic Integration." In *The Economics of the European Community,* edited by A. El-Agraa. Oxford: Philip Allan.

Josling, T. 1984. "U.S. and EC Farm Policies: An Eclectic Comparison." In *Price and Market Policies in European Agriculture,* edited by K. Thomson and R. Warren. Department of Agricultural Economics, University of Newcastle-upon-Tyne.

Josling, T. 1986. "Agricultural Policies and World Trade." In *Europe, America and the World Economy,* edited by L. Tsoukalis. Oxford: Basil Blackwell for the College of Europe.

Josling, T., and J. Harris. 1976. "Europe's Green Money." *The Three Banks Review* (March).

Kaldor, N. 1971. "The Truth about the Dynamic Effects." *New Statesman,* 12 March.

Kang, T. 1989. *Is Korea the Next Japan?* New York: Free Press.

Kaufmann, H. 1985. *Germany's International Monetary Policy and the European Monetary System.* New York: Columbia University Press.

Kay, J. 1988. "Europe without Fiscal Frontiers: An Assessment." *European Management Journal* 6 (Winter).

Keating, M., and B. Jones. 1985. *Regions in the Community.* Oxford: Clarendon.

Kenen, P. 1969. "The Theory of Optimum/Currency Areas: An Eclectic View." In *Monetary Problems of the International Economy,* edited by R. Murdell and A. Swoboda. Chicago: University of Chicago Press.

Kennedy, P. 1989. *The Rise and Fall of the Great Powers.* New York: Vintage Books.

Kerr, A. 1980. *The Common Market and How It Works.* Oxford: Pergamon Press.

King, K. 1982. *U.S. Monetary Policy and European Responses in the 1980s.* London: Routledge & Kegan Paul.

Kirkland, R., Jr. 1986. "Europe's New Managers." *Fortune,* 29 September.

Klassen, L., and W. Molle. 1983. *Industrial Mobility and Migration in the European Community.* Aldershot, England: Gower.

Kotkin, J., and S. Baer-Sinnott. 1989. "Hotspots." *Inc.* 11, no. 3 (March).

Krauss, M., ed. 1973. *The Economics of Integrations.* London: Allen and Unwin.

Kreinin, M. 1974. *Trade Relations of the EEC.* London: Praeger.

Kruse, D. 1980. *Monetary Integration in Western Europe: EMU, EMS, and Beyond.* London: Butterworths.

Labich, K. 1989. "The Best Cities for Business." *Fortune,* 23 October.

Laguette, S-P. 1987. *Lawyers in the European Community.* Luxembourg: Office of Official Publications of the European Communities.

Langeheine, B., and U. Weinstock. 1985. "Graduated Integration: A Modest Path Towards Progress." *Journal of Common Market Studies* 23, no. 3 (March).

Lasok, D., and J. Bridge. 1987. *Law and Institutions of the European Communities*, 4th ed. London: Butterworths.

Lawrence, R., and C. Shultze, eds. 1987. *Barriers to European Growth: A Transatlantic View*. Washington: Brookings Institution.

Lawson, D. 1990. "Saying the Unsayable about the Germans." *The Spectator,* 14 July.

Layton, C. 1969. *European Advanced Technology*. London: Allen and Unwin.

Lee, R., and P. Ogden. 1976. *Economy and Society in the EEC*. Farnborough, England: Saxon House.

Leigh, M., and N. van Pragg. 1978. *The Mediterranean Challenge*. Sussex European Research paper, no. 2. University of Sussex, Sussex, England.

Leonard, D. 1988. *Pocket Guide to the European Community*. London: The Economist Publications.

Lewenhak, S. 1982. *The Role of the European Investment Bank*. London: Heinemann.

Line, T. 1988. "The Acquisition Route to a European Presence." *European Management Journal* (Winter).

Lombard Odier Group. 1989. *Project Europe: New Land of Opportunity*. Geneva: Lombard Odier Group.

Lodge, J., and V. Herman. 1978. *The European Parliament and the European Community*. London: Macmillan.

Lodge, J. 1983. *Institutions and Policies of the European Community*. London: Frances Pinter.

Lodge, J., ed. 1986. *European Union: The European Community in Search of a Future*. London: Macmillan.

The London Times. 1989. "No Sign of Softening on Delors Stance," 24 November.

Long, F., ed. 1980. *The Political Economy of EEC Relations with Africa, Caribbean and Pacific States*. Oxford: Pergamon.

Ludlow, P. 1982. *The Making of the European Monetary System*. London: Butterworths.

Ludvigsen Associates, Ltd. 1988. *The EC92 Automobile Sector*. Luxembourg: Office of Official Publications of the European Communities.

Lundgren, N. 1969. "Customs Unions of Industrialised West European Countries." In *Economic Integration in Europe*, edited by G. Denton. London: Weidenfeld and Nicholson.

M&A Europe. 1989a. "DRGs Double-Barreled Move into Europe." (March-April).

———. 1989b. "Carnaud Wins Metal Box as Greenmail Arrives in London." (March-April).

Mackel, C. 1978. "Green Money and the Common Agricultural Policy." *National Westminster Bank Quarterly Review* (February).

Maclennan, R. 1978. "Food Prices and the Common Agricultural Policy." *The Three Banks Review* (September).

Macsween, I. 1987. "The Common Fisheries Policy." *The Royal Bank of Scotland Review,* no. 154 (June).

Magee, S. 1972. "The Welfare Effects of Restrictions on U.S. Trade." *Brookings Papers on Economic Activity,* no. 3.

Magnifico, G. 1973. *European Monetary Unification.* London: Macmillan.

Mahotiére, S. de la. 1970. *Towards One Europe.* Harmondsworth, England: Penguin.

Malcolm, N. 1989a. "Europe's Unholy Godfathers." *The Spectator,* 23 September.

———. 1989b. "Mr. Kinnock Takes a Walk on the Supply Side." *The Spectator,* 7 October.

Management Europe. 1989a. "Akzo's Acquisition Policy." 8 May.

———. 1989b. "Amper: How the Prospect of 1992 Provoked Global Reach," 8 May.

———. 1989c. "How 3M Has Responded to 1992," 31 July.

———. 1989d. "Honda/Rover-Strains in the System," 1 December.

Management Today. "Business in Europe Awards 1989," May.

Marques-Mendes, A. 1987. *Economic Integration and Growth in Europe.* London: Croom Helm.

Marsh, J., and P. Swanney. 1980. *Agriculture and the European Community.* London: Allen and Unwin.

Masera, R., and R. Triffin, eds. 1984. *Europe's Money: Problems of European Monetary Co-ordination and Integration.* Oxford: Clarendon Press.

Mathijsen, P. 1985. *A Guide to European Community Law.* London: Sweet and Maxwell.

Maucher, H. 1989. "Global Strategies at Nestlé." *European Management Journal* 7 (Spring).

Mayne, R., ed. 1972. *Europe Tomorrow.* London: Fontana/Collins.

McGee, J. 1989. "1992: Moves Americans Must Make." *Harvard Business Review* (May/June).

McKinnon, R. 1963. "Optimum Currency Areas." *American Economic Review,* no. 53.

McQueen, M. 1977. *Britain, The EEC and the Developing World.* London: Heinemann.

Midland Bank. 1977. "European Monetary Union." *Midland Bank Review* (Winter).

———. 1986. "On Joining the EMS." *Midland Bank Review* (Winter).

———. 1987. "Setting Priorities for Science and Technology." *Midland Bank Review* (Winter).

Minc, A. 1989. *La Grande Illusion.* Paris: Grasset.

Minogue, K. 1989. "Europe's Passion for Cooperation." *Wall Street Journal,* 8 May.

Mintzberg, H. 1973. "Strategy Making in Three Modes." *California Management Review* 16 (Winter).

Morgan, A. 1980. "The Balance of Payments and British Membership of the EEC." In *Britain in Europe,* edited by W. Wallace. London: Heinemann.

———. 1984. "Protectionism and European Trade in Manufactures." *National Institute Economic Review,* no. 109 (August).

Morrison, C. 1989. *1992: The Leading Issues for European Companies.* Washington: The Conference Board.

Moussis, N. 1982. *Les Politiques de la Communauté Economique Européene.* Paris: Dalloz.

Mueller, J. 1988. *The Benefits of Completing the Internal Market for Telecommunications Equipment/Service in the Community.* Luxembourg: Office of Official Publications of the European Communities.

Mundell, R. 1961. "A Theory of Optimum Currency Areas." *American Economic Review,* no. 51.

Myrdal, G. 1957. *Economic Theory and Underdeveloped Regions.* London: Duckworth.

National Institute of Economic and Social Research. 1983. "The European Monetary System." *National Institute Economic Review* (February).

Nau, H. 1989. *Domestic Trade Policies and the Uruguay Round.* New York: Columbia University Press.

Nelson, M. 1989. "EC to Proceed with Work on Plan for Monetary Union." *Wall Street Journal,* 18 April.

Nerb, G. 1988. *The Completion of the Internal Market: A Survey of European Industry's Perception of the Likely Effects.* Luxembourg: Office of Official Publications of the European Communities.

Nicholson, F., and E. East. 1987. *From the Six to the Twelve: The Enlargement of the European Communities.* Harlow, England: Longman.

Nicoll, W. 1984. "The Luxembourg Compromise." *Journal of Common Market Studies* 23, no. 1 (September).

Noel, Emile. 1988. *Working Together: The Institutions of the European Community.* Luxembourg: Office of Official Publications of the European Communities.

Noll, R., and B. Owen. 1983. *The Political Economy of Deregulation.* Washington: American Enterprise Institute.

Noort, P. van den. 1983. "Agricultural Policy." In *Main Economic Policy Areas of the EEC,* edited by P. Coffey. The Hague: Martinus Nijhoff.

Oberreit, W. 1989. *1992: The Changing Legal Landscape for Doing Business in Europe.* New York: Practicing Law Institute.

Organization for Economic Cooperation and Development. 1989. *STI Review.* (April).

Ohmae, K. 1985. *Traid Power.* New York: Free Press.

Olson, M. 1971. *The Logic of Collective Action.* Cambridge: Harvard University Press.

———. 1982. *The Rise and Decline of Nations.* New Haven: Yale University Press.

———. 1987. "Economic Nationalism and Economic Progress." *The World Economy* 10, no. 3 (September): 241–64.

Open University. 1973. *The European Economic Community: History and Institutions, National and International Impact.* London: Open University Press.

Owen, N. 1983. *Economies of Scale, Competitiveness and Trade Patterns within the European Community*. Oxford: Oxford University Press.

Padoa-Schioppa, T. 1984. *Money, Economic Policy and Europe*. The European Perspective Series. European Commission, Brussels.

Palmer, M., and J. Lambert. 1968. *European Unity: A Survey of the European Organizations*. London: Allen and Unwin.

Parr, M., and J. Day. 1977. "Value Added Tax in the United Kingdom." *National Westminster Bank Quarterly Review* (May).

Pearce, J. 1981. *The Common Agricultural Policy*. Chathan House Paper, No. 13. London: Routledge and Kegan Paul.

Pearce, J., and J. Suttons. 1986. *Protection and Industrial Policy in Europe*. London: Routledge and Kegan Paul.

Peat-Marwick McLintock. 1988. *The "Cost of Non-Europe" for Business Services*. Luxembourg: Office of Official Publications of the European Communities.

Pelkmans, J. 1988. *The Internal Markets of North America: Fragmentation and Integration in the US and Canada*. Luxembourg: Office of Official Publications of the European Communities.

Pelkmans, J., and A. Winters. 1988. *Europe's Domestic Market*. Chatham House Paper, No. 43. The Royal Institute of International Affairs. London: Routledge.

Peltzman, S. 1976. "Toward a More General Theory of Regulation." *Journal of Law and Economics* (Spring).

Petith, H. 1977. "European Integration and the Terms of Trade." *Economic Journal* 87.

Pfaff, W. "Trade Bouts: Japan vs. Europe Is the Main Event." *International Herald Tribune* (date unknown).

Philip, A. 1988. "Management and 1992—Illusions and Reality." *European Management Journal* 6 (Winter).

Pinder, D. 1986. "Small Firms, Regional Development and the European Investment Bank." *Journal of Common Market Studies* 24, no. 3 (March).

———. 1987. "Is the Single European Act a Step Towards a Federal Europe?" *The Journal of Policy Studies* 7, part 4 (April).

Pöhl, K. O. 1989. "A Vision of a European Central Bank." *Wall Street Journal*, 15 July.

———. 1990. "Herr Pöhl Reviews Current Progress Towards European Monetary Union." *BIS Review*, 8 January.

Pollard, S. 1974. *European Economic Integration 1815–1970*. London: Thames and Hudson.

Pomfret, R. 1986. *Mediterranean Policy of the European Community*. London: Macmillan.

Postan, M. 1976. *An Economic History of Western Europe 1945–1964*. London: Methuen.

Posner, R. 1971. "Taxation by Regulation." *Bell Journal of Economics* (Spring).

Presley, J., and P. Coffey. 1974. *European Monetary Integration*. London: Macmillan.

Presley, J., and C. Dennis. 1976. *Currency Areas: Theory and Practice*. London: Macmillan.

Prest, A. 1983. "Fiscal Policy." In *Main Policy Areas of the EEC*, edited by P. Coffey. The Hague: Martinus Nijhoff.

Prestowitz, C., Jr. 1988. *Trading Places*. New York: Basic Books.

Price, V. 1988. *1992: Europe's Last Chance?* London: Institute of Economic Affairs.

Price Waterhouse. 1988. *The "Cost of Non-Europe" in Financial Services*. Luxembourg: Office of Official Publications of the European Communities.

Pridham, G. 1986. "European Elections, Political Parties and Trends of Internalization in Community Affairs." *Journal of Common Market Studies* 24, no. 4 (June).

Priebe, H. 1980. "German Agricultural Policy and the European Community." In *West Germany: A European and Global Power*, edited by W. Kohl and B. Basevi. Lexington, Mass.: D.C. Heath.

Pryce, R., ed. 1987. *The Dynamics of European Union*. London: Croom Helm.

Quelch, J., R. Buzzell, and E. Salama. 1989. *The Marketing Challenge of 1992*. Reading, Mass.: Addison-Wesley.

Quickel, S. 1989. "Target: Europe." *Business Month* (August).

Ransom, C. 1973. *The European Community and Eastern Europe*. London: Butterworths.

Redmond, J. 1987. "Trade Between China and the European Community: A New Relationship?" *National Westminster Bank Quarterly Review* (May).

Rezvin, P. 1977. "European Bureaucrats Are Writing the Rules Americans Will Live By." *Wall Street Journal*, 17 May.

———. 1988. "Welcome to Their Party." *Wall Street Journal*, 30 December.

———. 1990. "Fast Changing House of Europe Defies Single Blueprint." *Wall Street Journal*, 22 February.

Ritson, C. 1977. *Agricultural Economics*. St. Albans: Granada.

Roarty, M. 1987. "The Impact of the Common Agricultural Policy on Agricultural Trade and Development." *National Westminster Bank Quarterly Review* (February).

Robert Rhodes, J., ed. 1974. *Winston S. Churchill: His Complete Speeches 1897–1963*. London: Chelsea House Publishers.

Roberts, B. 1988. *Delors versus 1992?* Occasional paper, no. 1. The Bruges Group, London.

Robson, P. 1980. *The Economics of International Integration*. London: Allen and Unwin.

Rustlow, D., and T. Penrose. 1981. *Turkey and the Community: The Mediterranean Challenge*. Sussex European Research Centre paper 10. Brighton, England.

Scott, A. 1986. "Britain and the EMS: An Appraisal of the Report of the Treasury and Civil Service Committee." *Journal of Common Market Studies* 24, no. 3 (March).

Seers, D., and S. Vaitsos. 1980. *Integration and Unequal Development*. London: Macmillan.

Servan-Schreiber, J-J. 1968. *The American Challenge*. London: Hamish Hamilton.

Shanks, M. 1977. *European Social Policy Today and Tomorrow*. Oxford: Pergamon Press.

Sharp, M., ed. 1985. *Europe and the New Technologies*. London: Frances Pinter.

Sharp, M. 1985. *The New Biotechnology: European Governments in Search of a Strategy*. Sussex European paper, no. 15. University of Sussex, Sussex, England.

Shonfeld, A. 1973. *Europe: Journey to an Unknown Destination*. Harmondsworth, England: Penguin.

Sked, A. 1989. *Good Europeans?* Occasional paper no. 4 (November). London, England: The Bruges Group.

Slot, P., and M. van der Woude, eds. 1988. *Exploiting the Internal Market: Cooperation and Competition Toward 1992*. Deventer, The Netherlands: Kluwer Law and Taxation Publishers.

Smith, A. 1976. *An Inquiry into the Nature and Causes of the Wealth of Nations*. Chicago: University of Chicago Press.

Stertz, S., and S. Moore. 1989. "GM to Purchase 50 Percent Saab Stake for $500 Million." *Wall Street Journal*, 18 December.

Stevens, C., ed. 1984. *EEC and the Third World: A Survey*. No. 4, ODI/IDS, London: Hodder and Stoughton.

Stigler, G. 1971. "The Theory of Economic Regulation." *Bell Journal of Economics* (Spring).

Stone, N. 1989. "The Globalization of Europe: An Interview with Wisse Dekker." *Harvard Business Review* (May-June).

Strange, S. 1980. "Germany and the World Monetary System." In *West Germany: A European and Global Power*, edited by W. Kohl and G. Basevi. Lexington, Mass.: D.C. Heath.

Svennilson, I. 1954. *Growth and Stagnation in the European Economy*. Geneva: United Nations Economic Commission for Europe.

Swann, D. 1983. *Competition and Industrial Policy*. London: Methuen.

———. 1985. *The Economics of the Common Market*, 5th ed. Harmondsworth, England: Penguin.

Sweet & Maxwell. 1977. *European Community Treaties*, 3rd ed. London: Sweet & Maxwell.

Tarditi, S. 1984. "Price Policies and European Economic Integration." In *Price and Market Policies in European Agriculture*, edited by K. Thomson and R. Warren. Dept. of Agricultural Economics, University of Newcastle-upon-Tyne.

Taylor, P. 1983. *The Limits of European Integration*. London: Croom Helm.

Thatcher, M. 1988. *Britain and Europe*. London: Text of speech delivered in Bruges, Conservative Political Centre, September.

Tipton, F., and R. Aldrich. 1987. *An Economic and Social History of Europe: From 1939 to the Present*. Baltimore: Johns Hopkins University Press.

Toman, B. 1989. "Guinness Plans to Buy Stake on 16.8 Percent in Dior." *Wall Street Journal* 7 April.

Treaties Establishing the European Communities, abridged ed. 1987. Luxembourg: Office of Official Publications of the European Communities.

Tsoukalis, L. 1977a. *The Politics and Economics of European Monetary Integration.* London: Allen and Unwin.

Tsoukalis, L., ed. 1977b. *The European Community and Its Mediterranean Enlargement.* London: Allen and Unwin.

———. 1986. *Europe, America and the World Economy.* Oxford: Basil Blackwell for the College of Europe.

Tugendhat, C. 1988. *Making Sense of Europe.* New York: Columbia University Press.

Tulder, R. van, and G. Junne. 1988. *European Multinationals in Core Technologies.* New York: John Wiley & Sons.

Turner, G. 1986. "Inside Europe's Giant Companies: Cultural Revolution at Philips." *Long Range Planning* 19/4, no. 98 (August).

United Nations. 1949. *ECE in Action.* New York: United Nations.

———. 1988. *Statistical Yearbook, 1985/86.* New York: United Nations.

U.S. House of Representatives. 1989. *European Community's 1992 Economic Integration Plan.* Report by the Subcommittee on International Economic Policy and Trade of the Committee on Foreign Affairs.

U.S. President's Committee on Foreign Aid. 1947. *European Recovery and American Aid.* Washington: U.S. Government Printing Office.

Utne, A. 1986. "EFTA's Importance as a Trading Partner for the EC." *EFTA Bulletin* 27 (October-December).

Vandamme, J. 1987. "The Tindeman's Report (1975–76)." In *The Dynamics of European Union,* edited by R. Pryce. New York: Croom Helm.

Vanhove, N., and L. Klassen. 1980. *Regional Policy: A European Approach.* Farnborough, England: Saxon House.

Vernon, R., and D. Spar. 1989. *Beyond Globalism.* New York: Free Press.

Wallace, H. 1985. *Europe: The Challenge of Diversity.* London: Routledge and Kegan Paul.

Wallace, H., W. Wallace, and C. Webb, eds. 1977. *Policy-Making in the European Communities.* London: John Wiley.

Wallace, W., ed. 1980. *Britain in Europe.* London: Heinemann.

Whitby, M., ed. 1979. *The Net Cost and Benefit of EEC Membership.* London: Wye College.

White, L. 1989. "Federal Express: Managing Ahead for 1992 is Risky." *Business Month* (August).

Williams, M. 1977. *Teaching European Studies.* London: Heinemann.

Winters, A. 1987. "Britain in Europe: A Survey of Quantitative Trade Studies." *Journal of Common Market Studies* 25, no. 4 (June).

Wolferen, K. van. 1989. *The Enigma of Japanese Power.* New York: Alfred A. Knopf.

WS Atkins Management Consultants. 1988. *The "Cost of Non-Europe" in Public-*

Sector Procurement, 2 vols. Luxembourg: Office of Official Publications of the European Communities.

Yannopoulos, G. 1985. "EC External Commercial Policies and East-West Trade in Europe." *Journal of Common Market Studies* 26, no. 1 (September).

Yannopoulos, G., ed. 1986. *Greece and the EEC.* Basingstoke, England: Macmillan.

Ypersele, J. van. 1984. *The European Monetary System: Origins, Operations and Outlook.* Luxembourg: Office of Official Publications of the European Communities.

———. 1985. *The European Monetary System.* Cambridge, England: Woodhead-Faulkner.

Zis, G. 1984. "The European Monetary System 1979–1984: An Assessment." *Journal of Common Market Studies* 23, no. 1 (September).

Index

About the Authors

Timothy M. Devinney is a member of the faculty at the John E. Anderson Graduate School of Management, University of California, Los Angeles. He has previously taught at the Owen Graduate School of Management, Vanderbilt University, and was a visiting professor at Universität Ulm and Universität Hamburg, both in Germany. He received his B.Sc. from Carnegie Mellon University in psychology and holds an M.A. in public policy studies, an M.B.A. in economics and statistics, and a Ph.D. in business economics, all from the University of Chicago. Professor Devinney is an applied economist whose work covers diverse topics such as firm pricing decisions, the role of bank screening policies and bank customer relations, the impact of taxation on firms' investment choices, and game theory. His previous publications include two books, *Issues in Pricing* and *Rationing in a Theory of the Banking Firm,* and articles in journals such as *Management Science, Journal of Business, Journal of Economic Psychology, Strategic Management Journal, Journal of Institutional and Theoretical Economics, Journal of Product Innovation Management,* and *Journal of Marketing.*

William C. Hightower, Sr., is assistant director of business development for Emerson Motor Company, a division of Emerson Electric Company, St. Louis, a leading Fortune 100 company with worldwide operations. He is a graduate of the Owen

Graduate School of Management, Vanderbilt University and received his B.Sc. from the University of South Alabama with additional coursework in Europe. Mr. Hightower also contributed to "1992 and the International Financial System" a paper presented at the Lucky-Goldstar Conference in Seoul, South Korea in 1989.